John Hamlin Dewey

The Way, the Truth and the Life

A hand book of Christian theosophy, healing, and psychic culture, a new education, based upon the ideal and method of the Christ

John Hamlin Dewey

The Way, the Truth and the Life
A hand book of Christian theosophy, healing, and psychic culture, a new education, based upon the ideal and method of the Christ

ISBN/EAN: 9783337037963

Printed in Europe, USA, Canada, Australia, Japan

Cover: Foto ©Lupo / pixelio.de

More available books at **www.hansebooks.com**

The Way, the Truth and the Life

A Hand Book

OF

Christian Theosophy,

Healing, & Psychic Culture,

A New Education,

Based upon the Ideal and Method of the Christ,

BY

J. H. Dewey, M. D.

Published by the Author,
Buffalo, N. Y.
1888.

To all
seekers after the light,
freedom and mastery of the perfect life,
to all who look and labor for the realization
of the Christ Ideal of the Kingdom of God and the
Brotherhood of man on earth, this
book is respectfully and heartily
inscribed, by the
AUTHOR.

"I am the way, the truth and the life; no man cometh unto the Father but by me."

"I am the door: by me if any man enter in, he shall be saved, and shall go in and out, and find pasture."

"I am the light of the world: he that followeth me shall not walk in darkness but shall have the light of life"

"To this end was I born and for this cause came I into the world, that I should bear witness unto the truth. Every one that is of the truth heareth my voice."

"Verily, verily, I say unto you, He that believeth on me, the works that I do shall he do also; and greater than these shall he do; because I go unto the Father."

"Ye therefore shall be perfect, as your father in heaven is perfect."—THE CHRIST.

PREFACE.

In the early days of the modern "Faith Cure," "Prayer Cure" and "Mind Cure" movement, several remarkable instances of "Prayer Cure" of undoubted genuineness came under our observation. Being actively engaged in the practice of medicine, and holding at the time a thoroughly materialistic philosophy of life, these extraordinary facts of experience indicating a source of healing power hitherto unrecognized, challenged our careful consideration, and led to a full, practical and experimental study of the law and principle upon which they were based. To this end every phase of experience in this direction was carefully noted and considered, and no well authenticated fact overlooked.

Believing that all cases of healing through purely mental or spiritual influence, whether classed under the head of "Faith Cure," "Prayer Cure," "Metaphysical" or "Christian Science Healing," etc., involve the operation of the same law and principle, we have subjected the facts, claims and theories presented under all these heads, to a candid and rigid examination in connection with a careful study of the relations of mind and body, to determine if possible the specific nature of the conditions and processes involved.

Finding the most remarkable developments connected with specific religious experiences, and apparent super-mundane influence, we were led to the further study of the exceptional experiences and teaching of the so-called "Seers" and "Prophets" who have moulded the religious thought and life of a large portion of the human race. This led to the specific study of the life and teaching of him whom many of the most enlightened minds of the western world have united in accepting as the one supreme man, the Christ or God-anointed Teacher of mankind.

Though beginning this investigation in the most critical and questioning spirit, the candid study of the spiritual as well as the physical constitution of man, in the light of these exceptional experiences and inspired teachings, led to the clear and grateful recognition of diviner possibilities for him than the philosophies of the world had ever dreamed of. We were led to the most profound conviction, that the brightest fore-gleams of millennial glory which ever dazzled the anointed vision of ancient seer or prophet, were but the faintest shadows of the possible reality.

The greatness, majesty and perfection of being which the unbiased study of the recorded life and words of Jesus revealed, won both mind and heart, and imprinted on the soul a divine Ideal never to be effaced as an ideal, until realized in personal experience. The transcendent possibilities for man, opened to the world in the actual experience as well as the illuminated teaching of Jesus, proved both a revelation and a revolution to our own thought and experience.

Through an enlightened understanding and from what we have already realized in personal experience, we are fully persuaded that the law of FAITH as announced by Jesus and exemplified in his life, is the supreme law and method of all divine realization for man, of which physical healing is the most external and superficial manifestation.

We fully accept the ideal perfection of man as a child of God, held up and emphasized by Jesus, and actualized in his own experience before the world, as the legitimate goal of all human ambition and effort.

We have become thoroughly convinced, that a clear understanding and practical application of the principle and specific method involved in this supreme law and power of faith, will secure the speedy emancipation of man from the thralldom and limitations of the sensuous life, and bring the full realization of that larger freedom and understanding for which he instinctively yearns and seeks.

Having found the key, as we believe, to the true understanding and practical working of the principle and method established by the Christ, in their specific application to the changed conditions of modern life and thought, we have sought to unfold and illustrate the same in the most simple, practical and specific manner possible.

The book has been written under a press of other duties and many interruptions, with the one desire of helping those who are seeking the perfect way of life, by giving them the light which we have found in this study of the "Model Man," and of our common nature in the light of his example. We have pursued this study independent of any theological bias, and ask the reader to follow us in the same manner, as fully as possible.

The mission of Jesus as the Christ, it would seem, was not so much to teach a philosophy, as to establish a method, by which all might come to the immediate, intuitive knowledge of the truth, each for himself, by an inward illumination, precisely as he, their true leader and example had done. "He spake as one having authority, and not as the Scribes." Their appeal was to the law and testimony as written in books. He spake from the living authority of an inward revelation, and assured his disciples that upon this rock he would build his Church, against which the gates of hell should not prevail. "Blessed art thou Simon Bar Jona, for flesh and blood hath not revealed it unto thee, but my Father which is in heaven."

This experience of a direct and immediate revelation of God, to the soul of His child, is the only solid and enduring foundation possible, for a true Church of the Spirit. And such a Church of Spiritual illumination, of immediate and perpetual revelation, is the only practical realization or fulfilment of the predicted result which was to follow the advent of the Messiah, as shadowed forth in the Messianic prophecies. "This is the covenant that I will make with the house of Israel. After those days saith the Lord, I will put my law in their inward parts and write it in their hearts; and will be their God and they shall be my people. And they shall teach no more every man his neighbor and every man his brother, saying, Know the Lord: for they shall all know me from the least of them unto the greatest of them saith the Lord: for I will forgive their iniquity and I will remember their sin no more." "The Comforter, which is the Holy Spirit," "even the Spirit of truth which proceedeth from the Father," "shall teach you all things," and "will guide you into all truth." This was the acknowledged source of the marvelous wisdom and spiritual insight of the young, unlettered, but divine Galilean. "And the Jews marveled, saying, How knoweth this man letters, having never learned?" "And they were astonished at his doctrine, for his word was with power."

As the "Model Man," Jesus lifted up the true Ideal before the world, the ideal or pattern of the true life for man, and by living it in the flesh, demonstrated its possibility for all mankind. The great forerunner had predicted that through his coming, "The crooked shall be made straight, and the rough ways shall be made smooth. And all flesh shall see the salvation of God." Only as the true and perfect Example and Teacher, could he consistently and without presumption say, "I am the way, the truth, and the life; no man cometh unto the Father but by me." "I am the door, by me if any man enter in he shall be saved, and go in and out and find pasture." "I am the light of the world; he that followeth me shall not walk in darkness, but shall have the light of life."

If the gospel story of his life be essentially true, that life justified this claim. If both the claim and the record be false, the Ideal and the inspiration to noble effort it awakens, still remain the grandest and divinest we have. With this conclusion, however, we are brought to face the problem of a greater miracle, viz.: how "a brace of Galilean fishermen" could conjure, out of their uncultured brains, or the depths of their imagination, the perfection of a character they had never known. If this be so, "Lowly and unlettered though they were, they yet painted a beauty they had never seen, and invented a character they could not comprehend; nay, lifted up a shadow which the learned of earth were widely destined to mistake for the eternal substance; which for many centuries has fixed the gaze of the enlightened world, and been confessed the radiant ideal of mankind. If you believe this, demur at miracles no more."

The claim and the record of the Christ accepted, the supreme lesson of that wonderful life has yet, sadly enough, been practically lost to the world through the misconception, perverted teaching, and the narrow and materialistic faith of the Church which bears his name. By losing sight of his humanity, in its contemplation of his divinity, and holding him up as a vicarious substitute instead of an example for all men, the Church has wholly misinterpreted the nature and purpose of his work, and so of the character of the salvation opened to the world in him.

In its deification of the man, it has set him apart from humanity as another order of being, and thus practically neutralized the transforming influence which his example would otherwise exert upon his brethren. That he was fully and absolutely human, the veritable "Son of man," no sane mind will deny. That he was also fully and absolutely divine, the veritable "Son of God," we with equal positiveness claim and affirm. The divinity of his nature and character cannot be exaggerated. The law of self, or of self-love which rules the common life of man, was entirely displaced in him by the law of impartial and universal love and ministration, which rules the divine life. The spirit which recognizes the Brotherhood and identifies the life and interests of the individual with those of the race, and seeks and recognizes the personal good only in the good of all, is the spirit which is of God. This was the law of his life and the secret of his greatness and perfection. This was the insignia and demonstration of his divinity. When manifest in man it is the Spirit of the All-Father in His child. All that was possible to be incarnated of the Divine Nature and attributes in a human life and personality, was manifest in him, literally "God manifest in the flesh."

This incarnation of the Divine in Jesus, however, but reveals and demonstrates the innate capacity of our common humanity as the off-spring of God, for receiving into its unfolding life the full Spirit of the Father, and becoming divine, as illustrated in the life of our great Exemplar. The recognition and emphasis of this fact, were the vital element and supreme message of his teaching; together with the law and conditions of its realization in human experience. The possibility of this divine perfection of man, he based upon the fact of the divine sonship of man. "Ye therefore shall be perfect, even as your Father in heaven is perfect."

We have no theology, old or new, to offer, and no desire to jostle any man's theological belief. Let every one be fully persuaded in his own mind, and accord the same right to all. Our earnest desire and effort in this book is to recall our age, if possible, to the divine Ideal and Method opened to the world in the Christ, and bring to bear such light as the experimental efforts of men on the various planes of human activity furnish, as an aid to their true interpretation to our practical age.

The work of the incarnate Christ, as announced by the angel to the parents of Jesus, was not specifically to save men from the *effects* of their sins in the world to come, but to save them "*from their sins*" in the world that now is. "He shall save his people from their sins." The true work of Christian Theosophy, therefore, is not to prepare men for another world *per se*, but to help them to the perfect life here and now, as there is no other salvation from sin but the perfect life. "Ye therefore shall be perfect, as your Father in heaven is perfect." Surely the perfect life in this world is the best and only preparation for any future world. The thought of the world needs to be turned to the true preparation for life in this world, and this can be attained only through the method of the Christ, "Seek ye first the kingdom of God and His righteousness, and all these things" [of this life] "shall be added unto you."

The term Theosophy signifies Divine Wisdom. The practical study of Theosophy implies the true method of attaining divine wisdom, supremacy and perfection of being. To reveal and establish this method as well as to lift up the divine Ideal of attainment for man on earth, was the clearly-defined mission and supreme message of the Christ; and to carry this work forward to its full consummation, is the essential mission and character of the true Christian Theosophy.

The Theosophy of the Christ, therefore, embraces in its work the healing and perfection of the body, as well as the illumination and perfection of the soul of man as the child of God. In recognizing man as the child of God, necessarily partaking potentially of the Father's nature and attributes, it recognizes and appeals to his inherent ability to unfold into all the perfection of being which characterizes the Father's nature, to become perfect as He is perfect.

The only hope left for the Church to redeem her claim as the representative of Christ and his work in the world, after eighteen centuries of practical failure, is by breaking away from the traditional misconceptions and misguiding teaching of the past, and in the clearer light of our age re-study with unbiased minds the actual Christ of history, and then re-study man and his possibilities, in the light of his example and teaching.

Nothing will be lost by this process, but the errors and stumbling stones of tradition; while the pure gold of truth, freed from the clogging dross of creed and dogma, will be recovered in its incorruptible purity and imperishable beauty.

The solution of the great problems of God and man, of life and destiny, will be found in the life of this one transcendent Brother of mankind. The true THEO-SOPHIA, the wisdom of God, and "The Way, the Truth and the Life" for man as the child of God, stand revealed and exemplified in him. The eternal Logos or "Word was made flesh." Divinity was revealed in the human and the human made divine. The At-one-ment of man with God in the permanent consciousness of identy of nature as child with Parent, was undoubtedly for the first time fully realized in and by him, only however, to be re-produced from his example and leading, in the experience of the entire race of which he thus stands, not by arbitrary appointment, but by "natural selection," the living Spiritual Head.

There is no dispute here with the claim of theology for the manifest God in Christ, it is fully and gratefully accepted. We cannot stop, however, with this as an abstract proposition, but must accept, also, the logical outcome of this position, viz: that the manifestation of God in one man, demonstrates the possibility of a like manifestation in all men.

It will be conceded by every candid thinker, that whatever attributes of divinity became manifest in Jesus the acknowledged son of Mary, found organic expression in and through functions that were wholly and strictly human. No other understanding of the "Divine Incarnation" is possible. And what is this, but the practical demonstration in a living example of the claim put forth by the Christ himself, that man is the child of God, with an inherent ability to become perfect even as his Father in heaven is perfect?

Admitting that Jesus held the mastery of the conditions of life and death, that he wielded direct power over the forces of the physical world, that he really performed the extraordinary works recorded of him, we are then logically forced to recognize the same power latent in and therefore possible to all men. This was the positive teaching of Jesus himself, "Verily, verily I say unto you, He that believeth on me the works that I do shall he do also, and greater than these shall he do; because I go unto the Father."

We have as yet no complete anthropology or science of man; because man has been studied only in his undeveloped and imperfect conditions, and in the light of his physical and sensuous limitations. All exceptions to this in the fragmentary exhibitions of a higher level of life in the individual experiences of prophets and apostles, have been regarded as exceptional and abnormal, and therefore no example of a like possibility for all mankind. This is manifestly a great mistake. To form any adequate conception of human possibility we must study man at his best. Jesus alone has shown him at his best, and is, therefore, the representative man from whose example we may best judge of the inherent possibilities of all men. In him we have an unmistakable revelation of God's Ideal of a man, and of his purpose in and provision for all men.

In the teaching and example of Jesus, we have also a revelation —if our eyes are open to perceive it—and full illustration of the law and conditions through which this divine Ideal is to be realized in the universal experience of the race. The fact that such divine possibilities are implanted in the nature of man, is God's own pledge of their fulfillment, through the personal co-operation of man himself, in spirit and truth. The only salvation worthy of the name, is the fruition in man of his divinest possibilities as a child of God. The earnest, at least, of what these possibilities are, was made real to man in the personal experience of the Elder Brother, who could without presumption say, "To this end was I born, and for this cause came I into the world, that I should bear witness to the truth. Every one that is of the truth heareth my voice."

In the following pages Jesus as the Christ is recognized, first: As a literal example for all men; second: As the one Teacher of the Perfect Way of life, or Method of attaining both physical and spiritual perfection; and third: As a living continuous Personal influence and Power in the spiritual life of the race, in co-operation with all those who have risen into unity with his life in God, ever working for the emancipation of man from the dominion and limitations of flesh and sense, into spiritual freedom and supremacy—the glorious liberty of the children of God.

If the exposition of the law and specific processes set forth in the following pages for the higher education of man and the attainment of spiritual illumination and supremacy, shall help the reader to a larger ideal of life and the realization of a diviner experience in this world; if any are helped by this book to reach that higher life of freedom and inspired wisdom for which they yearn, the object of the writer will have been accomplished, and his prayer answered.

J. H. D.

MARCH, 1888.

NORMAL SEERSHIP

"When God creates the human soul, He communicates to it original and essential knowledge. The soul is the mirror of the universe, and is in connection with all things. She is lighted by a light from within; but the storms of passion, and the multitude of sensuous impressions, and the distractions of the world, darken this light whose beams are only shed when it burns alone, and all within is in peace and harmony. If we would abstract ourselves from all external influences and follow this light alone, we should find within ourselves true and unerring counsel. In this state of concentration the soul discriminates between all objects to which its observation is directed. It can unite itself with them—penetrate their properties—and, reaching up to God, through Him attain the most important truths."—VAN HELMONT.

THE TRUE PHYSICIAN.

"The God-elected physician will be accompanied by many signs and wonders for the schools; and whilst he uses his gifts for the alleviation of his neighbor's suffering, he will refer the glory of his cures to God. Pity is his guide. His heart will be truth and his knowledge understanding. Love will be his sister, and the truth of the Lord will enlighten his path. He will call upon the grace of God, and the desire of gain shall not possess him, for the Lord is rich and a free giver, and pays back an hundred fold with a heaped-up measure. He will make fruitful his work, and his hand shall be clothed in blessings. From his mouth shall flow comfort, and his voice shall be as a trumpet, at the sound of which disease shall banish. His feet shall bring gladness, and sickness shall dissolve before him like the snow in summer. Health shall follow his footsteps. These are the promises of the Lord to the holy one whom He hath chosen; these are the blessings reserved for him whose path is the path of mercy. Moreover the Holy Spirit shall enlighten him."—VAN HELMONT.

POSSIBILITIES OF MAN.

"For there is nothing covered that shall not be revealed; neither hid that shall not be known. Therefore whatsoever ye have spoken in darkness shall be heard in the light; and that which ye have spoken in the ear in closets shall be proclaimed upon the housetops." (Luke xii. 2.)

These words, with others of the Great Teacher, imply the existence of a latent power in man which, when awakened into activity and brought forth to take its true place in the mental economy, will enable the mind to penetrate all secrets, comprehend all truth, solve all mysteries, and receive by direct inspiration or revelation the very wisdom of God.

In one of his latest recorded conversations with his disciples, Jesus said: "These things have I spoken unto you while yet abiding with you. But the Comforter, even the Holy Spirit whom the Father will send in my name, *he shall teach you all things,* and bring to your remembrance all that I said unto you." "I have yet many things to say unto you but ye cannot bear them now. Howbeit when he, the Spirit of Truth is come, *he shall guide you into all the truth.*" And again: "Ye shall receive power, when the Holy Spirit is come upon you; and ye shall be my witnesses." In these remarkable words the Lord Christ affirms the supreme reality of an Illuminating Spirit and Power, which belong to man and may be realized by him and which will render him, at least in the sphere of the human, practically omniscient, omnipresent and omnipotent.

This great promise of the Christ, and the possibility it implies, is based upon, and involved in his fundamental doctrine of the Universal Fatherhood of God, and Brotherhood of Man. For if man is a child of God he necessarily partakes of the essential nature of the Father, and hence, the attributes of God exist potentially within him. And if potentially within him may and must by developement come forth in organic function. "God is Spirit," and the attributes of Spirit are Omniscience, Omnipresence, and Omnipotence. Spirit, then, is the inmost and essential nature of man in which inhere these attributes of Divinity.

This spiritual nature while latent constitutes the secret life of man, and the divine seed-germ of these transcendent possibilities deposited by the All-Loving Father in the organisms of men as His children. This spiritual life is to be brought forth and made manifest in the fruits of the Spirit when the organism of the soul shall have become sufficiently unfolded through the operation of the secret dynamic energy of the inward life to bear, in and of itself, the blossoming and fruitage of the Spirit.

Now while the growth or unfolding of an organism is from within, the symmetry, vigor and perfection of its development depend upon the corresponding co-ordination of external elements and conditions.

The first consciousness of man as we know him pertains almost exclusively, if not quite wholly, to his external being and conditions. In this sphere of his consciousness and personal activities, he has freedom of choice and volition. Because of this personal freedom and responsibility, it is left to him, as soon as he shall become conscious of the nature of his inward life and its divine possibilities, to adjust the external man and its conditions to a full co-ordination with the inward life in its unfolding effort to give complete organic expression of itself in external manifestation. Hence the time involved in the unfolding of his being and the bringing forth of his latent spiritual power to complete external expression, depends entirely upon the man himself. First, upon his *recognition* of this inward spiritual life and its possibilities, and then his intelligent co-operation therewith. This co-operation consists in the perfect adjustment of the outward man to the requirements of the inward life.

To open the understandings of men to this great truth, and make known this law of personal co-operation with divine power, for the realization in human experience of the full purpose of the Father in the existence of His children, has been the burden of the teaching, the inspired message of every true seer and prophet since the world began. One at least of these spiritually unfolded men, by the fulfilling of the law, brought the full realization of these divine possibilities into his own life before the world, a living example of the "Way, the Truth and the Life" for all man. From that divine altitude of experience he could truthfully say, "I am the light of the world; he that followeth me shall not walk in darkness, but shall have the light of life." "To this end was I born, and for this cause came I into the world, that I should bear witness unto the truth; every one that is of the truth heareth my voice."

The term Holy, according to Webster, signifies "whole, entire, complete." Hence, in these words of Jesus, "When the Holy Spirit has come upon you," he plainly referred to the full coming forth of the spiritual nature in organic expression, and the manifestation of its attributes in all the functions of the personal life—literally, "God manifest in the flesh." We can readily picture to our minds what the nature, character, and powers of man would be if the attributes of pure Spirit—WISDOM, GOODNESS, POWER—were only expressed in all the functions of his being. And is not this exactly what we do see in the life of Jesus, allowing the essential truth of the record we have of him? Do we not also see the same in greater or less degree in the seers, prophets, and apostles of the spiritual life, just in proportion as their spiritual unfoldment approached the level of its perfect development in him?

That these sons of God, the so-called seers and prophets of the race, are not mythical personages, but have lived and spoken their words of supposed inspired wisdom and authority, there can be no reasonable doubt, since the great religions of the world are based upon them. Indeed there can be no other basis for these religions, save the spiritual and inspirational nature of man, which, quickened and unfolded in greater or less degree in the exceptional and favored few, made them the seers and prophets that they were. The fact of the exceptional lives, and teachings of these men cannot be questioned, since their record is preserved to us, and sacredly cherished by millions of our race. The inspired wisdom and authority of their teaching may, however, be a legitimate subject of inquiry. Happily there is a very simple method of testing this question, and that is by the effect upon the personal life of those who accept these teachings and apply them.

But let these questions be decided as they may, there still remains the one supreme question—why the existence of these great religions at all? Are they not the result of an irrepressible instinct based upon a fundamental and indestructible element of human nature itself? Do not these religions demonstrate the intuitive recognition of a possible emancipation from the limitations which cripple and hamper the common life of man? Do they not reveal an inner prophetic sense of a possible exaltation of being in which the wings of higher powers, now beating against the prison bars of flesh and sense, shall have boundless freedom of activity and expanse? Yet however clearly the truth may have dawned on the minds of the great illuminated leaders, it must be confessed that the religious instinct, both in the priesthoods and the masses of the various religions of the world, have been but blind impulses in the main, and hence the ministers of religion but blind leaders of the blind. The forms and ceremonies of religion, even in the most enlightened of the christian sects, judging from their results, are largely but blind and inefficient efforts to adjust the external man to the strict and divine requirements of the inward life—(the spirit in man)—which, when truly accomplished, will bring the whole man under the direct guidance and immediate inspiration of the indwelling Presence of the Father, " For surely there is spirit in man and the inspiration of the Almighty maketh intelligent, (true rendering).

Let us then calmly and with unbiased minds study anew the great ideals which lie at the core of all religions, as they were held by the illuminated souls of the great leaders themselves. We shall doubtless find that however much these ideals may have been misapprehended by the masses, they have nevertheless most truly voiced the undeveloped and undefined spiritual instincts of the race. For, in spite of the terrible perversions and degrading superstitions which misapprehension and misinterpretation have engendered, these ideals have still been eagerly accepted and cherished by mankind. This is the one historic fact of supreme significance, and suggests, if it does not fully demonstrate, the divine reality which underlies it. Another fact of great significance and encouragement in this study is found in the greatness of soul, the nobility of character, and the purity and moral grandeur of life manifest in greater or less degree in the earthly career and labors of these exceptional men ; and also to a corresponding degree, in those who, seeking to follow them, have entered most fully into the true understanding and spirit of their teaching.

Should these spiritual geniuses of the race, the founders of the great religions, come to be fully and universally accepted as anointed sons of God, true seers and prophets, the world must also accept the lesson which this fact involves, that in their loftiest attainment, they but illustrate the slumbering and undeveloped possibilities of all men. And as there were differences of degree in the spiritual attainment of these exceptional lives, from the humblest seer up to that son of truth and righteousness which rose to full-orbed glory and illumination in the transcendent soul of the divine Galilean, we may be sure that none of these, even the

Lord Christ Himself, reached in earthly career the full limit of this possible divine attainment. Hence we may take the words of this supreme Teacher himself in their most literal as well as profoundest spiritual sense, " He that believeth in me, the works that I do shall he do also ; and greater than these shall he do, because I go unto the Father." " Ye therefore shall be perfect, even as your Father in heaven is perfect."

A thorough and enthusiastic re-study of the law of this divine realization for man, as disclosed in the inspired lives and teaching of these great spiritual Leaders, and especially in him who was truly the "light of the world," should be of the first importance to, and therefore the first step of, every true philanthropist who would labor most effectually for the emancipation and advancement of his race. The obvious fact that the traditional misapprehensions and misinterpretations of inspired teaching by the uninspired teachers and leaders of the world, have rendered the word of God of none effect, but emphasizes the importance of repudiating at once and fully the stumbling stones of tradition. It makes urgent the necessity of turning to drink anew and direct from the original fountain opened in the truly inspired lives and teaching of men "approved of God by signs and wonders which God did" by them among men; "Whom God anointed with the Holy Spirit and with power, who went about doing good, healing all that were oppressed with the devil," or evil; for God was with them.

The confusion of tongues in the religious teaching, the lo here and lo there on every hand, make a new departure absolutely imperative.

But right at this juncture comes an astounding claim professing to meet the demands of this very emergency, in the name of Oriental Theosophy. This claim is that the pure wisdom of God once possessed by the children of light in the virgin morning of the world, and which has shone into the souls of the seers and prophets of the ages with more or less clearness, has been fully preserved and sacredly guarded by a mystic brotherhood whose secret ranks have been maintained and perpetuated from century to century, by initiation from the faithful few which the ages have produced. It is claimed by representative Theosophists who are themselves initiates and students of this wisdom, that the secret brotherhood of "Mahatmas" are now ready, as the world itself is ripening for it, to open its treasures and divulge its secrets to such as are prepared to receive them. The study of this Theosophy itself, under the guidance of initiates, is proposed as a means of further preparation.

While we await the demonstration of the actual existence of this mighty brotherhood and their treasured wisdom, we may at least listen calmly and without prejudice to what their reputed representatives have to offer us. If they can help us, or open to us the esoteric wisdom of our own inspired oracles, we will thank them.

The following from an intelligent and representative theosophical author, will perhaps set this claim fairly before us:

"Every thoughtful observer of the times must have discovered that the creeds of the world are crumbling into dust. The advancement of science has undermined them. Here, not even the law of the survival of the fittest obtains; they are all full of error, all false, and must all go, soon or late. But back of all these is the everlasting truth, from which they sprung through man's ignorant attempt to formulate. The philosophy of Plato, the doctrines of the Essenes and Gnostics, entered largely into the Christian philosophy, but even these were veiled in mystery, to be comprehended only by the initiated like Paul.

"There always was the secret, esoteric interpretation for the initiated, and the letter of the law for the common people. This secret wisdom is no longer in the possession of the priesthood; their patent has therefore expired. The children of this generation are wiser in many things than the priests of old, and the amount of general and scientific information possessed by the people renders the old landmarks, the old methods, useless. The basis of religion must neither ignore nor do violence to philosophy, science, and the common sense of mankind. * * * *

"For the time being the old creeds must be laid aside, though the Christian retain his Christianity, the Jew his Judaism, the Buddhist and Mohammedan their peculiar faith, and if he choose, his own forms of worship, being required only to exercise that degree of courtesy and toleration toward others that he requires for himself, while the creeds and basis of all religions are passed under review, very soon it will be discovered that while the basis and inspiration are the same, the formulations only differ, and as these formulations are shown to be untrue and effete, they will be easily discarded one and all.

"It will then be seen that at the very beginning is achieved that basis of Brotherhood which all other methods have failed to attain. Presently we shall begin to learn the meaning of that old inscription written in letters of gold over the entrance of the temples, MAN, KNOW THYSELF. A new meaning will be given to that old saying, "The kingdom of heaven is within you," and we shall have grown philosophical enough to add, *so, also, is the kingdom of hell.*" * * *

"It is not proposed, be it observed, to replace Christianity by Buddhism, nor Buddhism by Mohammedism, nor both by Judaism, nor yet all three by Spiritualism, but to bring each of the old religions back to its esoteric origin, meaning and purity, and if they are found to be in essence ONE, shall we not have found the TRUE RELIGION OF HUMANITY? But just here appears the need of wisdom, not only to declare, but ability to demonstrate the esoteric basis of all religions, including lost records that shall put the matter beyond dispute.

Now suppose that at this stage of our proceedings, it were discovered that there are living men who possess just this knowledge and ability, and possess these records: men who had gone over all this ground, not by patching together fragments of different religions, but who possess a knowledge of science so profound as to dwarf into insignificance our boasted modern discoveries: who, living in communities far removed and purposely inaccessible to modern civilization, have preserved the priceless treasures of the past; who, removed from the vicious influences of modern civilization, and possessing knowledge of the laws of life, live to an age that to us seems incredible, transmitting from generation to generation of selected Neophites, their accumulated wisdom and priceless treasures; and who now at the completion of one of the world's GREAT CYCLES, for the first time in centuries give out to the world a part of their treasures; requiring no pledge, save only *allegiance to truth,* no price, save that he who receives shall as freely give, and so help along the reign of Universal Brotherhood among the races of men. These Brothers are willing and anxious to teach every earnest soul, and to demonstrate the truth of all the above propositions,

"TRUTH, and only TRUTH," being their motto, and that demonstrable and free to all who will investigate and receive it.

What I have supposed, is but a bare recital of that which has actually come to pass, and among the thousands over all the world, who have taken these Brothers at their word, I have not heard of one who has been disappointed or turned away.

I am aware that such a statement will strike many people as incredible, and they will be inclined to question the sanity of him who makes it; yet it is the barest outline of the simple truth."

What shall we say to these extraordinary claims? They are not put forth in the guise of fiction, but veritable fact. Neither are they presented by obscure and unknown men, but men of high attainment, honored and active in the walks of professional and literary life. They certainly furnish, to say the least, a striking illustration of the exalted ideals of human attainment and possibility which have inspired the souls of men in all ages and among various peoples.

In this modern revival of Oriental Theosophy, and the attempt to plant it in our western world and unite or blend it with our modern civilization, we possibly hear but the echo of a voice which first spoke from the Ancient of Days, and, may be, feel the touch of that mighty spirit of light and gladness, which flooded the

"Golden Age," when the "morning stars sang together and the sons of God shouted for joy," seeking to re-incarnate itself in the active life of these later days. Be that as it may, the nature and aim of Theosophy as presented by the author quoted, is certainly broad and comprehensive enough to satisfy the most cosmopolitan mind, since it proposes to bring the universal Brotherhood of mankind to a practical realization through a complete regeneration of the race. (See appendix No. 1.)

IS THE CHRIST TO BE SUPERSEDED?

While we wait for a fuller exposition and vindication of the methods by which these results are to be secured; and while the source of the wisdom and power by which these methods are conducted, remains involved in so much secrecy and mystery; while the problem of the very existence of the "Holy Brotherhood," still perplexes the minds of thousands of initiates in the lower degrees, and access to them can be had only through intermediates, will it not be quite as profitable for us to turn to the esoteric study of our own inspired oracles? But this is the very thing they have asked of us, only that they be allowed to guide us in this study, through initiation into the secrets of the hidden wisdom, as fast as we are prepared, through advancing degrees of initiation, to receive them, assuming that all truth is now in the possession of the Thibettan Brotherhood, who preside over and direct the movement.

But suppose we accept on trust these tremendous claims, join the ranks of the Orientals, enter the lodge rooms, and through loyalty to all requirements pass through the initiatory degrees, until at last we are prepared to enter the august Brotherhood itself; what then?

Shall we become so far removed from the conditions of common life that, like the Brothers themselves, we can only work for the world through intermediaries, and have to dwell in such seclusion until the masses have been lifted through advancing degrees of inspiration to that condition of illumination and understanding that shall qualify them for immediate communion and fellowship with us? But suppose again that all this claim is based on fact and is possible of realization; and that we are led through initiation under the guidance of intermediates,—who themselves are guided by a higher wisdom,—to the heart of all religions, shall we find anything deeper, broader, more comprehensive, than the ideal offered and the experience promised and illustrated by the Christ himself? Did he not bid his followers make disciples of *all* nations, and proclaim his gospel to every creature? And what was that gospel,—the good tidings of great joy that should be to all people,—but the Universal and eternal Fatherhood and perfect Providence of God, and the Divine Sonship Brotherhood, spiritual nature and transcendent possibilities of man? Is the Ideal of attainment and the method of its realization as now presented to the world by the mighty "Brothers of the Himivat," through their official channel of communication, the Theosophical Society, any advance or improvement upon that of the Christ preserved to us and the world by his chosen witnesses, as found in our own New Testament? Is not this very New Testament a clear record of the New Covenant which God made with mankind in the full revelation of Himself in Jesus Christ—His true and loyal Son—as the Father of all men, in fulfillment of the more ancient Hebrew prophecy? Did not the full realization of this Divine Sonship and the true spirit of Brotherhood begin in the personal experience of Jesus, and become extended to a striking degree in the experience of his immediate followers, in that early brotherhood of the Apostolic Church, "when the multitude of them that believed were of one heart, and of one soul; neither said any of them that aught of the things which he possessed was his own; but they had all things common"? Has not that ancient Hebrew prophecy been fulfilled in the personal experience of all from that day to this, to the full extent to which they have recognized Jesus as the Christ, the God-anointed Mediator of His New Covenant of Fatherhood and Sonship, and, following his leading of word and example, have entered into it in spirit and truth? Could there be any diviner experience vouchsafed to man than the full reproduction of the anointed life of Jesus in his followers, the lifting of the whole human race to the spiritual level of the personal life exemplified in him? Allowing all the treasured wisdom, knowledge, and power claimed for the Brothers, and their desire and offer to share it with the world, can it be anything above or beyond the Divine offer and promise of this New Covenant of the Father with His children through His Beloved because Loyal Son and our Divine Brother, to all who truly through his leadership, enter into it? Said the ancient prophet: * * * * "This shall be the covenant that I will make with the house of Israel; after those days, saith the Lord, I will put my law in their inward parts, and write it in their hearts, and will be their God and they shall be my people. And they shall teach no more every man his neighbor, and every man his brother, saying, Know the Lord: for they shall all know me, from the least of them unto the greatest of them, saith the Lord: for I will forgive their iniquity, and I will remember their sin no more." Can anything be more complete than this covenant when fully entered into and realized by man, who is left to perform his part? A covenant implies two or more parties to the bond of agreement. And again, as stated by St. Paul, "For we are a temple of the living God; even as God said, I will dwell in them, and walk in them; and I will be their God, and they shall be my people. Wherefore come ye out from among them, and be ye separate, saith the Lord, and touch no unclean thing; and I will receive you, and will be to you a Father, and ye shall be to me sons and daughters, saith the Lord Almighty." Then we have the prophetic vision by St. John of the final realization of this covenant of the Father with His human children in the universal experience of the race. "And I saw a new heaven and a new earth: for the first heaven and the first earth are passed away. * * * And I heard a great voice out of the throne saying, Behold, the tabernacle of God is with men, and he shall dwell with them, and they shall be his peoples, and God himself shall be with them, and be their God; and he shall wipe away every tear from their eyes; and death shall be no more; neither shall there be mourning, nor crying, nor pain, any more; the first things have passed away. And He that sitteth on the throne said, Behold I make all things new. * * * * He that overcometh shall inherit these things; and I will be his God, and he shall be my son."

Thus the first state of man, the carnal life of the flesh, out of the perversities of which come sin and sorrow, pain and death, that which constitutes the "first earth" or earthly life; and, also, its ideal of heaven or standard of happiness—sensual delight--which constitutes the first heaven, are to pass away, and be replaced by a new heaven, based upon communion and fellowship with the Father; and a new earth wherein dwelleth righteousness, based upon the coming forth and final supremacy of the spiritual life in man—a full realization of the New Covenant of the Divine Fatherhood and Sonship first fully opened to and realized in the world by Jesus as the Christ. Hence, it is but the reproduction of the personal attainment and experience of the Great Exemplar in his followers, in fulfillment of his emphatic promise: "If ye continue in my words [teaching], ye shall be my disciples indeed, and ye shall know the truth, and the truth shall make you free."

Does Oriental Theosophy propose to do anything more or better for us than this which we have seen offered to us in the Theosophy of the Christ? Can we be made sure that it would or could do even this for us? When the imprisoned John sent that question to him whom he himself, in an hour of inspiration, had prophesied was the promised Messiah, "Art thou he that should come, or look we for another? this was the convincing answer that the great Leader and Exemplar returned: "Go your way and tell John the things ye do hear and see: the blind receive their sight, and the lame walk, the lepers are cleansed, and the deaf hear, and the dead are raised up and the poor have good tidings preached to them. And blessed is he, whosoever shall find none occasion of stumbling in me." The wisdom of God and the power of God manifest in and through this loyal Son, was equal to the complete spiritual emancipation and healing of all those who turned to him for this blessing. And when he commissioned and sent forth his apostles to heal the sick and proclaim the good tidings, they went forth endowed with a high degree of the same power and wisdom, to witness for him in the carrying forward of his work.

So long as men were taught that they, each and all, had free access to this wisdom and power, the direct anointing or illumination and operation of the Holy Spirit in their own souls, without the need of any mediatorial hierarchy,, save the mediation of this knowledge opened to the world in Jesus the Christ, this mighty work of the apostolic church went forward unimpeded. But when ecclesiasticism lifted up its external standards of authority, as a substitute for the immediate revelation of God to the soul, and made the recognition of man-made creeds the basis of fellowship rather than the leading and inspiration of the Spirit, the illumination and Gifts of the Spirit declined; and its light was withdrawn from the world. These will return only with the renewal of the Apostolic life and doctrines. A return to the pure Theosophy of the Christ. Do these chosen representatives of the Thibettan Brotherhood who come to us with their high commission, come forth clothed with this needed Apostolic life and power, not only preaching the good tidings but engaging in direct works of beneficence and mercy, casting out devils and healing "all manner of sickness and all manner of disease among the people"? The doing of these was the answer of the Christ to the question, "Art thou he that should come, or do we look for another?" And these signs he affirmed, should follow them that believe and follow him. In his name and power they were to do these things.

These questions are asked in no spirit of opposition to any claim for the "Holy Brotherhood" and their treasured wisdom and power, nor to the Theosophical Society through which they are supposed to offer them to the world. We believe these men, whether deceived or not, are honest in the claims they make. But because these high claims remind us so fully of "the treasures of wisdom and knowledge," "the Power of God and the Wisdom of God," held and offered so full and free in the Theosophy of the Christ.

The writer already quoted points to the fact of the decline and almost utter extinction of the Apostolic life and power in the modern Church, as the very reason for the present necessity of opening to the world anew the treasured wisdom and power of the past, through this revival of Eastern Theosophy. He says:

"So long as the church, whether Catholic or Protestant, was dominant, so long as the ignorant masses were content to accept on faith the dicta of religion, we heard little of the conflict of religion and science. But the pendulum has swung from that blind superstition which fears and trembles but dares not question, to that crass materialism which dares not believe, and is too indifferent even to investigate. Our boasted liberty has degenerated into lawlessness; our national gods are Mammon and Materialism, twin monsters, whose insane votaries are forever clutching each others throat, and the *unholy trinity* that stares us in the face is *rum*, *riot*, and *ruin*. A doleful picture, indeed, but "'tis true, tis pity, and pity 'tis, 'tis true!' Every earnest, thoughtful soul, every true man and woman desires a remedy for this sad state into which we have fallen, this moral leprosy into which we are plunged. We are pointed to the churches and to the Christian religion, but alas! though many noble, earnest souls still cling to the forms, from which both life and soul have departed, though many are far better and few worse than their creeds, yet have these abuses in the body social and the body politic, not only grown apace with the churches, but they have crept into them, till the world is no nearer redemption to-day than it was a thousand years ago. We are pointed to the hospitals for the sick, infirmaries for the insane, homes for the orphans and the aged, as the work largely of organized church charity, yet beside these institutions flourish also alms-houses, penitentiaries, reform schools, Magdalen and foundling homes, institutions that are unknown and unneeded in many of those heathen countries to which we send missionaries. The very presence of these institutions is a confession that we do not know how to prevent crime, seduction, bastardy, insanity, and pauperage. [Was it not the angelic promise of the Christ, that he should save his people *from* their sins?] If we add to all this, the increase of crime, drunkenness, political and moral degradation, it may be well to inquire whither our boasted civilization tends? Had the organized churches presented an adequate remedy, backed by the power of divine truth, such a condition of things would have been impossible; but the trouble lies not in the nature and basis of that religion as originally laid down, and for the first three centuries exemplified, as will appear further on. 'Tis not because the churches are Christian, but because they are *un*-Christian, involved with the rest in Mammon-worship and materialism. * * * *

"These are the conditions that stare us in the face. Is

human life on this planet necessarily a failure? Are the nature, the ministry, and the destiny of man past finding out? Has not the time come for us to take counsel together?"

The essential truth of this picture cannot be denied. Some adequate remedy not now in the hands of the Christian Church is certainly called for. But will the magic of occultism, or the secret work of the lodge-rooms of the Theosophical society supply that remedy? Do these actually represent in modern form the working power of the Apostolic Church? Are the writings which the Theosophical society and the various "Chelahs" are now putting before the world, a good substitute for the New Testament? However, let us not refuse help and light from any source; but if, as this strong writer admits, the true life and power were lodged in the Christian Church of the first three centuries, can we do any better than return to the same divine fountain from which it drew its inspiration and its power, that rock of an inshining and indwelling Christ from which the Apostles drank, and following their successful example, drink at the same fountain and be ourselves renewed with its life-giving power?

This is not suggested in any spirit of sentimentality, or bias of a traditional prejudice, but a profound conviction that the mightiest revelation of God and the most momentous truth of human experience lies in this direction, to which the very misapprehensions of tradition have blinded the eyes of our modern world. Surely what *has* been done may be repeated under like conditions forever.

The exceptional life and character of him whom millions of men have united to call the Christ, is not only a fact, but the one transcendent fact of human history. And the Apostolic Church based upon the life, teaching, and spirit of that wonderful and God-anointed man, was itself the mightiest power known to history. The unparalleled marvels and victories wrought by those humble but inspired followers of Jesus, were not achieved by the power of the sword, physical force, or intellectual greatness; but by a power mightier than the sword and all physical agencies combined; and greater far than intellect in its loftiest attainment, with all its boasted science and philosophy.

It was the simple power of the Spirit which transformed cowards into heroes, and profligates into saints, ready and glad, if need be, to wear the martyr's crown, and lay all upon the altar of humanity in testimony of the saving power of truth. A power that casts out devils—the demons of lust, drunkenness, and every form of vice, and heals by its simple touch, all manner of sickness and all manner of disease, cleanses both physical and moral leprosy, raises the dead in sin and doubt into the light and blessedness of a true life, in one word, transfigures humanity and enthrones the kingdom of God and the light and joy of heaven in human life and society on earth.

That was no new force in history. It was only a fuller realization of the life and power of God in the souls of men, called forth by the influence of the one transcendent example of him who, through his own supreme loyalty to the Father, had entered fully into and become one with Him in Spirit and in life.

The story of the mighty Brotherhood of Himavat may be a literal truth; and those who have become adepts under their mysterious guidance and inspiration, may in their seclusion from the world, or in secret temple service, be able to perform prodigies, and develop a marvelous degree of occult power. But whether true or not. for near two thousand years has stood before the world the actual example of one who openly demonstrated, in his consecrated life *among the needy* of the world, the possession of the extraordinary wisdom and the power now ascribed to the mysterious "Brothers," whose safety and continued existence seems to depend, in the present state of the world, on their seclusion from it. This royal Son of God and divine Brother of Humanity, was not ashamed to call us brethren; did not, while on the earth, hesitate to descend in personal ministration to the lowliest and meanest of mankind. The Apostolic brotherhood established by him, were accomplished adepts of a power and inspiration, which did not require for their attainment and exercise, the secret initiation and mysterious processes of the lodge-room. The process of their enduement with spiritual wisdom and power was as simple and open as it was divine and effectual. This will be examined further on. In passing, we wish briefly to consider the specific reason for the cessation or withdrawal of the Christ power from the life of the Church that bears his name.

For a satisfactory answer to this question, we need not seek to find the special time in the early history of the Church, when this cessation began. We have the simple record of the Christ and his teaching, as well as that of the Apostles; and we have the present life and teaching of their successors in name, also, before us. The contrast thus presented is all that is needed.

Jesus taught and exemplified in his own life the enthronement of the kingdom of God, and the *doing* of his will, or entire obedience to the law of the Spirit in the personal life on earth ; and promised that all who followed him in this, should "not walk in darkness but should *have*" [attain] "the light of life." They should do the works he did and even greater. The Apostles followed his teaching and example, and their victorious lives became a witness to the truth of his words.

The Church of to-day, on the contrary, teaches as the Church of the past for many centuries has taught, that the kingdom of God and heaven are to be found only in another world; that this life is a mere probation in which to prepare specifically for the next; the eternal destiny of the soul to be sealed at death for weal or woe; and that man is to be saved from the effects of sin or retribution in the world to come, not for any merit of his own from a righteous life here, but through the merits of a righteousness fulfilled for him by the Christ in his stead, to be imputed to him through his faith in these merits by substitution. Christ having by the offering and sacrifice of himself, satisfied divine justice and paid the penalty of the sinner's guilt for violated law, God, it is claimed, can now maintain the dignity of His law, and forgive the rebels through the vicarious sacrifice and suffering of His Holy Son, provided they repent and accept of this truce, by faith, before death. But mark, even this salvation is not to be *from sin in this world*, but from its *consequences* in the next. Hence, the Church of to-day is not specifically a life saving and perfecting power for this world, but a "soul-saving" institution from the hell of a future world; forgetting that the abolition of the hells in this life would render salvation from any possible hell of the future unnecessary.

This doctrine of vicarious substitution, both in form and spirit, is diametrically opposed to the positive teaching of Jesus, which makes righteousness itself salvation, obedience to the righteous law of God in the doing of the Father's will in the personal and social life.

"For I say unto you, That except *your* righteousness shall exceed the righteousness of the Scribes and Pharisees, ye shall in no case enter into the kingdom of heaven." "Why call ye me Lord, Lord, and *do* not the things which I say?" "Not every one that saith unto me, Lord, Lord, shall enter into the kingdom of heaven; but he that *doeth* the will of my Father which is in heaven." "Therefore, whosoever heareth these sayings of mine and *doeth* them, I will liken him unto a wise man, which built his house upon a rock," etc. "And every one that heareth these sayings of mine and *doeth* them *not*, shall be likened unto a foolish man which built his house upon the sand," etc.

These authoritative words of the Christ, with the whole Sermon on the Mount, from which they are taken, and the full tenor of all his teaching most unmistakably emphasize the *doing* of the Father's will, and unity with him in a righteous life, as the only salvation possible or desirable for mankind, while not a precept or parable of his can be brought to sustain in the slightest degree this doctrine of substitution. As though it were possible for the absolute justice and goodness of the All-Father to demand or accept the punishment of the innocent for the guilty, or could impute the righteousness of the sinless to the sinner, or accept any as righteous who are not really so. But as righteousness of life is secured only through personal obedience to the law of right, no man can become righteous before God, except by his own act of obedience. If this were possible in the economy of God, then the very idea of justice would be a delusion and a sham, and the thought and talk of a changeless moral order a pitiable and unmeaning farce.

So long as man dwells in a universe of law he must inevitably reap what he sows. If he sow to disobedience of a righteous law, he will reap the inexorable penalty; and when he sees his mistake and sin and sows again to repentance and reformation, he will reap in return the forgiveness and restoration which the infinite and changeless love of the Father eternally secures. This is the one great doctrine of Jesus, so fully emphasized in his parable of the prodigal son.

Surely salvation from sin in this life, by lifting man above the power of temptation, as promised by the Christ, and exemplified in his own life, would prevent all consequences of sin in this world or any other. And this is the only salvation worthy of the name.

How is this to be accomplished but by the perfection of human life itself, through the unfolding and bringing forth of the divine or spiritual nature in that life. This was the simple doctrine of Jesus, and its truth and power were demonstrated in his own life, and also in Apostolic experience. This was the basis of the marvelous power of the Apostolic Church, which was a practical school for the unfolding and education of the spiritual life and its higher powers, or gifts of the Spirit; not for the sake of personal advancement in the building up and expansion of the sensuous life, but for the perfection of character and the mastery of the world.

The modern Church, on the contrary, has become so absorbed in its frantic efforts to save souls from the consequences of sin in another world, as to allow the supreme work of bringing the personal and social life of men to perfection in this world, to sink into secondary importance, if not to neglect it altogether. Indeed, the Church has become so absorbed in, and wedded to its ecclesiastical machinery and methods, and so blinded by the misconceptions of its traditional theology and creeds, as to have almost, if not entirely lost the true conception of the nature of the Holy Spirit and its Gifts and work in man. Hence the power and work of the Spirit is so feebly manifest in its life and ministrations.

One thing only has saved the Church from utter destruction as a religious institution. It has preserved, cherished, translated into many tongues, and spread among the nations, that priceless record and treasury of inspired lives and words which the past has given us, among which is the simple, unadorned story of the Christ and his blessed ministrations and words of comfort and spiritual wisdom to the children of men.

But that which most of all is of unspeakable value to

the race, is the revelation which the Christ has given us, not only in words of more than earthly wisdom, but in the demonstration of his own life, of the loving universal Fatherhood and perfect Providence of God, and the divine possibilities of men as children of God, with the law for the realization of these possibilities, in the universal experience of mankind.

The misinterpretation and consequent misunderstanding of the sacred and priceless record,—through the blind teaching of a false theology,—has involved the world in bondage to the letter, by which it has failed to catch its spirit, in any large and free sense. In spite of this, however, the influence of the book and the story of that one exceptional and perfect life, has kept alive the hope, and fed the spiritual intuitions and aspirations of mankind.

For this let us give the Church full credit, while we seek to break the shackles of a false and paralyzing theology, and by emancipating it from that terrible nightmare of mediæval ignorance and superstition, restore the Church if possible to its original freedom and inspiration as the true channel of a saving power in and to the world.

The object of this book, however, is not to discuss the problems of theology, philosophy, or ethics; but to more specifically consider the spiritual nature of man and his exalted possibilities as a child of God in the light of the living example and inspired teaching of the model Man, and by the specific study of the higher human powers in that light, to develop and define the processes by which they are to be brought to their highest degree of functional activity and vigor, and man lifted through this higher spiritual education and development into that supremacy and perfection of being which is his birthright.

CHRIST THE PERFECT WAY.

Right on the threshold of this important study, there is need also of warning, lest we approach with the wrong motive. The vice and danger of occult study, is and has been the seeking of power for personal ends. If self-denial and ascetic practices are found necessary to the attainment of power, they are cheerfully entered upon, not for the perfection of character they may help to secure, but for the attainment of the higher power which a selfish ambition craves. The following, from "Nature and Aims of Theosophy," will bear reproducing here:

"For be it remembered, there were always both the right and left hand paths to which this wisdom [knowledge] held the key. The former leading to Nirvana or the at-one-ment of man, and the regeneration of the human race: the other, Black Magic, leading at first to occult power, but finally and inevitably to everlasting destruction. The motto of the first is, ALL FOR TRUTH, AND TRUTH FOR THE SAKE OF HUMANITY: the motto of the second, ALL FOR POWER, AND POWER FOR SELF, AND THE DEVIL TAKE HUMANITY."

That it is God's will and purpose that man should attain complete, yea absolute mastery over not only himself, but the outward world and all his environments, ought to be apparent to every thoughtful person who believes in the Divine Wisdom and Providence. It was the emphatic message of the Christ. "Fear not, little flock," he says, "for it is your Father's good pleasure to give you the kingdom." "Ye therefore shall be perfect, even as your Father in heaven is perfect."

The original and therefore changeless purpose of God in man's existence in this world—as reflected in the mind of the inspired author of Genesis,—is thus clearly defined: "And God said, Let us make man in our image, after our likeness, and let them have dominion over the fish of the sea, and over the fowls of the air, and over the cattle, and over *all the earth*, and over every living thing that moveth upon the earth."

Man's very position in nature, since he is the head and controlling center of the organic world, as the brain itself is the organic head and controlling center of the animal body, is the emphatic testimony of nature in corroboration of this truth. It was doubtless this vision of man's position in nature which led the psalmist to exclaim, "Thou hast made him a little lower than thyself" [New Ver.]; "and hast crowned him with glory and honor. Thou madest him to have dominion over the works of thy hands; thou hast put all things under his feet." Now while this is the evident destiny of man, and God's purpose concerning him, it is not reasonable to suppose that he could or should come into this supremacy of being in the Father's kingdom, and dominion over nature under the divine government, except through obedience to the righteous laws of the divine economy, which express the Father's perfect will and method, both in nature and in man. Without this, there would be opposing activities and discord, destructive to the well-being of man himself. It is to those only who in spirit are conformed to His image, and His likeness, that are to be given this dominion. The whole object and discipline of life, under the gracious government and perfect Providence of the Father, is to bring or unfold man into this image and likeness, that he may safely have and exercise this dominion.

God having given man freedom of choice and volition in the whole sphere of his personal activities, cannot, without interfering with that freedom, bring man to that perfection of being in his own image and after his likeness, which he has designed and provided for him, only through the consent and co-operation of the man himself.

But should man seek to unfold his powers and attain dominion over the forces of nature for selfish ends, without regard to the honor of the righteous laws and government of the Father, it would be an unholy ambition; and he would be in spirit both a thief and robber. And were he allowed to attain this mastery of power, he would inevitably wield it to the ultimate destruction of himself and others, or, at least, to the destruction of their well-being.

Thus we find the eternal and unchangeable laws of the Father's righteous government and providence wisely and beneficently hedged about with wholesome penalties for their violation, as the needful means of the primary education and discipline of His children, and a preparation for the wise use of power when they are thus made ready for its possession.

We have the example before us of the Son of Man, who through *perfect* obedience came into possession of this power, and we see him use it only for beneficent ends. Indeed, supreme power can be attained and wielded only through obedience to the law of its activity under God, and that is universal and absolute good. So the will that would use the power of God, must be at-one with the will of God, which is infinite and universal *good* will.

Jesus revealed the secret of his exceptional power and greatness, when he said, "It is my meat to do the will of Him that sent me, and to finish His work." We can realize how safe supreme power was in his hands. He would not even use it to overrule and coerce the free wills of his enemies to save his own life; but when they had crucified him, he used that power to reanimate his body for the comfort and restoration of the courage, faith, and spirit of his dismayed, mourning and dispirited disciples.

Surely he who controlled the winds and the waves of the tempest-tossed sea, could have controlled or paralyzed the wills of his crucifiers and enemies; but being at-one with the Father, he would not interfere with the freedom of one of his brethren.

Now all men, equally with Jesus, are sent into the world by the Father, to finish his work in themselves and in their race, by personal co-operation with His power in the functions of their life, in obedience to the perfect law of that life. When the full lesson of obedience to divine law is learned, and the spirit of obedience is established, man will rise through this obedience or co-operation, into that freedom and supremacy of personal life that divine law and order was ordained to establish.

Through an understanding and intelligent application of the supreme law of co-operation with divine power, for the working out of transcendent results in individual and social experience, there is practically no limit to human achievement in the direction of good.

It is only through this human co-operation with divine Wisdom and Goodness, that disease and vice, poverty and crime, and every form of evil is to be banished from our world, and the kingdom of heaven enthroned in human life and society on earth. But how can this be done, save by the cultivation and development of the spiritual part of our being, which is his nature in us, and which alone can lift us into his image and likeness, and enthrone the law and love of righteousness in our lives ?

"And being asked by the Pharisees when the kingdom of God cometh, he answered them and said: The kingdom of God cometh not with observation; neither shall they say, Lo here! or there! for lo, the kingdom of God is within you."

In these words Jesus sought to correct the false impression which then rested in the minds of the Jewish people, even of the higher classes; that the kingdom of God was to be an external order of things, in a Theocratic government to be established by external agencies.

By diverting the attention of men from seeking the exclusive manifestation of God externally, to the recognition and realization of His presence in the soul as the inward spirit and life, Jesus sought to transfer the centre and motive of human effort from the plane of the external and sensuous, to the higher and internal plane of the spiritual. The internal and spiritual, being the permanent element and the essential nature of the true man, the unfolding and bringing forth of its latent powers in the personal life, can but exalt and bring that life in all its inferior or subordinate and external functions, to their highest degree of perfection and use. The true education and development of man, therefore, is from within; not from without.

It was the direct exercise and bringing forth of the central, inward, spiritual power of the soul, that illuminated the mind of Jesus, and clothed him with that marvelous wisdom and power which so astonished and perplexed the people who, familiar with his history, knew that they were derived from no external education or advantage.

"Whence knoweth this man letters, having never learned?" said the Jews, as they listened to his marvelous teaching in the temple. "And coming into his own country he taught them in their synagogue, insomuch that they were astonished and said, "Whence hath this man this wisdom, and these mighty works? Is not this the carpenter's son? * * * Whence, then, hath this man all these things?" "And he came down to Capernaum, a city of Galilee, and taught them on the Sabbath day. And they were astonished at his teaching: for his word was with power." We are told further that "he needed none to testify of man; for he knew what was in man."

Here, then, we have the example of a man possessing immediate knowledge of men and things by direct intuition, independent of all external sources of information. From a purely spiritual source within his own being, which he recognized as the indwelling Spirit of the Father, we see him endowed with a wisdom and power transcending that of all other men of recorded history.

KNOWLEDGE AT FIRST HAND. 41

This supremely illuminated Teacher assures us that the same possibility is latent in all men, awaiting only the application of the method of calling it forth, instituted and exemplified by him. "Be not anxious, therefore," he says, "as to what ye shall eat, or what ye shall drink, or wherewithal ye shall be clothed. * * * For your heavenly Father knoweth that ye have need of all these things; but seek ye *first* His kingdom" [which is within you], "and His righteousness" [perfect way], "and all these things shall be added unto you."

It is believed by some that Jesus must have acquired his exceptional spiritual insight, wisdom and power, through initiation in some branch of the secret Brotherhood of the East. But there is no historical hint, nor shadow of internal evidence from his teaching to sustain this belief. Both the internal and external evidences are against this supposition. In the first place, he was too supremely loyal to truth not to acknowledge and honor the source of his wisdom and power. In reply to the question of the astonished Jews, who evidently knew that he had had no such advantage, "How knoweth this man letters, having never learned?" he said, "My teaching is not mine, but his that sent me. If any man willeth to do His will, he shall know of the teaching whether it be of God or whether I speak from myself." Again he said to his disciples, "Believe me that I am in the Father, and the Father in me." "The words that I say unto you I speak not from myself, but the Father abiding in me doeth His works." No words could be plainer than these. To the direct illumination of the indwelling Spirit of the Father, he attributed all his wisdom and power.

In the second place, his method of inducting others into the same condition of inward illumination, and the direct teaching of the Spirit, was not the method of the secret mystic Brotherhood. He instituted no secret orders or initiatory processes; but opened wide the door of direct and immediate access to God, to all mankind. He bade each man recognize God the universal Spirit and Providence as his heavenly Father and friend; and his own life as the indwelling Presence of the Father. To recognize himself as the immediate child of God and the special object of his love and care, and as such to consecrate himself in faith and loyalty to this divine relationship. He promised that all who did this should thus become immersed into the full Spirit of the Father, which should "teach them all things," "guide them into all truth," "show them things to come," and "give them a mouth, and a wisdom, which all their adversaries should not be able to withstand or gainsay:" would endue them with power from on high, to witness for him as the Christ in doing in his name, or under his instruction, the works he did, and even greater. This simple method was fully illustrated in his own life and his promise practically fulfilled in Apostolic experience. The secret of his full induction into the spiritual life is revealed in the simple story of his open and public consecration, through John's baptism at Jordan; when coming out of the water, we are told "he prayed, and as he prayed the heavens were opened unto him, and the Spirit descended and abode upon him." Then was he led also into the wilderness, or a solitary place, by the Spirit, to be tempted of the adversary; that is to meet and vanquish at once and forever the temptations of the flesh and the selfish and sensuous life, the character of which was clearly revealed in the temptations which the record describes. When the victory was complete, it is written: "He returned in the power of the Spirit into Galilee, preaching the gospel of the kingdom of God," etc. The story of Pentecost illustrates the descent of the Spirit into and upon the personal lives of the disciples, and the corresponding experience of multitudes under their teaching. Illustrated also in the experience of Saul of Tarsus on his way to and at Damascus; where he gave himself in earnest prayer, in full consecration to the inspiration and leading of the Spirit.

Numerous experiments in modern times have demonstrated the possibility of educating the mind into a practical knowledge and mastery even of history, physical science, the arts, etc., by the development and exercise of the intuitive powers, independent of external observation and study, examples of which are given in the appendix.

In another place will be found a description of the essential and specific processes for the successful cultivation and exercise of the higher psychic powers, as the rudiments of, and an introduction to this higher spiritual education of man.

The supreme law of personal co-operation with divine power for the working out of transcendent results in human experience, and the principle on which it is based,—Faith,—were clearly taught by the Christ, and its certain and practical working fully exemplified and demonstrated both in his own and Apostolic experience before the world. The full and universal understanding and practical application of this great law and principle, however, adapted to the conditions of modern life in the higher education and perfection of mankind, is yet to come. It is hoped that the suggestions of this book may prove a step in this direction.

TRUE BASIS OF THE HIGHER EDUCATION.

There are three successive planes of consciousness and life, upon which man may dwell in the exercise of his faculties while in the flesh, each distinct and separate from the other, by discreet degrees or steps from the outward to the inward, from the lower to the higher. On one or the other of these, each man will and must locate and seek the treasures of his heart. Which shall it be?

The first is the plane of the physical senses, on which the existence of man as a conscious personality begins; and in the sphere of which he becomes individualized, and the several faculties of the mental, moral and social departments of his nature established in functional activity.

His consciousness of being on any plane of his development, is the result of the combined activity of all his faculties; and the report which these faculties give to consciousness, will depend upon the character of the sphere in which, and the plane on which, they are exercised.

As long as the activities of the soul are confined to the sphere of the outward world on the plane of the physical senses, man will be conscious only of this world and its phenomena; and failing to recognize any other realm, from sensible experience of his own, he is likely to deny the actual and even the possible existence of anything super-sensuous, however much others may testify to a higher experience. This constitutes the external man, whose standard of truth is the testimony of the physical senses and his deductions based upon them. This is also the sphere of physical science and sensational philosophy, and even the external and sensuous forms of religion.

The second is the plane of the occult; the sphere of the purely psychic functions and forces. The development of the sixth sense opens this sphere to the consciousness of man, by awaking the activity of his faculties on this interior and higher or super-sensuous plane, which by the observation and study of its phenomena, becomes a familiar and legitimate sphere of human consciousness and activity. This is the normal sphere of true and legitimate occultism.

The third is the plane of the purely Spiritual and Divine; the deepest and highest or most interior sphere of man's being, consciousness and activity; in which he comes to dwell and act in perfect unity and oneness with the Father. It is "the kingdom of God" which Jesus preached, the attainment of which he enjoined his followers to make the treasure of their heart, and so the supreme object of life and effort. This is reached by the opening of the deepest, inmost or seventh sense. It is the opening of the seventh seal of the book of life; first accomplished by the "lion of the tribe of Juda," which made him the Christ, or Divine Man. Our great forerunner who having himself entered in, opened and led the way for us to follow and attain the true Theo-Sophia,—the Wisdom of God. The specific steps which lead to the opening of these higher senses, and finally to the divine attainment, are the special subjects of consideration in subsequent pages.

As there are three distinct planes of human activity and consciousness, so man himself is a three-fold being. There are three distinct spheres of being or realms of activity that meet and are represented in him. On the one and lower side he is linked with the sphere of the animal, which touches and blend with his own; and on the other, the inward and higher side he is linked with the sphere of the purely spiritual, which is Divine.

The elements of the animal nature, which meet and mingle with his own, are spontaneously active and prominent in his life, because he begins his existence and the individualization of his powers as a personal identity, on this plane. The animal nature seems to have been as much a necessity, as a matrix for the depositing of the seed-germs of the human powers, and their evolution, as was the mineral kingdom for the vegetable.

The elements or attributes of the Divine Nature which meet and dwell within his own, are, on the contrary, so far as he and his faculties are concerned, latent; because the spiritual condition of a divine manhood is something to be attained by all men ; just as the qualities and possibilities of physical and intellectual manhood are latent in the child, awaiting development. The spiritual nature is to be brought forth and assume its rightful supremacy in the personal life, through illumination of all the faculties, by transferring the seat or centre of activity of the rational and moral powers from the plane of the external and sensuous life, to the internal and spiritual, as will be seen further on.

While the consciousness and the activities of man are confined to the sphere of the sensuous life, he is but an intellectual and moral animal. At his highest development and best estate on this plane, he is yet in the childhood stage of his true career as a child of God. He is in bondage to the fleshly life, dependent upon and the subject of physical conditions. He is still under the law of the animal life in which sensation is the standard of good and evil. His highest law of social and political economy, therefore, will be the law of expediency ; and his highest sense of justice, that of exact equivalents; the "pound of flesh," and "an eye for an eye."

That which constitutes the man proper, and separates him from the animal kingdom, is the possession of a rational and moral nature, capable of an indefinite unfolding, which makes of him a progressive being. The lines of his intellectual powers converge to a focus which we call reason; while the corresponding lines of his moral sensibilities converge to the focus we call conscience. As long, therefore, as reason depends wholly upon the impressions derived from the outward world through the five physical senses, for its knowledge *of* the world, making the testimony of the senses its standard of truth,—and conscience depends upon experience for its knowledge of good and evil, and upon external enlightenment for its standard of right,—just so long will man remain an intellectual and moral animal; because he is ruled by the law of the animal life. But when the intellectual and moral powers are lifted up to the plane of the spiritual, by transferring the centre of their activity from the outward to the inward life, they become illuminated by the light of the Spirit. The eye of reason is then opened to the clear vision of truth, and becomes INTUITION; and the heart of conscience is opened to the pure love of good and the clear sense of duty, and becomes INSPIRATION.

Pure Spirit, or God, is the inmost or central life of man, as he is of Nature. Man is the only being on our planet with faculties capable of recognizing the Divinity within. By his own desire and volition he has power to call it forth by uniting or entering into and becoming one with it. Thus the animal and sensuous part of his nature is also lifted up and transformed after the pattern of the indwelling divinity.

The state of savage animality, is but the infant stage of race development, and the most civilized condition of the sensuous life is still the stage of childhood. Even the opening of the sixth sense and the development and activity of the psychic powers upon this plane, the lifting of the mind from its dependence upon the external senses to the higher plane of the inward vision, and the mastery of occult science, may still measure but the immature period of its youth; but the true divine manhood of the individual and the race, begins only with the coming forth of the spiritual nature and the complete dominance of the spiritual life.

Thus man, as man, stands between two worlds, and partakes in a degree of the nature of both; the animal below and the Divine above. He has the ability, therefore, to unite and become identified with either. By uniting and blending with that which is within, he rises into all the freedom and perfection of divinity, and becomes a god, uplifting and perfecting all that is beneath him. In uniting and blending with the animal on the plane of the external, he falls into bondage and degradation; and becomes in comparison, a worm crawling in the dust.

> "The chain of being is complete in man,
> In man is matter's last gradation lost;
> The next step is Spirit! Deity!

Perhaps this three-fold nature and relationship of man will be better apprehended, by presenting the statement in another form, based upon the classification of St. Paul, Swedenborg and many other seers, as "body, soul and spirit," recognizing both a physical and spiritual body. In this classification, the soul is regarded as the real, permanent, self-conscious personality, inseparably united with an indestructible spiritual body, constituting a permanent and complete organism of which the physical body is but the external counterpart and material covering. The physical organs are the negative pole of corresponding invisible organs, which are composed of an ethereal semi-spiritual substance, constituting the active centre of those attractive and repellant forces that maintain the unceasing processes of nutrition and excretion in the physical body. The nervous system forms the medium through which these forces find organic expression and balance of vital activity, and the great nerve centres become the seat of the modifying and co-ordinating influence of mental action.

As the animal nature is conjoined with the life of man in the physical body, so there is also an animal soul which constitutes the animal nature in man. This animal soul dwells wholly in the physical or sensuous life, and is a necessity to the existence and perpetuation of the physical body. It supplies the physical appetites, propensities and impulses, so essential to the repair and reproduction of the body itself. Evil comes, not from the presence and activity of these functions, but from allowing their activity to predominate over the higher demands of the human soul.

The spirit in man is the indwelling, animating life of the soul, and of its indestructible organism, we call the spiritual body or form. It is the focalization of God, the universal Spirit in the soul of man, as His child. As the brain is the great co-ordinating centre and controlling organ of the physical body, so the rational and moral powers of the soul constitute the co-ordinating and controlling centre of the spiritual organism. Hence when the human soul gains and asserts its rightful and normal supremacy over the animal soul, the spiritual organism will also dominate the physical. The rational and moral powers, at the centre and throne of being, receiving their light and power from the Spirit within, will then hold absolute dominion over the entire domain of the personal life and its environments.

Substance in the form and condition of that which we call matter, seems to have been a necessity for the projection, condensation and individualization of Spirit into form and personal identity. Could the Universal Spirit otherwise re-produce itself in individual offspring, who must be differentiated from the parent source in form, though existing in, and being one in spirit with, the universal Life?

SPIRIT AND MATTER. 53

Spirit in its essence being abstract, impersonal and universal, requires some form of materiality and its limitations, to give a concrete individual expression of itself.

Form and limitation are absolutely essential to individuality; and these are impossible without the conditions of what we call materiality, however fine or ethereal this material may be. This must of necessity be a form or mode of substance separate and distinct from that which constitutes Spirit, in its naked essence. Hence the physical as well as the spiritual organism, was a necessity for the individualization of the soul and the establishment of its various powers and functions.

In the process of individualization or gestation and birth under the conditions of materiality and its limitations, the spirit becomes for the time, obscured. It awakes to consciousness as the faculties of the soul become individualized in the corresponding bodily organs, and unfolds as these organs become perfected through development as organic instruments or channels of the soul's activities. As these activities are at first and primarily on the most external and purely physical and sensuous plane, the physical senses being the avenues of their contact and communication with the outward world, they are thus under the temporary dominion of the animal life, which came to organic perfection before the human soul could be brought forth. Some one has said, "Spirit sleeps in the mineral, breathes in the vegetable, dreams in the animal, and comes to consciousness in man."

As before remarked: the human cousciousness is the result of the combined impressions derived from the activity of the soul's powers in contact with its recognized environment.

As the soul first wakens to the consciousness of its individual self-hood on the plane of the external and sensuous life, through the primary exercise of its faculties on this plane, its first consciousness is necessarily only of the external world. Its first birth into conscious life and self-hood as a personal spiritual identity, is on this plane. Hence the necessity of that higher spiritual birth announced by the Master, "Verily, verily I say unto you, ye must be born again." Except a man be born from above he cannot see or enter into the kingdom of God. The soul is therefore to be born into the consciousness of the spiritual life through the awakening and activity of its faculties on the inner and higher plane of the spiritual, by the opening and development of the inner senses of the spiritual organism which relate to that realm.

All physical development is but an external manifestation of a corresponding interior and invisible activity; and all physical forms represent corresponding spiritual realities.

The external atmosphere so essential to the existence

and activity of the physical body and its organs, and as a medium of communication with other bodies through the senses, must therefore represent a corresresponding internal atmosphere or ethereal medium, equally essential and vital to the activities of the spiritual organism and *its* senses. This is a necessity also as a medium of communication with the spiritual and internal organisms of other bodies, and the interior life of all things.

Whether this interior, ethereal medium of psychic vibration and spiritual activity be the "Space Ether" of the physical scientists, or not, its existence is as certain as the law of correspondence. It is an absolute necessity to the existence and activity of spiritual organisms.

As the existence of spiritual organisms cannot in the nature of the case be demonstrated to the senses, the spiritual instincts of the soul and the universal concordant testimony of seers, must be appealed to as evidence; and hence the necessity of the oracular manner in which this subject is treated.

The spiritual organism of man admitted, the interior atmosphere or ether, becomes an organic necessity for the full development and play of its activities, and as a medium of communication with corresponding spiritual organisms, and with the interior life and condition of all beings and things, animate or inanimate.

This ether, sometimes called the "Astral Fluid," being

vastly more subtle and diffused than the outward atmosphere, not only fills the inter-planetary spaces, but penetrates the densest substances, fills the interstices of all matter and holds its supposed atoms and molecules in its encircling sphere, something as worlds are embosomed in the soft embrace of their atmospheres.

The sphere of this "Astral Fluid" or spiritual ether, embraces the entire realm of the super-sensuous and the occult. It is the medium for the activities of the purely psychic powers and forces, and hence the medium of the silent communication of mind with mind,

It is the medium through which the soul comes in contact with, impresses itself upon, and in turn, receives impressions from the interior life and condition of all things and beings within the sphere of its personal activities.

The external senses are but the focalization of the mind outwardly, in and through the nerves and organs of sense. The physical organs do not see, hear, feel, etc.; the mind sees, hears, feels, tastes and smells in and through these organs.

As there is an internal organism with a corresponding medium of communication, when the perceptive powers of the mind are sufficiently individualized, unfolded and disciplined through external focalization, they may be turned within and become focalized inwardly, where they become a unit of activity, and develop the one all-inclusive sixth sense.

The "Astral Fluid" being the medium of an inner light, sound, sense of touch, taste, smell, etc., to the soul, the mind by this inward focalization of sense and its concentrated unity of action in a single direction, can produce on this medium, the vibrations of light, sound, feeling, taste, smell, etc., at will, and receive the same from all other objects with which it is in this inner communication. If it desire light it creates it by the vibration of that desire; so of sound, feeling, etc. The wonders of trance and somnambulism demonstrate this. The trance does nothing to secure this result but to lock up the external avenues of sense, and shut off from the mind all impressions from the outward world through the senses. The mind being thus liberated from its entanglement with sensuous impressions, and the attentien focalized inwardly, the all-inclusive sixth sense is awakened and the mind enters at once through this into untrammeled freedom of super-sensuous activity.

We have discovered and demonstrated that this inward focalization can be perfectly effected without the abnormal conditions of either trance or somnambulism; and without the full suspension of external consciousness. It is effected by the simple transfer of the attention from the external to the internal plane of mental activity, from the external to the internal medium of communication and contact.

Normal seership, or the inward vision in the normal waking state, is thus developed and made practical in daily life.

The development and exercise of the mental powers on this super-sensuous plane in the sphere of the occult, through the awakening of the all-inclusive sixth or psychometric sense, is as normal and legitimate as is the corresponding activity on the outward plane of the purely physical senses.

When this inward focalization is complete, the mind attains absolute supremacy over the body, and acquires perfect control over its sensations and functions. It can suspend or create sensation at will, in the whole or any part of the body. It can also control the memory, and retain or banish any impression at pleasure. These achievements, if there were no other reached by this process, would prove of incalculable benefit to the world.

But these are the least and simplest results of this attainment. The higher attainment of occult knowledge and power, the development of Intuition, the psychometric sense, clairvoyant vision, inner hearing, etc., etc., thus reached, so open the avenues to a higher education, and enlarge the boundaries of human consciousness and activity, as to fairly dwarf into insignificance the achievements of external science.

This condition gives the mind free access to knowledge at first hand ; and will ultimately render a thousand cumbrous external appliances entirely unnecessary and useless. Among these will be the telephone and telegraph ; as direct communication between mind and mind at any distance, will be the simplest matter of common experience.

Many of these things are now and have been for a long time, a common experience with eastern adepts, if any reliance is to be placed upon the accordant testimony of travelers.

This subtle medium of communication between mind and mind embraces the interior organism, and touches the springs of life in all structures, from the simplest plant up through animals to man. Hence in this state of inward concentration, man has the inherent ability to direct his attention to the internal condition of any being, plant, animal or man, and by focalizing the image or picture of his own thought or intense desire upon them, affect them for good or ill according to the nature of his desire and purpose. The vibrations from the thought of Jesus, focalized upon the fig tree, and penetrating to the springs of its life, so dried them up that it withered in a single night. That he had equal power to unseal and renew the springs of life, was demonstrated by the innumerable cases of immediate healing and restoration recorded of him.

He most positively affirmed the same power within

reach of all men, through the perfect following of his instruction.

There is a mental alchemy normal and legitimate to man, which when attained and employed to wise and useful ends, will make of him a true magician. But this power may also be attained and employed to base and selfish purposes, and for this reason the great master magicians of the ages have kept the method of attainment a secret, opening it to none except through initiation, in which the qualifications of the neophite for receiving this secret were put to the severest test.

The development and exercise of occult power to selfish ends, constitute "Black Magic." Mediumship, Necromancy, and Sorcery, are all perversions of the psychic powers of the sixth sense.

The development and exercise of all the psychic powers of this inner sense, may be attained under the motives of the selfish life; but the evil of their perversion will correspond in magnitude with the greatness of the attainment. If one sow to the selfish life in the use of these powers, he will of that life, sooner or later, reap destruction; but if he sow to the Spirit, he will of the Spirit reap the life everlasting; because it is a life forever held to the divine service of universal good.

Though all these powers of the sixth sense were attained, possessed and exercised by Jesus, this was not the plane on which he dwelt and exercised them.

He dwelt on and wrought and spake from the still higher and more interior plane of the Spirit.

The law of the spiritual life is universal and impartial love and ministration. No one can enter into that life without becoming transformed into the likeness and character of the Christ. Neither can one enter into and thus become transformed by this life except he desire it, even to the sacrifice of all else. No one, therefore, can come under the inspiration and dominion of the law of this life, without full emancipation from the law and motives of the selfish life. Hence, to seek and attain first the kingdom of God and his righteousness, which is the plane of the Spirit and its perfect life, all liability of perversion of any power is put out of the question. This includes also the possession of all the higher gifts.

This was the method of the Christ. Seek first the true life and all useful gifts will open to the soul as needed. In his method, therefore, there was no need or place for the secrecy and initiation instituted by the "Brothers." In the Theosophy of the Christ, there is no place for the motives of the selfish life to seek power for power's sake, but only to seek the true and perfect life, and through this the useful Gifts that come as the legitimate fruit of that life. True Christian Theosophy is the immediate life and revelation of God in the soul of man, as his true and loyal child.

Occultism and magic may be attained and mastered through obedience to the law of psychic development under the impulsion of self-will. But the kingdom of the Spirit can be entered only by the laying down of self-will, and the union of the soul with the one universal will of the Spirit, which is the will of God—infinite good-will.

The pugilist can as effectually train and develop his muscular power for the prize ring, as the athlete who trains and developes his powers for useful service, so long as he observes the law of physical development. So the unprincipled lawyer will as effectually develop his intellectual keenness and power, whereby to defeat the ends of justice, for selfish motives, as he who trains himself for the opposite course, so long as the law of intellectual culture is observed.

For the same reason all the psychic powers of the sixth sense may be developed and exercised, and a high degree of occult science mastered, with a selfish motive, so long as the simple law of psychic culture is observed. But in all these cases, physical, intellectual and psychical, the misuse of acquired knowledge and power, will sooner or later involve the actor in the ruin of the evil his perversion inevitably brings. No permanent good can, in the very nature of things, be attained and held, save in conformity to the law of truth and right. And as truth and right are designed to secure the perfect good of all, and can result in nothing else, to ignore these under any circumstances, and for any supposed immediate benefit, is a mistaken policy even from the standpoint of selfishness. "Righteousness exalteth a nation," says the proverb, "but sin is a reproach to any people." The same is true of individuals. But the eyes of a mind blinded by selfishness cannot always see the truth; and the selfish heart is deceitful above all things. So "there is a way that *seemeth* right unto a man, but the end thereof are the ways of death." There is no security nor safety save in righteousness of life; and there is no surety of this, save under the law of the Spirit.

The purely spiritual in man is the deepest, highest and divinest element of his being. Its cultivation, development and supremacy, therefore, in his life, can but exalt and ennoble that life. Indeed, the true destiny of man on earth cannot be achieved, nor the perfect life attained in this world or any other, save under the direct inspiration, guidance and power of the Spirit.

No greater mistake is possible, than the notion incurred by false religious teaching concerning God and the spiritual life, that the cultivation and dominance of the spiritual nature will destroy all the normal and legitimate pleasures of this world. The full supremacy and control by the spiritual, will not destroy or suspend a single function of mind or body; but on the contrary, it will, by preventing perversion, hold every function to its true and highest use, and bring the whole man, body and soul, to the highest degree of organic perfection and vigorous activity. It will destroy selfishness, subordinating the animal to the nobler supremacy of the human powers, and supply the motives of a perfect life. It will immeasurably deepen and expand the sphere of activity and enjoyment to man in all the normal and legitimate relations of his domestic and social nature. "Lord, who shall abide in thy tabernacle?" sings the Psalmist, "who shall dwell in thy holy hill? He that walketh uprightly, and worketh righteousness, and speaketh the truth in his heart." "And he shall be like a tree planted by the rivers of water, that bringeth forth his fruit in his season; his leaf also shall not wither; and whatsoever he doeth shall prosper."

The seeking of the spiritual life or kingdom of God, was not designed to be left until death approaches, but to be the crowning glory of life from childhood. "Suffer little children to come unto me," said the Christ, "and forbid them not, for of such is the kingdom of heaven."

As the spiritual nature is the deepest, noblest and most essential part of man, it is impossible for him to live his true and perfect life without it. While this has been the essential message of all inspired teaching since the world began, it was the especial mission of the Christ to exemplify this truth before the world,

The universal carnality of the fleshly mind has prevented the world from entering into the full understanding of inspired teaching, and hence the distorted views set forth in the great mass of religious teaching.

The cultivation and development of the spiritual nature, or of the human powers on the plane of the spiritual life, is as normal and simple a matter as the cultivation of music or any branch of art or science.

Jesus was no recluse or ascetic. He mingled freely with all classes of people, and entered into all their rational enjoyments and festivities. The charge of the exclusive and self-righteous Pharisees against him was that he was "a gluttonous man, a wine bibber, a friend of Publicans and sinners." "This man receiveth sinners and eateth with them," said they, reproachfully.

The kingdom of God, or the spiritual life as exemplified in him, did not forbid nor destroy any rational or legitimate enjoyment of life, but came to make man glad and joyful by the presence of a divine Guest, in all the legitimate activities of life. "For God sent not his Son into the world to condemn the world, but that the world through him might be saved;" saved to its true and perfect order. Man can be saved to the perfect life, only through his emancipation from the dominion of the fleshly and animal life, into the freedom and power of the spiritual, "The glorious liberty of the children of God."

As long as men do not recognize the existence of

God and his divine government in the world, they will and can have no motive for the laying down of self-will. But when God as Omnipresent Spirit and Providence, is recognized as the one supreme reality of the Universe, and the spirit in man as the only interpreter of the Being and Will, or Law of God, to the soul, he will have the true motive to seek the immediate inspiration and guidance of the Spirit. To make his will one with the divine and universal Will, and his personal life at-one with the Father's, that he may "be perfect even as the Father in heaven is perfect."

When this reconciliation or at-one-ment is effected, there will be no seeking physical power in such a life for the prize ring, no intellectual development for expert rascality, nor seeking mental illumination and supremacy for the purposes of Black Magic, no perversion of any department or power of our being; but the development and perfection of them all and their full legitimate application, to the ends for which they were given.

Man was endowed with the higher psychic powers for a wise and beneficent purpose, and hence their cultivation and wise use is a duty as well as a privilege. The sphere of a true occultism is as legitimate as that of physical science; and when made universal, will vastly extend the sphere and power of human activity, usefulness and enjoyment.

Neither are the higher psychic powers of the soul,

and the attainment of occult science and knowledge, any more liable to perversion than those of physical science or the bodily functions. Being a higher attainment, however, the perversion when made, brings the greater evil. Hence the wisdom and importance of the caution already given, to all who would enter upon this occult study.

So while we seek in the following pages to unfold in a clear and simple manner, the specific law and conditions for the attainment of mental illumination and supremacy, and the direct processes of psychic culture in the higher education, as they have been opened to us, we would specially emphasize the injunction of the Master: "Seek ye *first* the kingdom of God and his righteousness, and all these things shall be added unto you."

MAN A MICROCOSM,

AND WHAT IT INVOLVES.

Man is undoubtedly a microcosm. His three-fold nature,—body, soul and spirit,—has its correspondence in the three-fold character of the Macrocosm. These are, the visible universe of physical phenomena, the inner world of invisible realities, and the Divine Inmost, the realm of pure Spirit, the central inmost life of all beings and things, the throne of absolute Being,—the kingdom of God.

The external world of phenomena and form, is penetrated by and held within the embrace of the inner world of corresponding spiritual forms and invisible realities, of which the outward world is but the external manifestation and expression. This in turn is interpenetrated by and held within the embrace of the all-animating, sustaining, indestructible life and changeless being of God.

The inner world of active life and being, is the real world behind the veil of materiality through which it is manifest, an ever-present though invisible reality—invisible to the physical senses.

Thus, where there is a visible plant or tree there is an internal, invisible organism which is the real plant or tree of which the external is but the outward manifestation and physical expression. This inner organism is in turn the organized expression of its own essential life, the secret working of the divine inmost—the manifestation of God.

Life is not the product of organized matter. The organization of matter, the transformation of inert material into living substance, is a manifestation of an omnific spiritual energy, operating from within outwardly through an internal to an external organism; the internal being the specialized activity of the one universal Life of an Omnipresent Deity. The same is true of animal and man.

First, then, we have the outward physical world, which to the physical senses seems the only world. Then we have the inner or soul realm, the world of internal organisms and active forces, which though invisible to outward sense, is an everywhere present reality. This is the realm of the occult, in which the spiritual ether or inner atmosphere, is the medium of inward vibration and communication. It is the world not only of those internal organisms and active forces connected with outward forms and phenomena, but also of all living beings who have finished their immediate connection with the outward world, and casting off the shell of materiality, continue their existence as independent and indestructible spiritual organisms in the soul world.

In this realm, the human soul exists as an internal spiritual organism, as actually and fully while yet robed in flesh, as when finally disconnected therefrom. With this realm of internal realities, man is capable—as soon as his various faculties and powers become fairly individualized and established in functional activity—of coming into conscious communication through the awakening of what we have called the sixth sense, which is latent—when not active—in all men. Even some animals have given evidence of the possession of this sense.

This sense is awakened, as before intimated, by the inward focalization of the outward senses, in which act the five become one all-inclusive inward sense, the spontaneous manifestation of which in so many individuals—though not generally understood—has by common consent been named a "sixth sense." When this inward focalization is effected, the soul can see, hear, feel, taste or smell the objects and things of the inner world, as perfectly,—but with a vastly wider range of activity—as in the most familiar and easy play of the senses on the plane of the outward. In the state of inward concentration the mind can accurately perceive, and read with absolute certainty the internal or real character, quality and condition of all persons and things to which its observation is directed.

Finally, within and behind the soul world, behind and above all personalities and things, is the inmost and eternal realm of the Divine, Impersonal and Absolute, the all-animating, sustaining Life and ubiquitous Presence of Deity, the infinite within, the sphere of inextinguishable Light, of ineffable Blessedness, and unutterable Beatitude of Being,—the kingdom of God.

Man as a microcosm, is a re-production in miniature of the three-fold Macrocosm; a child of the infinite Father and Mother; the universe itself being a living organism, in which Wisdom and Love are conjoined in eternal Fatherhood and Motherhood, the life-giving, life-sustaining and directing power of all existence.

The inmost life or spirit in man is, therefore, the specialization of the infinite Spirit or Parent Life in the soul of man as its offspring in organized activity, for the reproduction of the Divine Nature in children, capable of unfolding in this image and likeness, and so of entering into and dwelling in conscious communion, fellowship and unity of life with the divine Wisdom and Goodness.

Thus man by virtue of his three-fold nature is vitally related to, and can enter into conscious communication with the corresponding three-fold spheres of the great Macrocosm, around, within and above himself, of which he is a living part, each sphere being essentially reproduced and represented in him.

Man in his inmost and essential life is one with God. In the combination of his faculties and functions which constitute his organism and form, he is a personal identity and individuality, and as such, differentiated from the Parent Life in the consciousness of this personality.

This substantial organism of combined powers and functions, was a necessity for the establishment of a separate and distinct personal consciousness. The evident object, therefore, of the existence, development and perfection of the human organism,—beginning with the more external and ephemeral, and rising to the internal and indestructible,—is for the bringing forth and external embodiment of the attributes of pure Spirit, in the self-conscious personalities of men as children of eternal Love and Providence.

It is the coming forth of that which is within and permanent, to dominate and use that which is without, for the development and perfection of the organism, and the extension of the sphere and dominion of the personal life. This constitutes true growth in man, in harmony with the divine and universal order.

The human consciousness, however, being at first awakened only to the recognition of the outward world by the combined activities of the mental faculties on that plane, must be brought to the recognition, also, of this higher truth before the soul in the exercise of its freedom of choice and volition, can intelligently co-operate with the indwelling Spirit of the Father to this end.

Man certainly has the inherent capacity, by virtue of his three-fold nature, not only to dwell in the outward world and become familiar with and possess its treasures, but also to step behind and within the veil of materiality, and master the secrets and possess the treasures of occult knowledge and power, and also to enter into communion with the master spirits of the ages who have attained victory, honor and immortality in the world of mind.

Infinitely more and above all else, is that supreme possibility—when man shall awake to its full recognition and set his heart upon its realization—of entering through his inmost or spiritual nature, into conscious unity of life, and unfettered communion and fellowship with the Father; and with the vast and mighty Brotherhood of those who have risen into this conscious oneness of life in God.

Through this inward communion and fellowship, by thus partaking consciously of the One Supreme Life, he will bring the fulness of the Divine into every part of his being, and crown every power of mind and heart with its supreme attributes of wisdom, goodness and power.

This will confer on him all the gifts of the Spirit, and clothe him with power to overcome and enter into his dominion and thus fulfill his destiny as a child of God.

It was this experience that constituted the opening of the heavens—the sphere of the Divine—unto Jesus; and the descent and continuance of the Spirit upon him,—into and upon all the powers of his being. This is what is meant in the New Testament by "the gift of the Holy Spirit." This is "the promise of the Father, which," said Jesus, "ye have heard from me: for John indeed baptized with water, but ye shal be baptized with the Holy Spirit."

This also makes clear the full significance of that promise of Jesus to his disciples: "Ye shall receive power when the Holy Spirit is come upon you, and ye shall be my witnesses," etc. Also, that statement concerning the Christ himself: "And Jesus returned in the power of the Spirit into Galilee: and there went out a fame of him through all the region round about." "He came into Galilee preaching" this very "gospel of the kingdom of God, and saying, The time is fulfilled, and the kingdom of God is at hand, repent ye," that is, turn about, "and believe in the gospel." "And Jesus went about all Galilee, teaching in their synagogues, and preaching the gospel of the kingdom, and healing all manner of sickness, and all manner of disease among the people. And his fame went throughout all

Syria: and they brought unto him all sick people that were taken with divers diseases and torments, and those which were possessed with devils, and those which were lunatic, and those that had the palsy; and he healed them."

This illustrates something of the nature of the power conferred on man by the Spirit, as exemplified in the personal experience of him who first preached it in all its fulness and significance.

This was not to be the exceptional experience of the Christ, but was to be fulfilled in the experience of *all* his faithful followers and disciples. "These signs shall follow them that believe," etc. Through faith, and loyalty to him in his teaching and example, they were to do the works he did, and even greater. This at least was his positive assurance; and its practical realization in Apostolic experience demonstrates both its truth, and its possibility for all. "And by the hands of the Apostles," we read, "were many signs and wonders wrought among the people. * * * And believers were the more added to the Lord, multitudes both of men and women. Insomuch that they brought forth the sick into the streets, and laid them on beds and couches, that at the least the shadow of Peter passing by might overshadow some of them. There came also a multitude out of the cities round about unto Jerusalem, bringing sick folks, and them which were vexed with unclean spirits; and they were healed, *every one.*"

The cause of the decline of the gifts and power of the Spirit since Apostolic times, has already been noticed.

In spite, however, of the paralyzing influence of a despotic ecclesiasticism, instances of a corresponding experience have not been wanting in the lives of a faithful few, through all the intervening centuries from that day to our own; in which there are happily abundant signs on every hand of a revival of the Apostolic faith and spirit. Theological dogmatism and priestly arrogance are fast losing their hold on the mind of to-day, through the rapidly growing spirit of independent thinking on matters of religion, as well as the common affairs of life.

Happily no theological belief, no intellectual training, no attainment of occult knowledge is needed, as a preparation for "the gift of the Holy Spirit;" but the supreme desire of the heart to be at-one with the Father in spirit and purpose, the will to do his will, and complete his work in the personal life and the life of the race.

Many have sought the gifts and power of the Spirit not for the honoring of the Father and the cause of humanity, in a righteous and consecrated life, but for personal ambition and the gratification of self-will. Indeed there is such a thing as self-will in the vaulting ambition and subtlety of the selfish spirit, asserting its oneness with God, but practically making self that one. The world has had and still has abundant illustrations of such insane assumption and fanaticism in its would-be leaders.

It has been said that this was the delusion and fanaticism of him whom we have called the Christ. But it should be remembered that humility was the one supreme characteristic of Jesus. That he ever sank his personality in the principle and the cause he gave himself in life and death to establish. While he claimed unity with the Father, it was first and last, through the subordination of his own will to the will of the Father. "It is my meat to do the will of him that sent me, and to finish his work."

In his deep and full recognition of the eternal supremacy of the Father, he sought through unreserved consecration to the cause of truth and righteousness, to honor the Father's name and government in his life and work. "I can do nothing of myself," he said; "the Father abiding in me doeth his work."

The divine law of exaltation through humility, which he proclaimed, was fully exemplified in his own humble and consecrated life. "Whosoever exalteth himself shall be abased; and he that humbleth himself shall be exalted."

Because he gave himself in entire and unreserved consecration to the service of humanity in the name and spirit of the universal Fatherhood of God, and the divine Sonship and Brotherhood of mankind, making himself "servant of all." "God hath made this same Jesus both Lord and Christ."

The ability to acquire deep truths and attain occult knowledge and power, is native to man as already shown, and will be further illustrated in another place; but when such attainment is turned to the promotion of self instead of the universal good, sooner or later it will involve that self in utter defeat; and the depth of the fall will correspond to the height of previous attainment. "For whosoever will save his life," or self, "shall lose it," but "whosoever shall lose his life for my sake and the gospel's, the same shall save it."

Let every seeker after the higher life and its achievements and victories, seek first the full baptism of the Holy Spirit, which is free and open to the weak and the strong, the lowly and the great alike; laying down self-will that it may be merged into and become one with the universal and impersonal will of the spiritual life, which makes the interests and demands of the neighbor and self, one and the same.

This will remove all liability of perverting any gift or power, through the selfish spirit, and by opening the consciousness to the in-dwelling light and power of God in the personal life, will lift the soul to the supremest height of conscious power and divine guidance, and enable it to bring all the faculties of its nature, external and internal, to their highest degree of perfection and activity.

Having considered the law of permanent spiritual achievement, we will close this part of the subject by presenting the true key to the higher education and attainment it involves.

The key to success in the line of all mental and spiritual achievement, is CONTROL OF THE ATTENTION. The ability to concentrate and hold the attention upon any given point at will, and resist all diverting tendencies and desires, is an absolute necessity to high attainment and rapid progress. Happily this is an art that all may acquire by resolution and persevering effort. The very practice itself is a wholesome and efficient mental discipline.

The key to this acquisition, and its subsequent application to all future achievement, is DESIRE and FAITH. Desire is prayer, and the only true and real prayer; so that all men pray whether aware of this truth or not. It is simply a question of the prayer being wise or foolish; since all earnest prayer is, in a sense, and a very practical sense, answered. As a man sows so shall he reap, is an inevitable law, and every desire focalized in thought is a seed sown.

As desire is prayer, so faith is the expression or exercise of confidence and trust. Hence an earnest desire focalized in thought with confidence and trust, that is, in the full assurance of its realization in experience, is the prayer of faith. And, "according to your faith be it done unto you," is the divine provision. "Therefore," said Jesus, "what things soever ye desire and ask for, when ye pray, believe that ye receive them and ye shall have them."

The true basis for this confidence and trust, or "assurance of FAITH," is the recognition of the supreme fact that every normal and legitimate desire or demand of our lives, is infinitely provided for in the Divine Economy, and will be fully met under the proper conditions. The law of demand and supply is as universal as the law of gravitation, but like all laws, operates under and through established conditions.

Some prayers belong to the realm of mental alchemy, and are answered through the operations of the silent forces of mind and Spirit; others belong to the sphere of external effort, and are answered only through such effort. In both cases it is human co-operation with divine law. The desire for physical healing, for spiritual illumination, pardon for sin and wrong-doing (except when against a fellow-being), when fully focalized in thought, with perfect confidence and trust in the supreme power within, is fully met and answered in the subtle alchemy of mind and spirit. The fulness and immediateness of the answer will correspond with the strength of the desire and the faith in which it is focalized or expressed,

"In God we live, move and have our being." The spirit, which is the inmost or essence of our being, is the focalization of God in us, and is, therefore, potential with his omnific energy and wisdom, to be evoked and called forth by the inward concentration of desire and confidence—the prayer of faith. "The prayer of faith shall save the sick, and the Lord shall raise him up; and if he have committed sins they shall be forgiven him." The power is of God, who "is able to do exceeding abundantly above all that we ask or think, according to the power that worketh in us," but the desire and faith, or personal co-operation, are with us.

It is just as essential that we should put forth this prayer of faith for healing, or for spiritual illumination, to secure the result, as it is that we should put forth the proper effort to secure food for the demands of nutrition, or for the supply of any other necessity. "If any of you lack wisdom, let him ask of God, who giveth to all liberally and upbraideth not; and it shall be given him. But let him ask in faith, nothing doubting; for he that doubteth is like a surge of the sea, driven by the wind and tossed."

If the desire be for the healing of another, the exorcising of an evil habit or enslaving appetite, the lifting of a deep sorrow or heavy burden from the soul of one that is cast down, the conversion of a sinner, the promotion of a humane enterprise, the moving of others to deeds of justice or benevolence, or the securing of any good by the moving of men and women to such impulses, etc., we have but to silently and intently focalize this desire with perfect confidence, upon the one supreme Spirit which embraces all, and is focalized in each, to secure this result. The spirit within clothes every true desire, when expressed in faith, with power to accomplish its end.

All these things are within the sphere of a true mental and spiritual alchemy, and are readily effected by the silent and potent forces of mind and spirit, set in operation by earnest desire and faith. If there is a work for us to perform, whether by brain or muscle, the concentration of desire and faith upon the inward spirit, calls forth and fully endows us with the power and wisdom to accomplish the work.

We should remember that every faculty and power of our being has its roots in the inward spirit, and so can take on a divine activity, that the central life and power of every faculty is spirit, and that spirit in man is so much of God in us. Whatever God does for us, therefore, he must do in and through the activities of his life in the functions of our own being, from the spirit within. Realizing this we shall not look out and away for a far-off God, but shall turn within and find him at the centre of our own being, our own essential life—an indwelling God.

We have but to recognize this supreme yet simple truth, and to put forth our efforts and exercise every power, in full confidence of his strength to sustain us in every good word and work, to realize the fulness of that help.

The spirit within us is the stored life and energy of God, to be liberated and brought forth into every faculty and function of our being, through the concentration of desire and faith upon it, which this understanding enables us to do.

Whether it be for the illumination of the mind, the enlightenment of the moral sense, the healing of the body, or the clothing of our whole being with a superhuman energy, for some extraordinary emergency or unusual work, the needed supply is ever ready in the spirit, or God within.

If we realize that God is within our life by his spirit for this purpose, through our co-operation with him by desire and faith, and if we realize further, that without this co-operation, or by the indulgence of doubt or distrust, we shut this out, we can readily see that the whole matter lies in our own hands.

Results will correspond with our recognition, desire and trust on the one hand, or ignorance, doubt and fear on the other. We limit the divine activity within us, or in the functions of our life, by our doubts and fears, and open ourselves to, and call it forth in its fulness, by our desire and faith. Truly, "As a man thinketh in his heart, so is he."

Thought is of the head, but desire is of the heart; and desire is the motive power of the life. Thought is awakened by desire, and may become either its servant or its master; and desire in turn may be awakened by thought.

Desire is the prompter of all effort, and "as a man thinketh" and desires, so will be his effort. His application and perseverence will be in proportion to the strength of his desire and faith, or confidence of final success. However strong the desire, if he indulge in doubt of his ability to succeed, and think only of failure, his effort will be correspondingly inefficient, and the result a failure.

As a man's thinking in his heart determines the result of all his efforts, the importance of the cultivation and exercise of faith, as enjoined by the Master, cannot be over-estimated.

The true basis for this faith is the understanding and realization of the supreme truth, that through true mental co-operation, the spirit within clothes every normal desire and its legitimate efforts with divine power of attainment. "Have faith in God," who operates in man only in and through the spirit within him, "and nothing shall be impossible unto you," was the positive affirmation of the Christ. Hence, also, the importance of training the desires of the heart for the true riches. "For where thy treasure is, there will thy heart be also." "Keep thy heart with all diligence; for out of *it* are the issues of life." "Ye cannot serve God and Mammon."

The concentration of attention in desire and faith, upon any legitimate object, is the key to all achievement and attainment. The realization in thought of the potential energies of the human spirit, and the concentration of attention, desire and faith, in the appropriate effort to bring them forth in the development of a God-like life and character, is the true work of a child of God. "Be not therefore anxious, saying, What shall we eat? or, What shall we drink? or, Wherewithal shall we be clothed? For after all these things do the Gentiles seek; for your heavenly Father knoweth that ye have need of all these things. But seek ye first his kingdom and his righteousness; and all these things shall be added unto you."

The method of education and attainment adopted by the world, is external and sensuous; but the method introduced and successfully practiced by the Christ and his Apostles, was internal and spiritual.

The absolute mastery of the external and physical can be attained only by first securing the supremacy of the internal and spiritual. "Seek first the kingdom of God," etc., which is this spiritual supremacy.

God, as pure Spiritual Being, is the Supreme Power and arbiter of the Macrocosm, and rules it absolutely from within. So man as the child of God must come to the realization of his own spiritual being, and rule from within, before he can become the absolute master and arbiter of the microcosm—to which he is appointed. "Ye therefore shall be perfect as your Father in heaven is perfect."

ELEMENTS OF CHRISTIAN THEOSOPHY.

That "God is," and that he "is Spirit"; and that man is the direct offspring of God, and, therefore, in his essential being spiritual and divine, is the root proposition of Christian Theosophy, from which all its deductions concerning the life, powers and destiny of man are drawn.

"God is Spirit," not a spirit—an individuality among other individualities—but Eternal and Primordial Substance and Being, omniscient, omnipotent, omnipresent, and as such both Personal and Impersonal. As impersonal Being he is the original self-existent substance of Life, Intelligence, Goodness and Power, from which all existence and subsistence are derived. As Divine Personality he is the illuminating Presence and sustaining Power of all conscious Being, the eternal, all-embracing Ego, Consciousness or I AM of the universe, holding unceasing vigilance and care over all his dependent creation; a Providence and Economy which is absolute and perfect, wanting nothing, so that not a sparrow can fall nor a single hair perish, without his knowledge and care.

The recognition and realization of this truth is indispensable to a true understanding and progress. Without this understanding, man, as a rational and morally responsible being, could not intelligently co-operate with the divine Providence to promote in himself that perfection which belongs to him as a child of God. "Ye therefore shall be perfect as your Father in heaven is perfect."

This recognition of the supremacy and absolute perfection of the Father, and the consequent subordination and dependence of his human children, tend to induce in man a true spirit of humility and self-abnegation. Only through this spirit, the Christ assures us, can he rise to the realization of divine fellowship and mastery.

This paradoxical law of divine realization for man— the yielding up those things which seem to constitute his life on the subordinate and outward planes of his being, that he may find his true life in oneness with the divine life, is based upon the recognition by man of the absolute perfection of the divine wisdom, and the relative imperfection of his own, which leads him to choose to do the Father's will instead of his own, because he believes in and trusts the Father's perfect wisdom and goodness. He need not believe it right merely because the Father wills it, but he does need to believe the Father wills it because it is right. This is genuine faith in God, and prompts to that obedience to his righteous law of life which serves to unite the free life of man with God, and exalt him to the full realization of his destiny as a child of God—absolute supremacy in the Father's kingdom.

GENESIS OF MATTER.

If we accept the Christian affirmation that in God we live, move and have our being, we must admit that all being exists in him alone, and that its manifold forms are so many modes or conditions of spiritual manifestation. Hence that which we call matter, and which in its primordial condition is invisible and impalpable substance, may be considered as the precipitation or condensation, so to speak, from their original etherealized condition in Spirit of the elements from which the material universe is formed.

Thus matter may be regarded as a mode or condition of spiritual substance, made visible and tangible to sense for the specific ends and purposes of creation, but capable of returning to its original, invisible and impalpable state in Spirit when these ends shall have been accomplished. "For the invisible things of him since the creation of the world are clearly seen, being perceived through the things that are made, even his eternal power and divinity." "For the things which are seen are temporal [temporary states of being]; but the things which are not seen are eternal."

CREATION.

Creation may be defined as the thought of God differentiating itself into the innumerable forms which constitute creation. Man is the ultimate of this differentiation, having the potential attributes of the Father.

THE HUMAN EGO AND ITS EVOLUTION.

The Ego of man is the I Am of self-consciousness existing in organic relations with the material orders beneath him, and the spiritual ranks above him. In proportion, therefore, as this ego becomes absorbed in the things of the outward world, and the purely physical sense of life, does the soul become mundane, conscious only of the outward world as it appears to the sensuous vision, and deems it the only reality.

On this plane of consciousness, the indwelling divinity is limited in its manifestation or organic expression, to the purely sensuous sphere, and the soul or self-conscious personality becomes imprisoned in the body, and held in bondage to flesh and sense. That which was made and designed for service, becomes the master through the voluntary servitude of the real master himself.

On the other hand, as man awakes to the recognition of his spiritual nature, and becomes absorbed in the eternal realities of spiritual being, he becomes conscious of the life of God in which he is insphered, and thus of his own inherent divinity and essential identity of being, with the Father. Through this opening of the spiritual consciousness and understanding, he merges into light, freedom and power. The soul then asserts its supremacy, achieves its emancipation from the limitations of flesh, sense and the animal or purely sensuous life, and rises into the glorious liberty of the sons of God.

BODY, SOUL, SPIRIT,

AND THE RELATION OF THE HUMAN EGO TO THE DIVINE EGO.

As the informing, animating and sustaining life of the soul is pure Spirit, the physical body is constructed by, and held in this life of the soul around the indestructible spiritual organism as a medium of communication and contact with the outer world, while the soul is acquiring its primary education and discipline in the school of the senses. The body and its senses become subordinated to the soul and its service just in proportion as the soul itself comes to realize its true relation to them.

The human soul is a self-conscious spiritual identity, endowed with rational, moral and inspirational powers, being differentiated from, yet existing in, the Divine Being.

The pure spirit which animates and illumines the soul, is the focalization or inshining radiance of the Divine Consciousness—"the bright Effluence of bright Essence increate"—which, when realized by man brings him into unity with the Father. "Surely there is Spirit in man and the inspiration of the Almighty maketh intelligent." "Know ye not that ye are a temple of God, and that the spirit of God dwelleth in you?"

"Thus, the soul is the ego of the body, the spirit is the ego of the soul, and God is the Ego of the spirit." These three are one, one in nature, and should be one in fact or consciousness. The perfect wisdom and goodness of the Father rule the spirit, WHICH BEING ALWAYS AT-ONE WITH GOD, is the true light and guide of the soul. "The true light, which lighteth every man coming into the world."

THE DUALITY OF MAN,

AND HIS RELATION TO THE WORLD WITHOUT AND THE WORLD WITHIN.

The material body, in which the soul is individualized and differentiated from the Father, is begotten and transmitted through human parentage on the plane of animal generation, and consequently is subject to the law of the animal life. Hence the organic senses, tendencies, and limitations of the external man, are the proper subjects of external education and discipline. But the internal and real man, the soul itself with its divine possibilities, as already intimated, is the direct offspring of God, and, therefore, the subject of a divine education under the inspiration and guidance of the Father.

The birth of the soul into its first consciousness of personal existence is, however, within the sphere and on the plane of the senses. Hence in this primary condition it is conscious of purely physical sensations alone. But as it unfolds, there come to it vague but positive intimations of a possible condition of conscious activity vastly transcending the limitations of the senses. These super-sensuous hints and impressions kindle inextinguishable aspirations in the soul after a higher freedom and supremacy, and happy is that man whose faith and hope in a higher condition of being lead to practical efforts for its attainment. "For he that seeketh findeth," are the words of inspired wisdom and authority.

The permanent awakening of the soul to this higher spiritual consciousness, or the spiritual sense of being constitutes the second or spiritual birth, referred to by Jesus in his conversation with Nicodemus, by which man comes into a full realization of his divine sonship and transcendent possibilities.

THE PERMANENT BASIS OF CONSCIOUSNESS,
AND THE TRUE EDUCATION IT SUGGESTS.

The first object then, of all true education should be to establish the conditions whereby the spirit may enlighten and rule the soul and the soul in its spiritual consciousness and supremacy rule the body, and so the perfect will of the Father be done on earth as it is in heaven. In this way only will the true education and destiny of man on earth be achieved.

The evolution of the human ego as it emerges from the conditions of materiality on the plane of animal life, is step by step up the successive stages of an ever-opening and expanding consciousness. These successive heights of consciousness to which the soul is lifted by its unfolding life, are not outward, as at first it may appear, but inward. Through them the soul attains higher and still higher altitudes of vision and comprehension of the outward, until it reaches the central, divine and permanent ego, and conscious unity with the Father.

From the first motions of the personal life at the dawn of conscious being, it is in reality the central, spiritual or divine ego unfolding from within, as the organic conditions of brain and body yield to its transforming and perfecting power, and become more and more fitted to give expression to its attributes of intelligence, affection, aspiration, and worship.

In this process of soul development, the Father is forever giving himself to his children, and seeking through their own consent and co-operation to reproduce himself in them.

As fast as they feel and obey the influence of his spirit, does he work in and through them "both to will and to do of his good pleasure."

While the personal sense of permanent being, which forms the basis of self-consciousness, must proceed from the central and divine indwelling life, the immediate consciousness is the product of the combined activity of the various faculties of the soul. But, as the physical senses are the avenues through which the impressions of the outward world flow in to awaken the psychic functions of the brain, and the senses themselves are based in the animal life, the influence of the animal nature is more sensibly felt on the plane of primary self-consciousness, than the inward spirit to which it stands as a resisting power.

THE LIMITS OF HUMAN RESPONSIBILITY.

The sphere of self-consciousness and volition, is the true sphere of personal responsibility, because there is within it conscious freedom of choice in the mode and direction of the personal activities. Man is at liberty to turn within and receive and follow the leading of the spirit, or free to yield to the solicitations of the animal nature.

Every man is conscious of these apparently conflicting tendencies of his nature, and that his choice entails personal responsibility. He feels a sense of defeat and degradation when he has yielded to the animal against the protest of the spirit. He feels also a sense of dignity and noble achievement when through spiritual inspiration he has subdued and overcome the clamor for personal indulgence and won a victory over his lower nature. Thus is verified the Apostolic statement that the flesh lusteth against the spirit and the spirit against the flesh, and the fact of personal responsibility vindicated in the universal experience of mankind.

The only pathway to human achievement or true development and progress, is therefore disclosed to the personal consciousness of men, the truth of which universal experience is a perpetual confirmation. This highway of holiness is entire consecration to God and personal co-operation with his Spirit in the inward life, in overcoming the resistance of the animal and the physical, bringing them into complete subjection to the soul, and perfecting the body as an organic instrument for the higher activities of the soul, in the work of achieving complete mastery over all environments.

This emphasizes the importance of the early and proper training of the human will in the supreme lesson of life, obedience to and co-operation with established laws. The Master himself attained his transcendent life, and achieved his marvelous victories through this perfect obedience to the divine voice within. He said of himself, "It is my meat to do the will of him that sent me, and to finish his work." In this he stands as "the way, the truth and the life" for all men. Each man has thus to finish the Father's work in and through himself, by this personal co-operation.

In this way man gains the mastery not only of his own physical organism, but may measurably control the phenomena of the outward world by which he is environed. Thus is fulfilled the purpose of the Father in his existence, as reflected in the inspired vision of the writer of Genesis, as previously quoted.

FINAL ANALYSIS OF THE HUMAN CONSTITUTION.

In this analysis of man as "Spirit, soul and body," authorized by St. Paul the Christian Hierophant, we recognize the Spirit as the indwelling, informing and sustaining energy of life, or the creative, enlightening and redeeming power of God in the Life.

That which we call the soul is the organic personality, or that combination of psychical organs and powers, differentiated from, yet existing in the Divine Being, and whose co-ordinated activities constitute the self-conscious and pre-conscious personal life.

The physical body is the external counterpart and material envelope of the spiritual organism, derived from the outward world, woven into and held around the indestructible spiritual form by the indwelling and divine energy of life, as a flexible covering and organic instrument through which the soul comes in contact with and handles the grosser elements of the physical world, while acquiring its earthly education and discipline.

The physical senses and the organic functions of the animal life previously unfolded and perfected, serve as a matrix for the deposit and individualization of the human powers; something as the mineral kingdom preceded and became a matrix for the seed-germs, and the evolution of the vegetable kingdom. The unfolding attributes of the human soul, therefore, were not evolved from the animal nature and the sensuous life, but were involved and potential in the divine germs of faculty and function as deposited direct from the Father into the animal life as a matrix.

The soul being the real organic man, destined to an endless career of unfolding life and progress, the body is but its first necessary material tenement or house, to be cast off when the soul itself, with its ethereal body, is ready to leave its chrysalis state and rise into the spiritual spheres.

The symmetry and beauty of the spiritual body at the dissolution we call death, corresponds to the degree of spirituality the soul has attained at the time of this separation; and the physical body is, in an important sense, an index to the inward development, becoming grosser or more refined, according to the corresponding state or condition of the soul itself.

Remembering that what we call matter is but a temporary mode or condition of spiritual substance or elements, the spiritual body may be thought of as composed of the ethereal elements which, in a grosser form, enter into the composition of the physical body. These may be condensed direct from spirit, or appropriated from the spiritualized elements of the physical body. Indeed, both of these sources undoubtedly contribute to it, the nucleus being deposited from the primal fountain of Spirit, and the elaboration and perfection of the organism being brought about by the union of both.

Hence it is not difficult to imagine a time coming in the evolution and development of the spiritual life of the race, when the physical body itself shall become so refined, and transmuted into the etherealized condition of spiritual substance, as to become one with the inward and permanent body of the soul, and, like that of the Christ and others of sacred history, pass from the outward plane of existence without dissolution, through a glorious translation, into the spiritual realms of light and immortality, the eternal and beatific home of the "spirits of just men made perfect." This would be but the carrying forward and culmination of the process by which the whole organic world has been built up from the earliest crude forms of the vegetable and animal kingdoms, to its culmination in the marvelously complex and finely tuned organism of the human body.

Mineral substance is transformed into vegetable substance by the vital chemistry of vegetable life, the vegetable into animal tissue by the higher chemistry of animal life, and both vegetable and animal substance into the finer tissues of the human flesh, by the still higher chemistry of human life. Why, then, may not the yet higher chemistry of spiritual life, or human life on the plane of the spiritual, carry this process of transformation forward, in the ultimate transmutation of the physical into a spiritual body? Would this be anything more than the quickening and concentration of the process daily going on in the human organism, by which the most highly spiritualized elements of the physical body are incorporated into the permanent spiritualized body of the soul? High inspired authority testifies that "the last enemy that shall be destroyed is death," and death in the sense of absolute destruction, is possible only to physical form.

The decay of a single physical organ, the amputation of a limb, or the dissolution and casting off of the entire body, does not change or affect in the least the spiritual body or the soul's organic powers, as these are independent of and in no way subject to the laws and conditions of the material world, and have only a temporary relation to that world.

While the spiritual organism gives form to the physical body and its organs, it is itself formed from within by the flowing forth and embodiment in spiritual substance of the ultimate elements and principles that inhere in spirit *per se*. As such it is a living, indestructible organism, with an inherent capacity for an endless unfoldment of being from the infinite within toward the comprehension and mastery of the infinite without. It has, therefore, the ability to appropriate to its use all the without that is essential to its own progress as an organic personality, beginning with the elementary form of the physical body, and the possible transformation or transmutation of its ultimate elements into the spiritual body itself.

THE ORDER OF HUMAN EVOLUTION.

In the individualization and evolution of the human soul and its various powers, life and physical organization precede sensation, as sensation precedes intelligence and volition, and with these, gives birth to consciousness. Consciousness is the permanent registration of the degree or level which the evolution of the soul's powers has at any time reached. The first consciousness of life therefore was of a purely animal existence, or life in the senses; then followed the higher consciousness of personality and moral accountability, a sense of existence and responsibility, distinct from and vastly transcending the highest possible level of the brute creation. With the unfolding and expansion of this consciousness, came also a dim foreshadowing of a still higher possible range and level of conscious life, out of which should spring the thought of personal immortality on a more spiritual plane of being.

With the evolution of the latent functions of the spirit in the superior faculties of the soul, will dawn the higher spiritual consciousness, and the assertion of the inmost or divine Ego in man, God manifest in the flesh.

Just as the automatic instincts of the animal life prefigured the higher volition and understanding of man, so the reason and conscience prefigure the intuitive wisdom and goodness or divinity of the spiritual nature which these powers of the soul shall take on through spiritual illumination, when the soul awakes to its divine possibilities, and in the exercise of its moral freedom, turns to the true source of its life, light and power—the kingdom of God which is within. Says a popular writer:

"In the common every-day existence, the soul is like one standing with his back to the light, who contemplates the shadows of objects and supposes them to be real. The conceptions of the actual truth are, nevertheless, not entirely extinguished. The higher nature may be asleep, but there are dreams."

Yes, *dreams*, but the dream is the assumption that the changing and evanescent phenomena of the material world are the only reality, when in very truth these are but the shadows of the real and permanent kingdom of being, which is spiritual and eternal.

Awaking first to consciousness in the sphere of the senses, man even after the birth of the higher consciousness, which comes with this unfolding of the reason and moral sense, is prone to linger and cling to the outward and physical world as the only reality; while the inspiration, intuition, and ideals of the spirit, which ever and anon, flash upon the soul, he regards as shadowy, visionary and unreal.

Again the writer already quoted says:

"The moral nature, however, which renders us conscious of right and wrong, is no more an emanation of the corporeal organism, nor has it any bestial antecedent. A stream may rise no higher than its fountain. The mind has its perception of justice in it, as an inheritance from the world of ABSOLUTE JUSTICE. Being of an essence kindred, and even homogeneous with the Deity, it has its home in that world, and is capable of beholding eternal realities. Its affinities are all there, and it yearns, even amid the seductions of sense and material ambitions, for that nobler form of life."

The Apostle Paul, in accord with many seers and spiritual philosophers, refers to man in his entirety as a three-fold being—"spirit, soul, and body." Says Ireneus:

"There are three things of which the entire man consists, namely: Flesh, soul and spirit; the one, the spirit, giving form; the other, the flesh, receiving form. The soul is intermediate between the two; sometimes it follows the spirit and is elevated by it, and sometimes it follows the flesh and so falls into earthly concupiscences."

Says Origen:

"If the soul renounce the flesh and join with the spirit, it will itself become spiritual; but if it cast itself down to the desires of the flesh, it will itself degenerate into the body."

Says the late Prof. Crocker, in his summary of Platonic psychology:

"Thus the soul as a composite nature is on the one side linked to the eternal world, its essence being generated of that ineffable element which constitutes the real, the immutable, and the permanent. It is a beam of the eternal Sun, a spark of the Divinity, an emanation from God. On the other side it is linked to the phenomenal or sensible world, its emotive part being formed of that which is relative and phenomenal. The soul of man stands mid-way between the eternal and the contingent, the real, and the phenomenal; and as such it is the moderator between, and the interpreter of both."

It is evident from the very nature of God, and of the human soul, that God can be found and known by man, or be revealed to him, only in and through the spirit that is in man; because the spirit in man is the divine ego, and the only interpreter of God. It is the centralization or focalization of God in man, therefore the only direct avenue through which a manifestation or revelation of God is possible to the soul.

The physical universe is but the shadow or external and symbolic representation of the spiritual universe. Hence until we recognize God in and through the spirit that is our own inmost being, and see him as the supreme and eternal reality of universal being, we have not found and do not know the truth of the universe itself, nor of our own being. "Except a man be born of the spirit, he cannot enter into the kingdom of God." That is, except the consciousness and the understanding of being are begotten of the spirit, and not—as in the external state of man—of the senses, he can neither see nor enter into the reality of being, termed in the Scripture the eternal life. "And this is life eternal to know" (understand, be concious of) "thee, the only true God, and Jesus Christ, whom thou hast sent."

"But as it is written, Things which eye saw not and

ear heard not, and which entered not into the heart of man.

"Whatsoever things God prepared for them that love him.

"But unto us God revealed them through the Spirit: for the Spirit searches all things, yea, the deep things of God. * * * * Now the natural" (sensuous) "man receiveth not the things of the Spirit of God; for they are foolishness unto him; and he cannot know them, because they are spiritually judged. But he that is spiritual judgeth all things and he himself is judged of no man."

The Apostle Paul, like his Master before him, evidently spake that which he knew from experience, and testified of that which he had seen, with the opened eyes of the spiritual understanding. "Every man's words who speaks from that life," says Emerson, "must sound vain to those who do not dwell in the same thought on their part." Says another: "They only truly worship in whom something responds to the divine and comprehends it."

Says the quaint Iamblichos:

"In the contemplation of blessed spectacles, the soul reciprocates another life, is active with another energy, goes forward as not being of the order of men on earth; or, perhaps, speaking more correctly, it abandons its own life, and partakes of the most blessed energy of the gods."

Says the great apostle again, "Ye are not in the flesh but in the spirit, if so be that the Spirit of God dwelleth in you." That is, in the consciousness and understanding which constitutes the man proper. So Emerson says: "The simplest person, who in his integrity worships God, becomes God."

The secret of God, or of knowing and entering into his perfect life, is for man to recognize his actual presence in the inward spirit which constitutes the real life and light of the soul, and seek unity therewith. The fact that a few of our race, while yet in the body, have thus found and become one with the Father, demonstrates its possibility for all. Such " have powers and energies as well as spiritual and moral excellencies, infinitely superior to those of common men." "They are the spiritual in whom is developed the divine nature, who are born from above, the intelligent who intuitively know the truth and are free, who are in law and therefore above law, who are a law to themselves, and therefore cannot sin."

Says the Perfect Way:

"The object set before the saint is so to live as to render the soul luminous and consolidate with the spirit, that thereby the spirit may be perpetually one with the soul, and thus eternize its individuality. For individuality appertains to the soul, inasmuch as it consists in separateness, which it is the function of soul substance to accomplish in respect of spirit. Thus, though eternal and immaculate in her substance, the soul acquires individuality by being born in matter and time; and within her is conceived the divine element which, divided from God, is yet God and man."

"God is spirit, or essential substance, and is impersonal, if the term person be taken in its etymological sense, but personal in the highest and truest sense if the conception be of essential conciousness. For God has no limitation.

"Spirit is essential and perfect in itself, having neither beginning nor end. Soul is secondary and perfected, being begotten of the spirit. Spirit is the first principle and is abstract. Soul is the derivative, and is, therefore, concrete.

"The essential principle of personality—that which constitutes personality in its highest sense—is consciousness, is spirit; and this is God. Wherefore the highest and innermost principle of every monad is God. But the primary principle—being naked essence—could not be separated off into individuals, unless contained and limited by a secondary principle. This principle — being derived — is, necessarily, evolved. Spirit, therefore, is projected into the condition of matter in order that soul may be evolved thereby. Soul is begotten in matter by means of polarization; and spirit, of which all matter consists, returns to its essential nature in soul—this being the medium in which spirit is individualized—and from abstract becomes concrete; so that by means of creation, God, the One, becomes God, the Many."

In the present consciousness of a large portion of the human race, the animal and the human blend, while in many the animal largely predominates, and in but few is the higher spiritual or God-consciousness recognized at all; and when recognized as such, it is even then too often thought to be only for the chosen few, the seers, apostles and prophets of the race.

Nevertheless, these stand as beacon lights, pointing

the way for all to follow, and at the same time are demonstrations of the possibility for all, that is of the spiritual nature in all waiting recognition and development. The supreme head of all these sons of God, who stood upon the very summit of this divine realization, says to all the brethren of his race, "I am the light of the world, he that followeth me shall not walk in darknes, but shall have the light of life." "Verily, verily I say unto you, he that believeth on me, the works that I do shall he do also; and greater than these shall he do, because I go unto the Father."

Thus the actual unfolding of man is from within outward—evolution—while his apparent growth is from the plane of the animal without, inward to the spiritual. Hence when man comes to recognize the higher possibilities of his being, and discovers that these are to unfold from within, he will cease his vain and useless struggles after emancipation through external, arbitrary and vicarious means and measures, and turn to the radiant centre of divine light and power within, and, uniting with the Spirit, rise to the consciousness of oneness with God through the Spirit. As he thus emerges into the light of the God-consciousness, he attains that spiritual supremacy and personal mastery which this consciousness imparts.

It is only through personal attainment of spiritual supremacy and identification of life with God, that man is raised above the power of temptation, and so above the possibility of sin and disease, because only through this supremacy the animal nature and the body itself become also transformed by the spiritual life to which they are thus conjoined, and in which they are thus held. "Because the creature itself also shall be delivered from the bondage of corruption into the glorious liberty of the children of God."

By the loss or want of the true understanding of his being, the attention, thought and desires of man are confined so fully to the external and sensuous condition of life, that he is brought into bondage thereto, and becomes the subject instead of the master of his material environments. Out of this dominance of the law of the animal and sensuous life over that of the spiritual in him, comes all the sin, sickness, vice, crime, violence, despotism, poverty, ignorance and superstition which have cast their hateful shadow over an otherwise beautiful world

So shall the true understanding of his being and destiny enable man to achieve his spiritual emancipation and banish forever from our world the darkness and suffering of sin, sickness and every form of evil, by enthroning the light of truth, and the power of love in the personal and social life of all mankind. Then will God's kingdom have come and his will be done on earth as it is in heaven, in the realization of the divine Sonship and universal Brotherhood of man in the eternal Fatherhood of God.

The Law and Rational Basis

—OF—

Mental and Faith Healing Practically Considered.

That "all manner of disease and all manner of sickness," even in their apparently most hopeless forms and phases were healed by a purely mental or spiritual influence or action, under the ministry of Christ and his Apostles, is believed by thousands. According to the record, these experiences of healing were not exceptional, but were a matter of common and daily occurrence. In the majority, if not all the cases, the restoration was immediate; not progressive or gradual.

That many cases of disease in its various forms pronounced utterly hopeless by good medical authority, have been cured in our own times by a purely mental or spiritual process, thousands of reliable witnesses are ready to testify, amongst which are plenty of those thus restored. Some have been immediate and apparently miraculous, while a much larger per cent. have been gradual, some slow and others remarkably rapid, yet all absolutely healed. Some of these were healed apparently in direct answer to prayer, others at the shrine of some canonized saint, or the touch of some saintly relic, or from the water of a blessed and sacred spring, etc., and come under the head of prayer and faith cure; and others still by a direct process of what is very properly called mental treatment, under the various schools of "Mental Healers." Numerous failures occur under the efforts of all these various branches of modern Faith and Mental Healing. As no tabulated reports are given of the proportion of success and failure, the relative success of the different methods cannot be accurately given.

So far as our own observation extends, these seem to be about equally divided. There are certainly remarkable successes as well as failures with them all. One fact, however, is established beyond dispute, a fact of great significance and importance. Cases absolutely beyond the reach of medical skill, and *pronounced* incurable by the highest medical authority, have been cured under these various methods, and in so short a period as to have all the appearance of the miraculous. These modern instances confirm the probable truth of the record of the Christ and Apostolic Healing. They certainly demonstrate the action of a law and principle, by which such perfect results are possible through a perfect understanding and application of the law and principle involved.

That the religious opinions held by the healer or

the healed has nothing whatever to do with the result, save so far as they serve to stimulate faith, is demonstrated by the fact that equally good illustrations occur under nearly every form of religious belief; and some under no religious belief at all.

That these remarkable results are effected through the operation of some law of mental action as universal as the existence of the human mind, whether this law be understood or not, is obvious to all rational thinking. Jesus, whose success was absolute, never failing in his effort, so far as the record goes, recognized this by ascribing the marvellous cures wrought under his hands to the exercise of faith. "Thy faith hath made thee whole," was a common remark to the one healed. He doubtless understood this law, the secret of which is found in his doctrine of Faith.

The majority of those healed by the "Prayer Cure," or "Faith Cure," believe it to have been the result of a miraculous interposition of divine grace, though some believe it to be the result of a powerful impression of the mind upon the vital processes under the influence of faith awakened by a religious experience.

The law and conditions of this mental action have already been briefly pointed out in a previous chapter, and will be considered from another standpoint in this.

The founder of the modern school of "Metaphysical Healing," Dr. E. P. Quimby, of Portland, Me., a remarkably successful practitioner, believed that he had discovered the true secret and law of all mental healing. This secret was, the *non reality* of disease itself. He believed that he had discovered and demonstrated (by his success based on this discovery) that what men called disease was wholly a delusion of the mind; that in the nature of things there could be no disease, hence that to discover the fact of this delusion in one's self, or to awaken another to the recognition of it, is to utterly banish disease or error from the life. This is essentially the working basis of the purely "Metaphysical" method.

Whether disease be a delusion of the mind or a fact of actual experience, that it is often cured by a certain positive attitude of mind, induced by an acceptance of this doctrine, is itself a demonstration of the power of mind to overcome and banish the apparent disease from the body.

Whether this doctrine be a satisfactory explanation of the law on which the results are based, each must decide for himself. One thing is certain,—it is the attitude of mind and not the doctrine, that secures the result, though the doctrine, when accepted, may bring about the attitude of mind which effects the cure. It is that supreme state of mind which Jesus termed Faith, and emphasized so fully. As this doctrine cannot readily be brought into universal acceptance, if a more satisfactory basis can be presented which can be very generally accepted, and by which this attitude of mind can be more widely and generally induced, will it not be wise and prudent to adopt and apply it, until at least something still more comprehensive and perfect is presented? Such a basis we seek to present in this chapter.

Without discussing the reality or non-reality of the physical world, it has, at least, the appearance of a past and present reality; and in this chapter we will accept the appearance for the fact.

Disease we will define as a disturbed or deranged condition of vital action, to which all physical organisms, whether of plant, animal or man, are liable under abnormal conditions, and which in animals and men, often causes great suffering and distress. To remove the disturbance and restore the balance of harmony in the vital processes, is to remove the disease and restore the health of the sufferer.

There is an inherent tendency in the principle of life in all organisms, whether of plant, animal or man, to spontaneously react against the disturbance, recover the lost balance, and in case of injury to the organs or tissues, either from disease or accident, to heal and restore the injured parts. This takes place in plants, the same precisely as in animals and man, and therefore is independent of mental action one way or the other. It is the spontaneous and automatic action of the healing function of life itself.

In plant and animal the process of healing and recuperation is always gradual; never immediate nor instantaneous, yet may be hastened or hindered by external conditions. The influence of external conditions is the same also upon the healing processes in man. But the active influence of mental states upon the vital processes, and especially upon the healing function of life, is very great and may be made almost absolute. *Fear* which engenders distrust and despondency, is *the one* demoralizing mental state, and faith, which gives assurance, confidence and trusting expectancy, is the one restoring and sustaining mental state. The problem of mental influence on health and disease is involved in these two opposing states.

The functions of life as manifest in the processes of growth, repair, and reproduction, are spontaneous and automatic, and exist and operate independent of thought and mental influence, the same in man as in the plant; but where mind exists and is active, as in man, with free powers of choice and volition, it becomes the most direct and potent power, to disturb the vital processes and induce disease, or to sustain them in their highest vigor, and so prevent or cure disease. It is through this direct influence of mental states over the vital processes, that immediate healing occurs so often in man, while it is always gradual in animals and plants.

It has been demonstrated, however, that the human

mind is capable of affecting the vital processes and the springs of life in animals and plants, by the concentration of attention in desire and faith upon them also to this end. The law and conditions of exercising this influence were illustrated in a previous chapter.

The "Metaphysical" theory starts out with the assumption, that all supposed bodily conditions, whether of health or disease, are *wholly* the reflection of mental states, and therefore that the mind, and not the body is the only proper subject of consideration and treatment.

While the mind is capable of inducing nearly if not quite all forms of disease, it obviously cannot produce a sliver in the flesh, nor mangle the body as from a railroad disaster, or other external catastrophe; neither do all bodily derangements originate in mind any more than do injuries from accidents, etc. In cases of disease or injuries, however, from external and physical causes, the mind is just as potent in quickening the restoration and healing action of life, as though the disease itself originated in mental disturbance.

With these explanations we may proceed to consider the physical as well as the spiritual basis of healing through mental action and supremacy, without being misunderstood. Our object is not to discuss theories as such, pro or con, but to consider the one law operating under all these theories; for as Spirit and Life are one, there can be but one law of health and healing though many conditions may be involved.

There is but one power of healing, and that is lodged in the life of the individual; the same in plants and animals as in man. This power may be disturbed and its normal action prevented by various influences and conditions, and by the operation of the same law it may be quickened and reinforced by the appropriate influences and conditions.

On the recognition of this principle all medical and hygienic measures are based, whether they be wise or foolish. Mental or Faith healing is but the substitution of mental therapeutics for the external measures of the other schools, medical and hygienic.

If, as we think, it has been fully demonstrated in experience, the mind itself in its various states and moods, is the most potent agent known in its direct influence upon the vital processes of the organism in which it is manifest, either to exalt or depress, derange or restore; then the mental therapeutists are destined sooner or later to supplant all other schools.

Every honest experimental effort in this direction should be encouraged; not opposed and ridiculed, as is too apt to be the case, from the stand-point of time-honored traditional bigotry and error, set with a flint-like prejudice against all advancing innovations.

It is hardly possible to introduce an error under the head of mental therapeutics, so absurd in its nature, or disastrous in its results, as many which have been taught in the name of science, and indorsed and cherished by all the most popular medical colleges of the world.

The one strong feature of the "Metaphysical" school is its full recognition and positive affirmation of the absolute supremacy of mind over all supposed physical laws and conditions. This is practically true, and hence a truth of supreme importance. But the mind even in this supremacy, must operate in obedience to certain established laws and conditions. Through ignorance it is itself brought into bondage even to physical conditions, and is liberated only through enlightenment. It can assert and maintain its freedom only as it understands and obeys the law of its freedom and supremacy.

Faith is the attitude of mind which crowns it with supreme power, but there must be a rational and demonstrable basis for the exercise of this faith. Faith is not credulity nor a blind adherence to creed and dogma, nor acceptance of any arbitrary authority whatever. This is superstition. True faith is perfect confidence and trust in the unvarying operation of recognized and established laws.

The economy of the universe is perfect, being established in divine harmony and order which is universal and complete. The law and conditions of mental supremacy are a part of this order and cannot be ignored or violated with impunity. The action of mind is not exempt from law. The faith which crowns the mind with its supreme authority and power must be based upon a full understanding and practical application of the law of this supremacy. This law was undoubtedly recognized by Jesus, and also by his immediate followers.

The opening of the spiritual understanding, by the bringing forth of the spiritual nature in man, discloses this law and its conditions so clearly to the mind, that it is enabled at once to assert and achieve its supremacy, as illustrated in the Christ and Apostolic experience. But if absolute supremacy be a possibility of mind in its relation to the physical body, then the law of that supremacy is established in the nature and constitution of things, and is a subject of intellectual discovery and understanding; and thus understood becomes the rational basis for the intelligent exercise of faith.

The specific processes for the development of intuition, and the opening of the spiritual understanding through which final and complete supremacy is attained, will be considered further on. At present we are to consider the determining facts of the organic world as seen from the standpoint of external observation and study.

It will be found that a careful study of these leads up to the certain and necessary recognition of the rightful and legitimate supremacy of the mind over the body,

BASIS OF MENTAL AND FAITH HEALING. 121

and discloses the law and conditions of that supremacy. The practical application of the principles involved in this discovery, will be the special subject of another chapter.

LIFE AND ITS CHARACTERISTICS.

The first great fact which attracts our attention in the outward world, as of primary significance to our subject, is the manifestation of life. If we seek for its origin in material conditions, we are baffled from the very start. Throughout the history of its development on our planet, there is not a single fact to show life to be the result of chemical action, or of any combined activity of the forces of the inorganic world. Carefully conducted experiments have dissipated forever the dream of its spontaneous generation. Everywhere life is begotten of life, and so far as human research has gone, life only can beget life, and we are forced to recognize it as the manifestation of a power above and behind all the elements, forces and conditions of the material world.

Light, heat, magnetism, electricity and chemical affinity were all active upon our globe ages before life appeared, and when life came a new kingdom was born, and a new world of marvelous possibilities opened into being.

Life everywhere is now the one supreme energy of the world, to which all other forms of force are subservient, and though we may not absolutely define its nature and origin, we must accept its transcendent nature as a fact. The unfolding developments of the organic world, from the simplest structures of the vegetable and animal kingdoms up to the noblest and most complex, are a complete demonstration of this.

Life is an omnific energy, and is not the product of organization, but is itself the organizing power. Its very first manifestation is the conversion of inert matter into living substance, in which its creative power is manifest.

Before life appeared upon the globe, matter existed in an unorganized state. The nearest approach to organization was crystallization; but there was no life in crystalline bodies. We know nothing of life from the external standpoint of observation, save as it is manifest in organic structures; and here it is manifest in the processes of growth, repair, and re-production; an entire reversal of the processes of the mineral kingdom. The formation of earth, rocks, metals, crystals, etc., is the result of precipitation or deposit and aggregation of like elements; while the living structures of the organic world grow and unfold from within, by the appropriation and assimilation of elements from without. The inert elements of the inorganic world become transformed and incorporated into the substance of living organisms by the vital chemistry and economy of life, losing the characteristics of mineral substance and passing into the elements of vegetable or animal tissue.

Again, just as the forces of the inorganic world were active on our globe, ages before life was manifest, so life itself appeared and was active in the transformation of matter and the building up and perfection of organic structures in the vegetable and mineral worlds, ages before conscious mind appeared in a living organism to look out upon, observe and study its phenomena. Indeed the development of the vegetable and animal kingdoms were the necessary preparation for the bringing forth of a structure suitable for the individualization and establishing of the powers of consciousness, thought and volition, or concrete mind, in organic function. Even then such organism had first to be built up and prepared as an organic instrument for mind by the automatic or involuntary functions of the pre-conscious life.

Again we repeat: the developed animal nature was as much a necessity for the deposit and evolution of the strictly human powers of mind and soul, as was the mineral kingdom for the deposit of the seed-germs and the evolution of vegetable life. The previous development of the vegetable and animal kingdoms, was also necessary to prepare the world as a fit abode for man, when the fulness of time should come for his advent.

The purely physical functions of life, that is, of growth, repair and reproduction,—by which all physical organisms, including the human body, are built up, sustained, healed, and reproduced,—are wholly automatic, and belong to the sphere of what may be called the involuntary and pre-conscious life; since it comes to full activity prior to the evolution of mind or the appearance of consciousness and volition. Life thus far is purely vegetative, and practically the same in plant, animal and man; the vegetable kingdom being wholly included in its sphere.

All that we know of life up to this point, is through the observation of these functions, which are always present and spontaneously active in individual organisms, wherever life is manifest; that is, construction, re-construction, and healing; and therefore can never be separated from life in organic structures. The exhibition of energy without these functions and processes would not be life. It is these functions in activity which constitute life in its primary manifestation.

The physical functions of life which were first manifest in the simplest forms of the vegetable and animal kingdoms, thus remain and become more fully unfolded and established as we ascend the scale of being from the earliest plants and animals to man. By the very exhibition of these functions in the transformation of inorganic substance into the organic, and the building up thereby and repair of living structures prior to the advent of organic thought and volition, the absolute supremacy of life as such over the material elements it uses for this purpose, and therefore over the organism it constructs, is fully demonstrated. "Is not the life more than the food, and the body than the raiment?"

If, previous to the advent of thought and conscious volition, through its purely automatic and physical functions, life had not absolute supremacy over matter, taking from the inorganic world its elements as needed, and returning them when they had served their purpose, the organic structures which constitute the vegetable and animal kingdoms would have been an utter impossibility. The very existence of these kingdoms stands as an unanswerable demonstration of the absolute supremacy of life over the elements it uses and the organisms it constructs through its purely automatic functions; and this independent of thought and volition in the organisms. Matter being thus subordinate to the supreme energy of life, and completely subject to the transforming power of its vital chemistry, the consideration of *its* essential character and origin is unnecessary to the practical development and application of this doctrine of the supremacy of life.

THE DETERMINING PRINCIPLE OF LIFE.

In the study of life and its characteristics, as manifest in the building up of the organic world, we find it to be the operation of a creative energy that takes hold of and transmutes inert matter into living substance, out of which it constructs the various organs and tissues essential to living bodies.

We see it converting the elements it uses for this purpose, into the infinite variety of substances which are found in the organic world, and constructing the innumerable variety of forms which constitute the living bodies of plants, animals and men.

Its power to transform matter from one form of substance into another in the building of organic structures, and endowing them with life, distinguishes it from all other forms of force, and demonstrates its origin to be above and behind the material world.

The question next arises, what determines the infinite variety of substance and form into which this higher energy is continually converting the elements of the material world? This leads to the observation and recognition of another universal fact of especial significance to our subject.

We find a specific germinal principle of life, endowed with individuality of character and function, behind the force of life in all living organisms, which directs its operation and determines the character of the organism. From this central controlling principle which constitutes the soul of the organism, radiates the transforming energy of that vital chemistry of life, which weaves the unfolding structure into the pattern or ideal furnished by the essential characteristics of this principle, or indwelling soul.

The correspondence between the organic structure and the character of its controlling principle of life, is always unvarying and complete. We can with unfailing accuracy determine by the outward form, the character of the germ or soul of any plant or animal with which we are familiar, and also the form, in turn, by the character of the germ. The wheat germ never produces anything but the wheat stalk, and the multiplied reproduction of itself in grains of wheat, and so of corn and every other form of life.

A variety of seed may be planted in the same soil, at the same time, and be subject to precisely the same care and conditions, and from the very same elements the controlling principle or soul of each builds up a structure for itself exactly corresponding with its own character and quality of being, and thus differing from the others both in form of structure and character, and quality of substance thus created. This important fact, with the law and principle it involves, is universal and without exception throughout the whole range of organic structures from plant to man.

The one supreme energy of life is doubtless the

same in all, but the central controlling principle of life, or soul of the organism, differing in each, directs this force with automatic accuracy and skill in the construction of a form exactly corresponding with its own characteristics and necessities.

These observations establish beyond all question two great universal facts and principles, which it is of the utmost importance that man should understand and practically apply in daily life, as they are calculated to secure his highest well-being. These are, first: the absolute supremacy of the one universal life-force over the material it uses in the building up, maintenance, repair and healing of living bodies; and, second: that this living energy which operates with automatic accuracy and certainty in any direction it is turned, is entirely subservient to the demands of the soul of each organism, whether of plant animal or man, and hence that the characteristics of the indwelling soul, whether a conscious entity or not, determines both the quality of organic substance, and the form of structure it shall have.

The soul of every organism, even before the appearance of consciousness and volition, is the architect of that body, and its inherent characteristics form the pattern into which the life-force, which is the builder thereof, weaves the structure. This is true of the very lowest and simplest organisms, as well as the highest. Shall not then the soul of man, endowed with consciousness and power of intelligent choice and volition, become, when fully enlightened, the absolute master and supreme arbiter of his own being, including his body and its environments? The question in the face of these universal and supreme facts is its own sufficient answer.

Man is the culmination of all that preceded him in the organic world, hence the essential characteristics of the forms of life which preceded him are of necessity represented in him, in connection with the higher attributes of humanity which lift him infinitely above and separate him from them by an impassable gulf, and make of him another and distinct order of being.

Soul, with its living energy, as we have seen, is not the product of physical organism, but the originator and creator of organism, each living body of plant or animal being but the external embodiment, in form and function, of its indwelling and controlling principle of life, which being above and behind materiality, is the expression of that which is spiritual and transcendent.

The human soul being endowed with the nobler attributes of the rational, moral and inspirational powers which make man a progressive being, with power of intelligent choice and volition, embraces within the sphere of its activities, not only the involuntary and automatic functions of the pre-conscious life, but the higher functions of consciousness and volition.

The involuntary functions of the soul build up and sustain the body as an organic instrument for the higher activities of the rational, moral and inspirational or spiritual powers, while the true growth and development of man consists in the unfolding and perfection of these higher powers, of which the external and physical organs are but the instruments of service in their relation to the outward world.

As a stream can rise no higher than its source, this coming forth of consciousness and volition in man, as the culmination of the rising stream and unfolding development of life in the organic world, is itself a demonstration of an original sphere or realm of intelligence and life, within and behind the world of form and phenomena, as the source from which he sprang; and for this we have no better name than Spirit,—and Spirit is God.

Since the constitution of the human soul is progressive in its nature and character, and its higher powers are but the organic evolution of the attributes of spiritual and absolute being, their development and training should give him intelligent control and actual mastery of all his physical relations and environments. If this be true, a practical knowledge of his own constitution, spiritual, as well as physical, will certainly enable him to achieve this mastery.

Man being the ultimate of creation and the highest form of organic life possible to our planet, and standing thus at the head of the organic world, he is by nature and position its rightful lord and sovereign. Though the last to be brought forth, he becomes the first in position and importance, and by virtue of his progressive nature, he is to unfold and bring to perfection in his own powers the supreme attributes of life and spirit, and thus become God-like in nature and character, a true son or complete re-production of God, perfect even as his Father in heaven is perfect.

So in the development of the physical organism, the brain is the last organ to be brought forth under the automatic processes and involuntary functions of the pre-conscious life, but when completed and its functions established, it becomes the first in position and importance, the central, co-ordinating and controlling organ of the body. It thus receives impressions from all parts of the body and sends them to all parts, and being the physical organ of the free powers of consciousness and volition, the active states of the mind being centered in the brain are through the brain focalized upon the body, and of necessity affects its processes according to the character of the mental states.

The human body, it is true, like those of plants and animals, is built up, sustained and repaired by the purely automatic functions of the involuntary life, which act spontaneously, and entirely independent of thought and volition, as perfectly in the idiot and plant as in the most intelligent man; as perfectly when will and consciousness are asleep as when awake and active. The intimate relation which exists, however, between the brain and the organs of vitality, and the corresponding relations between the voluntary and the involuntary powers of the soul, render it impossible that the active states of mentality being thus focalized upon the body, should not affect for good or ill the automatic functions and processes of life. Hence the great importance, nay, the imperative necessity, of a practical understanding of the law of this relationship, and an intelligent self-control acquired by man, that through such understanding and control he may maintain his health and vigor, and rise to the supreme heights of his power, perfection and mastery of being.

As the kingdoms below man and the world without, are represented in him, when he has full control of the elements and forces of the animal and physical within, he will find himself in possession of

THE KEY

To the mastery of the animal kingdom, and the rude forces and elements of the world without.

As the full-grown oak existed potentially in the germ of the acorn, so all the attributes and qualities that ever have been or ever can be brought forth in a living organism, existed from the first, latent in the pre-conscious life of the soul of that organism. Hence all the

BASIS OF MENTAL AND FAITH HEALING.

higher powers of the mind and soul of man were from the first latent in his pre-conscious life, and furnished the pattern into which the automatic functions wove or constructed the body and its organs for their use.

From this it will be readily seen, that if the mind while latent is thus influential in furnishing the model or pattern for the construction of its own physical organs, when it at last wakes to conscious activity, it must exert a still more potent and direct influence over the constructive, re-constructive and healing processes of vitality, not only in its own organ, the brain, but the entire body.

Hence, also, the soul in the exercise of its free powers of consciousness and volition, must have a body exactly corresponding to its own ideal of what the body is or shall be. The ideal of the mind concerning the body and its limitations, is of necessity reflected upon the body, and forms the mold into which the automatic functions are continually reconstructing the new-forming tissue, and the human being, whether conscious of the fact or not, is actually making his outward man after and into the pattern furnished by his own mind and thought. Truly, "as a man thinketh in his heart, so is he."

The preceding consideration of the determining facts and principles of the organic world ought to be sufficient to establish the following fundamental propositions:

First—That organic life, as a creative energy on our planet, preceded the evolution of mind in the order of manifestation.

Second—That this pre-conscious life which built up the vegetable and animal worlds before man and mind appeared, is still the specific constructing, sustaining and healing energy of all living organisms, including the physical body of man, and operates independent of concrete mind.

Third—That this operative force of life has absolute power under proper conditions, over the material it uses and the organisms it constructs; *i. e.*, it has power to convert the elements it uses into any kind and quality of substance, and to build up any form of structure required by plant, animal or man.

Fourth—That each individual organism is endowed with a germinal controlling principle of life, which constitutes the soul of the organism, the special characteristics of which, form the ideal or pattern into which the automatic life-force weaves the body, and so determines the character and quality of the substance, and the form of the structure it shall have.

Fifth—That when self-conscious mind, endowed with freedom of choice and volition, at length comes forth as in man, it has a controlling influence, and whether conscious of the fact or not, does exert that influence over the life-force in the constructive, re-constructive and healing processes in its own physical instrument, the body.

Sixth—That by the recognition of these facts and the understanding of the law they involve, man may intelligently direct this creative energy of life to the construction of an organism to suit his own highest ideal and desire; and if he make God's Ideal his own, it will be made absolutely perfect.

Seventh—That when man has thus learned to specifically direct the force of life in the control of the elements in his own organism, and acquired the mastery of that organism, he may then accumulate power within himself to master and control the elements and forces of the world outside himself; but as this is to be acquired through co-operation with divine power, he can attain absolute control over himself and that which is below only by first becoming at-one with the Divine, which is within and above him.

The direct and positive assurance of this divine possibility, has not only been given by seer and prophet, but Nature herself has for ages, in the most suggestive manner, given the same hint. Right before our eyes this

MIRACLE OF LIFE,

The transformation of inert matter into the infinite variety of living substances of the vegetable and animal worlds, is perpetually repeated. We see the soul of each organism absolutely determining the character of its own physical structure, and when we come to man, we see the ideals, dominant convictions and impressions of his mind, which constitute the practical faith of the soul, wrought out in his physical body and its conditions. Is it not time that attention be called to these facts, and men awakened to the study and understanding of the law of this mental influence over bodily states, that they may intelligently apply it to the abolition of disease, the preservation of health, and the complete perfection of man in all his organic conditions and relations?

Herein is established the firm and rational basis for the exercise of an intelligent faith, and the construction of a demonstrable science of health and healing through mental supremacy. The power of the soul over the body is absolute. Man can, and actually does have the kind of body he himself has chosen, not by the temporary moods and fluctuating desires and resolutions of his soul, but by the prevailing ideals and convictions of his mind concerning the body and its limitations.

The power of mental supremacy cannot be overstated, nor its importance over-estimated. If true, it is certainly the most important truth for man to know in this world; because his health and well-being depend upon it, and his personal destiny is involved in it. The health and organic perfection of his physical body are thus actually within his own keeping.

Herein is to be found the key to that great law of faith to which the Lord Christ attributed a practically omnipotent power. "All things are possible to him that believeth." "According to your faith be it done unto you." The whole being, psychical as well as physical, is embraced in the operation of this great governing principle—the molding power of the ideas, convictions, and faith of the soul. That this is true the foregoing considerations demonstrate in the abstract; while the personal experience of every one who will carefully observe and analyze the relation of his own dominant mental states to his prevailing bodily conditions, will confirm this abstract testimony.

Men do not rise above the level of their own ideals, either physically, mentally, or morally; neither will they put forth effort to attain that which they believe to be beyond their reach ; accordingly the spontaneous activities of life within them are bounded by the measure which they have set to their mental conviction and ideal of what that limit is or should be. "Whatsoever ye shall bind on earth [said the Christ], shall be bound in heaven ; and whatsoever ye shall loose on earth shall be loosed in heaven." Whatever we bind in the outward man by our thought, binds the operation of the inward life to it ; and whatever limitation we set to the development and activity of the soul by our own ideal, not only binds the operation of the indwelling spirit to that measure, but restricts the effort to attain it.

Both the life of the body and the light of the soul spring from the spirit within, which is the Shekina of God's indwelling presence and power. Faith is the key that unlocks this store-house of God, and opens its exhaustless resources unto him who holds and uses this key. "Know ye not that ye are a temple of God, and that the spirit of God dwelleth in you?" Thus the spirit, or God in man, is an inward fountain of infinite possibilities. Man limits the divine inspiration and activity in his soul, however, just as he limits the spontaneous and harmonious activities of life in his body, by the limitations he imposes from the standard he himself sets up. His ideal of to-day becomes his actual for to-morrow. Hence, if he gird the loins of his mind to-day and hold them so, he will find to-morrow the loins of his body correspondingly girded. If fear and distrust concerning the body possess and hold the mind to-day, a corresponding physical demoralization will ensue to-morrow. Recognize the power of disease over the life in your own body, and you thereby give it this power. Deny the power of disease in the presence of that life, and you destroy its force, and set the restoring and healing power of life in authority. Recognize God as the potency of your life in soul and body, and you are thereby clothed with power to overcome and cast out in his name every evil, and to dwell secure forever in the consciousness of his protecting power and providence. "In God we live, move, and have our being." He is therefore the life or inmost of our life, as he is the essential life of all things. The absolute Being of God, which includes within itself every form of life, admits of no possible imperfection.

How, then, it will be asked, is disease or imperfection possible in what we call our life, since God is that life, or our existence is only in his perfect life? The answer to this seeming paradox is simple and inevitable:

THERE IS NO IMPERFECTION.

What we call disease and death is the manifestation of a perfect law. The law or force of gravitation works as perfectly when a man walks off a precipice and is dashed to destruction, as when it enables him to perform his proper work.

So the law of God in the personal life and its automatic processes of vitality, works as perfectly when constructing and re-constructing the body into the imperfect ideals or patterns furnished by the free powers of the mind, as when it constructs a perfect body after a perfect model. The law operates as legitimately also when taking on deranged action called disease, through the false or deranged habits of life which in our freedom of choice we adopt, as when it produces perfect health and symmetry of body. "Know ye not that ye are a temple of God, and that the Spirit of God dwelleth in you? If any man defile the temple of God, him shall God destroy; for the temple of God is holy [perfect], which temple ye are." The same law which when obeyed builds up and perfects, must of necessity, when violated, tear down and destroy. Without this power to obey or violate law, to interfere or to co-operate with God in our life, we should be mere automatons, without individuality or personal responsibility; having no share in the working out of our destiny, and no participation with God as our Father in his work within us, and so for as we are concerned, life itself would have no significance whatever.

The tremendous responsibility which the conferring of this freedom upon us involves, is, nevertheless, attended with infinite advantage as well. For when we shall have fully and finally learned to observe the law of co-operation with the Father, in the working out of that unutterably grand and exalted destiny which he has designed and provided for us as his children, we shall enjoy the unspeakable satisfaction of a sense of our share in the achievement and victory won.

The infinite goodness and wisdom of the Father is displayed in this: that, while having absolute power in himself, he should bestow this marvelous freedom upon his children, making them the arbiters of their own destiny, and through their own free choice, participants in his perfection and supremacy of Being. The further exhibition of his absolute wisdom and goodness, as well as the exhaustless resources of his providence, are seen in the provision made for the restoration and healing of all who through ignorance or perversity have become separated from his divine order, whenever they shall come to themselves and seek restoration. His gracious providence is also seen in the missionary spirit which his indwelling love enkindles in all who have awakened to a conscious, living communion and fellowship with him in spirit and in truth, prompting them to speak and labor for the awakening and restoration of the spiritually blind and fallen of their kind. It came to Paul in the personal appearance of the risen Jesus, in that remarkable vision while he was yet called Saul, and outwardly an enemy of Jesus. "But arise, and stand upon thy feet: for to this end have I appeared unto thee, to appoint thee a minister and a witness both of the things wherein thou hast seen me, and of the things wherein I will appear unto thee; delivering thee from the people, and from the Gentiles, unto whom I send thee, to open their eyes, that they may turn from darkness to light, and from the power of Satan unto God, that they may receive remission of sins and an inheritance among them that are sanctified by faith in me."

By the realization of the

DIVINE IDEAL

In the human body, as well as the soul, every imperfection is cast out, and disease and deformity are rendered impossible. We are an actual part of his absolutely perfect life, because out of it we cannot exist. We are to consciously share or possess this life by simply recognizing it as ours, and being loyal to that claim. It is only through the admission of disease and imperfection in our bodies in thought, that either is possible to us. Cast out of the mind, by the higher and truer understanding of the perfect life in God, the thought of their possibility for the body, and we thereby destroy their power over us, since the body must of necessity represent the dominant convictions of the mind.

If, before we have reached this understanding, the enemy has already found a lodgment through our fear of him and ignorance of this law, such understanding emancipates us at once from fear, casts out the disease, and restores confidence and trust in the perfect life of God in us, and when thus recognized it restores the health itself. This faith and trust in the perfect life of God, and the fulfillment of this law, brings us into conformity therewith, and makes it one with us and we with it: it leaves no place for disease in fact, nor for the recognition of its possibility in thought, since no disease or imperfection can exist, or at least remain in our life, except through our recognition or permission of it.

Experience has proved that by thus ignoring and positively denying the claim and power of disease to hold a place in this life of God in us, through our understanding of the divine supremacy and perfection of that life, we actually destroy its power and thereby cast it out in his name.

If it be asked how this can apply to infants and other irresponsible persons, the reply is that individuals are bound up in the life of their families or communities, and the prevailing ideals or convictions of surrounding minds, directly affect for good or ill any individual that becomes the immediate object of their attention and solicitude. Especially is this true of infants and invalids, who are extremely sensitive to such influence. On this account many invalids have been actually forced into their graves through the blind fears and mistaken kindness of friends, who might have been saved through an understanding and practical or intelgent application of this law. Let this understanding become universal in any community, and the confidence of that community thereby established in the permanent conviction of the absolute perfection and supremacy of life, and the potency of its healing and restoring power, and

NO FATAL DISEASE

Would be possible to a single member of such community; for, should one through temporary fear come under bondage, the faith and confidence of the community would immediately restore his confidence and cast out the disease, and health would be the universal rule. The voice of the people would in very truth be the voice of God.

The principle involved in this law of health and healing for the body, applies with equal potency to the liberation and exaltation of the soul to its true position as the offspring of God, who is the only light or intelligence of the soul, as he is the only life and health of the body. The clear understanding of this great truth emancipates the soul from the thraldom and limitations of flesh and sense, by turning it from its dependence upon the mere light of the outward world—which is but reflected light—to the centre of divine radiance within, the inextinguishable light of consciousness. This emancipation opens and establishes the spiritual understanding and gives mental illumination, spiritual supremacy and personal mastery over all outward environments and relations; because it makes our life and the understanding of it one with the Father's, by lifting it to the plane of the spiritual which is divine and perfect. Hence in the understanding and practical application of this great fundamental principle and law of life, lies the secret of health, healing and physical perfection when applied to the body; and the illumination of the mind, the exaltation and perfection of the whole man in spiritual supremacy and personal mastery when applied to the soul. This the Christ assures us was the immediate source of his own transcendent wisdom and power, and his promised experience to all who should faithfully follow his example in making the realization of this kingdom of God and its perfect life the supreme end of their seeking. "He that followeth me shall not walk in darkness, but shall have the light of life."

This divine realization, however, does not lead men as some have taught, to utterly ignore and deny the reality and value of the senses, and their proper training in their own subordinate sphere. On the contrary we are assured by the Master himself, that our "Heavenly Father knoweth we have need of all these things;" but by ceasing to make the things of the outward world and sensuous life the end and aim of our being, and by subordinating them to the development and perfection of the nobler powers of the soul, "all these things shall be added unto you." This promise of the Christ finds abundant confirmation in the testimony and experience of every great seer and genius of inspiration since the world began.

Thus the absolute supremacy of life over its material organisms, and the elements of the physical world from which they are built up, demonstrates the spiritual origin and character of life itself; while the transcendency of its central, controlling principle in individual organisms, and especially the higher attributes of reason, conscience and spirituality in man, demonstrate the inherent divinity of the human soul, and therefore its transcendent possibilities and exalted destiny as the offspring of God—an organic receptacle of the Eternal Wisdom and Goodness.

THE LAW AND PRINCIPLE
—OF—
MENTAL AND FAITH HEALING PRACTICALLY APPLIED.

The fundamental principles of Health and Healing through Mental Supremacy having been fairly considered in a previous chapter, it is presumed that the student is now ready to consider their practical application to the development and perfection of organic power, and the cure of disease in himself and others.

The first condition of success in this ennobling science and art, is that attitude and disposition of mind termed FAITH. "All things are possible to him that believeth," said the great Teacher. This faith, to which the Master thus attributed such unlimited possibility, as previously shown, was neither a blind credulity, belief in dogma, nor a *careless indifference* to results; but an intelligent confidence and trust *reposed* in some person, principle or power, supposed to be trustworthy, with a positive expectation of corresponding results. As specifically applied by Jesus himself, it was a perfect confidence in God, and an unshaken trust in his providential order, which being accepted as perfect, is to be regarded as of necessity unchangeable. So that being once assured of an established law or provision of God in either the physical or moral world, we can rest assured of its spontaneous and perfect working whenever or wherever the conditions of its promised results are complied with. This is the "rest" or "assurance of faith." This is also the essential and practical faith that lies at the bases of all genuine seience and art, the recognition of and strict compliance with established law.

This is all that was essentially involved in the faith of the Christ and enjoined by him on his followers. Though his precepts and promises are widely regarded as resting wholly upon arbitrary authority, careful study shows them to be based upon the unalterable laws and principles of the physical and spiritual worlds, to both of which man stands related. "My teaching," he says, "is not mine, but his that sent me; if any man willeth to do his will," complies with the conditions of his law and providence in these things, "he shall know of the teaching, whether it be of God, or whether I speak from myself." In these grand words Jesus utterly repudiates all arbitrary authority as vested in himself, and refers to the unalterable principles of the Father's government as the only basis of authority, as well as for the exercise of all genuine faith. In this he anticipated the practical working basis of all scientific research and experiment. Those people who ridicule faith work, should remember that society, government, education and the ordinary business of life, would be impossible without its exercise. The promises of God should certainly be as trustworthy as the promises of men; why then ridicule the idea of their acceptance? "Have faith in God," in his unchangeable and perfect economy and providence, "and nothing shall be impossible unto you."

Convince any intelligent man that God has provided and established in the very constitution of things, a universal law of healing and restoration from disease and injury, as sure in its operation as the well known law of gravitation, and you give him at once the basis of a practical, working faith. "Faith without works is dead."

That such a law exists in the nature and functions of life has already been shown. This law is spontaneously manifest throughout the whole organic world, from plant to man, whenever injury or disease occurs in living structures. The perfect basis then for an intelligent and practical faith, or a working confidence in this divine law of healing, is found only in the true conception and understanding of life itself, and the organic relations of consciousness and volition to its automatic functions in the human organism.

The spiritual character and source of life, and its absolute supremacy over what is called matter, have been shown. Inert matter becomes living substance only as it is transformed and assimilated through the transcendent chemistry of organic life. The existence of the organic world is a perpetual demonstration of this supremacy. "Is not the life more than the food?" said Christ; more than the material it uses for the building up and repair of organic structures? To the illuminated mind of Jesus, life was the creative or constructing, re-constructing and healing power of all living bodies. It was the manifestation of the indwelling and overshadowing presence, power, and providence of the Father, who "is Spirit"—ubiquitous being. God is the one all-embracing life. "In him we live, and move, and have our being." Things exist only as they are held in his life. He who attained the most complete transcendency of personal life, said: "I can of myself do nothing." "The Father that dwelleth in me, he doeth the works." The same is true of every man. Jesus recognized and understood this truth, and exercised the free powers of his soul in conformity with this understanding, and thus realized in personal experience the working out of the Father's perfect ideal life.

Thus the life in every man holds within its mysterious bosom the potency of God. It is therefore instinct with the divine energy and unerring skill of him from whom it proceeds. It is equally true that man, through moral freedom, reason, and volition, has the power to apprehend this truth, and in the exercise of free will to co-operate with the Father in the Ideal and purpose of his life, and thus either to actualize them in the full organic perfection of his being, or antagonize them and bring disease and deformity upon himself. This power of the human soul to obey or violate the law of life in its own organism, and thus affect the results of its workings for good or ill to that organism, has already been fully shown.

In the bestowment of this freedom of choice and action upon his children, the Father, by the very conditions of the gift, is bound to respect the choice they make. Hence it is that we practically bind God, or limit the activity and power of his life within us to the measure of our own thought and faith. Hence, also, the significant words of Jesus already referred to, "Whatsoever ye shall bind on earth shall be bound in heaven, and whatsoever ye shall loose on earth shall be loosed in heaven." "Ye therefore shall be perfect, as your Father which is in heaven is perfect." Hence we have but to recognize and co-operate with the Father in working out this perfect Ideal and provision in our life, to "be perfect even as he is perfect."

With this understanding of the law and power of faith, we are prepared to confidently apply the principle involved to the healing and perfection of the body as an instrument of the soul, and also to the exaltation and perfection of the soul itself. When the art of self-healing by this mental process is fully acquired, the ability to apply it to the healing of others, through the power we have of affecting their minds and bodies by sympathetic contact and thought transferrence, will be developed according to our natural aptitude or "gift" for such a work. *Faith and courage are as contagious as fear and doubt.* Faith and courage, in a positive temperament, will always awaken and inspire the same feelings in others, even in the fearful and despondent. Abundant illustrations of this law in the commonest affairs of every-day life, will suggest themselves to the reader.

THE TRUE SECRET OF SELF-HEALING,

And relief from pain by the purely mental process or mental co-operation with the healing power of life, lies in completely withdrawing the attention from the disease and pain, and concentrating it in perfect confidence upon the healing action of life in the affected organ or part. The more complete this transfer of the attention, the more immediate and thorough will be the relief and healing. One half hour's entire forgetfulness of the disease, induced in this understanding, absolutely suspends its action and establishes the healing. In order to effectually do this, there must be the clear understanding of the truth that the healing power of life in the suffering parts is supreme, and, therefore, always greater than the disease or hurt, and will immediately overcome the disease and restore the parts when thus mentally co-operated with. This is absolute truth, but must be recognized and applied to be made true in personal experience. It should be remembered that the life-force is the constructing and controlling power of the organism, and therefore its healing and re-constructing functions are of necessity equal to any possible emergency of disease, obstruction or injury—where these have not reached the absolutely fatal point—when not weakened and interrupted by the fear and distrust of the mind itself. The supreme power of *Faith* to quicken, direct, and intensify the healing energy of life has already been shown and will be further illustrated.

It is a law of mind that "The concentration of attention in one direction inevitably suspends it in other directions." It is also a law of sensibility, that when the attention is diverted from any sensation as of pleasure or pain, hunger or thirst—whether normal or abnormal—the sensation becomes thereby weakened, and when fully diverted, entirely suspended. Sudden news, whether joyous or sad, coming to a person in the enjoyment of a feast, if sufficient to absorb his attention, will arrest the appetite and completely take away all desire for food. This is equally true of the sensations of hunger, thirst and fatigue. Concentrating and holding the attention upon any sensation or desire tends, on the other hand, to increase and intensify it. The recognition of the healing processes of life, and the concentration of attention in confidence, correspondingly quicken and intensify these processes. Hence as the concentration of attention in one direction inevitably suspends it in all others, and diverting attention from sensation tends to weaken and suspend it, just in proportion as the attention in any given case is diverted from the disease and concentrated upon the healing action of the indwelling life, does it quicken and exalt the healing process on the one hand, and correspondingly weaken and suspend the action of disease and mitigate suffering on the other.

With this understanding, let any one of firm resolution apply this principle to the various sensations of his body, whether of pain or pleasure, and especially to the morbid cravings of a depraved appetite, or even normal hunger, thirst, or fatigue, concentrating his attention upon the opposite of that which he is trying to suspend, and he will be surprised at the success of his experiment. In this way vicious habits, enslaving appetites, and abnormal desires of every kind are overcome, and a wonderful degree of personal control over the bodily sensations and functions is acquired. How many have lost the most intense toothache on their way to the dentist's, their whole attention being absorbed by the dread of the dentist's chair—an illustration of diverted attention.

Through this law of

SUSPENDING PAIN

And the action of disease, by transferring the attention from them to the healing and tranquilizing power of life, suffering from burns, scalds and severe injuries, may be immediately arrested, inflammation wholly prevented if attended to at once, and lacerated parts when brought into juxtaposition promptly healed. This has been demonstrated over and again in the experience of the writer, and also with his students. In case of dislocated joints, broken bones, lacerated wounds, etc., surgical aid and mechanical replacements are of course required, but the vital process of healing being automatic, is instinct with a higher wisdom and skill than any medical interference can possibly have, and needs but co-operation by the attention, trust and confidence of the mind, to do its work promptly and perfectly. Those who have never thought nor experimented in this direction, have no conception of the marvelous influence which this mental co-operation exerts over the vital processes to exalt and quicken them, and the equally depressing influences of fear and distrust to weaken and disturb them. No obstruction to the healing process is equal to the depressing influence of fear of injury and dread of disease, coupled with ignorance of the supremacy of the healing power of life. This fear may be so great as to almost, if not entirely suspend the healing action.

Hence the great importance of a universal recognition and understanding of this law, as these will destroy both the dread and fear of disease, and the fictitious power which they have given it. This also puts the key of healing and health into the hands of the people, by enabling them to enthrone the healing power in immediate and absolute supremacy in any and every case of disease and injury (not in the nature of the case fatal), by this mental co-operation with it. In the case of

SERIOUS INJURIES,

Let the attendants join with the patient in this transfer of attention from his suffering to the sustaining power and healing function of life, while waiting for surgical aid, and his suffering will be greatly mitigated if not entirely suspended, serious inflammation prevented, and when the needed replacements have been effected, the healing rapidly promoted. But so long as dense ignorance and corresponding fear of disease prevail in any community, the enlightened patient and the true healer will have to contend against mighty odds, because of their depressing influence upon mind and body. It is ignorance and fear which give to the disease its fictitious power over men. Even the Christ could do no "mighty work" in a certain place, save to put his hand on a few sick folk and heal them, "because of their unbelief."

It should be borne in mind, first, last and always,

that *there can be no disease where there is no life,* and THERE CAN BE NO LIFE WITHOUT THE HEALING POWER, which power is one of its indestructible functions, and is as universal and spontaneous in its operations as is gravitation itself. Neither can there be full mental co-operation with this potency of God in the healing power, without securing the immediate and certain result.

Hence there can be no disease nor injury without the spontaneous activity of the healing and restoring power of life, save where this activity is directly suppressed and interrupted by the depressing influence of the mind itself, as already described. It should also be remembered that this very spontaneous action of the healing energy of life may be as fully quickened and exalted by mental co-operation, as it is interrupted and suppressed by fear and distrust. The whole secret of this mental co-operation, then, lies in diverting the attention from the disease or hurt, and the fear of it, and concentrating it in perfect confidence upon the healing action of life in the affected part, with the understanding that THE HEALING POWER IS ABSOLUTE WHEN THUS RECOGNIZED AND CO-OPERATED WITH.

The remarkable effect of

DIVERTED ATTENTION

In suspending suffering even in severe injuries, was strikingly illustrated in the case of a man who had the top of his scalp and an ear nearly torn from his head in a railroad accident near Boston, who for a long time "worked heroically in rescuing others from the terrible wreck, wholly unconscious in the excitement of the occasion of the severity of his own injury, though covered with blood, supposing he had received only a slight hurt, until his attention was called to the fact, when he put his hand to his head, and the next moment fainted away."

In like manner soldiers in the excitement of battle often receive severe wounds unconsciously, because of their diverted attention. For the same reason the sense of fatigue from long and wearisome marches, will suddenly disappear on coming in sight of the enemy. There is good reason to believe that some of the martyrs, while burning at the stake, have so fully withdrawn from the sphere of sensation in exaltation of spirit, as to be nearly or wholly unconscious of physical suffering, while giving vent to their ecstacy in triumphant songs of victory, so long as the vocal organs remained to their use.

ILLUSTRATIVE CASES.

A lady who had passed through a single course in the writer's school, arose one morning with an unusually severe attack of sick-headache, to which she was subject, and which usually confined her for twenty-four hours or more in great prostration, the least noise or light adding to her distress. On finding herself in this dilemma, she thought herself too ill to attempt the effort of self-healing, but the second thought suggested, "If this teaching is good for anything, now is the time to apply it." So wrapping a shawl around her head to shut out the noise and light, she withdrew her thought and attention from her distress, and concentrated them upon the supremacy and healing power of life. Meditating upon the revelation of this wonderful power and possibility, she became *fully lost to everything else for a few moments*, even to her throbbing head and sick stomach, until called to herself by the ringing of the breakfast bell, when her nausea and suffering were entirely gone, and she sat down to the table as usual, eating her breakfast and remaining unusually bright and happy through the day. She has since had no return nor any symptom of her affliction. In like manner she cured herself of a long-standing weakness of the eyes.

A lady under great depression, having lost two children, suffered from continual anxiety about the two that were left her, lest they should be taken from her, entirely conquered her fear, and now exercises control over the health of her family. One morning a servant girl of hers having been kept awake all night with an excruciating neuralgia, was unable to attend to her usual duties. But later in the morning, unable to remain in bed from her suffering, she arose and tying a bandage tightly around her head attempted to walk about. At this the lady ventured to try her skill on the sufferer. Calling her by name she said confidently to her, "The healing power of life in your head is greater than the neuralgia, and will cast it out if you think of it in that way." The girl was so impressed with the statement, that in about ten minutes her pain had entirely disappeared, and taking off the bandage, she went about her work fully healed. A little son of this same lady, seven years old, readily heals himself and his schoolmates in this way, of headache, toothache, bruises, etc. In like manner the children of a number of families have thus caught the secret from their mothers, and practice it with great delight and success.

Pages could be filled with similar illustrations of prompt and immediate relief from pain, in cases of severe burns, scalds, bruises, etc., and from sudden attacks of disease in various forms. All these taken in season are promptly relieved by this method, and much suffering prevented. One case more will be mentioned because it illustrates so fully the benefit of this knowledge, and demonstrates the great value and simplicity of the method itself. A lady sustained a severe sprain in one of her ankles, from accidentally stepping into a hole on her way home from one of the evening classes. She was in great pain and could not at first put her foot to the ground. She thought she would have to be carried home and be laid up for some time. Presently, however, she rallied, and said to herself, "Now is the time to test this teaching. I ought to be healed at once." No sooner thought than done. She said to herself, "The healing power of God in my life is vastly greater than the injury, and can immediately restore health in the injured parts." Concentrating her whole attention upon the mental realization of the healing process in her ankle, she boldly and confidently put her foot squarely upon the ground, and in a few moments continued her walk home, several blocks away, the soreness and lameness rapidly disappearing, and before reaching home these were entirely gone, not even a tenderness being felt the next morning nor since. The pain was relieved at once. Without this knowledge she would doubtless have suffered for weeks. Another pupil, a lady in her eightieth year, achieved victories of immediate healing greater even than this. But this is so easily tested by any one who will give it a fair trial by experiment, that further illustration is deemed unnecessary.

The prompt and immediate relief and healing of long-standing and

CHRONIC DISEASES,

Especially if organic, require greater resolution. But in chronic ailments, where organic changes have taken place, time is required to effect the restoration, and the tendency to fall back into long-standing habits of thought and feeling, through the power of association, render it more difficult to hold the new ideal before the mind and appropriate at once the healing power of life. But the principle here enunciated holds good in chronic as well as in recent ailments, though the former demand a stronger resolution and more persistent effort. The rapidity of the cure will depend upon the tenacity with which the mental position is held. Numerous cases of the immediate healing of long-standing chronic diseases are reported. Many cases have occurred under the writer's hands, where even congenital defects have disappeared after a single treatment. The lady mentioned above, who healed herself of a sprained ankle, also cured herself of a life-long difficulty attended with almost constant pain, which had resisted all other treatment. This she did after her third lesson. She gave herself the first treatment without marked result, then a second before retiring for the night with considerable success, and on waking in the morning, she succeeded in getting entire mastery. Other members of the same class secured equally desirable results. One of them commenced treating an indolent tumor on the chest of her daughter, after the third lesson, and entirely removed it before the course of twelve lessons was finished. Any one who, in the understanding of this law, will enter upon the work with a fair degree of resolution and perseverance, can do all that these persons did.

In view of the powerful influence of the

MIND OVER THE BODY,

In extreme cases sufficient even to paralyze and destroy, it will be seen that we cannot think of any organ or part of the body as diseased or weak, without lowering its tone and tending to make it so. Nor can we fear an attack of disease without increasing our susceptibility to the disease we fear, and thus inviting the very evil we dread. On the other hand we cannot think of ourselves as proof against the action of disease, and *rest* in this confidence, even when exposed, without thereby increasing the vital power of resistance to disease and all disturbing influences, and thus helping to fortify the system against them. These truths are so self-evident that it seems almost foolish to repeat them, yet the philosophy of health and healing is so simple as to be entirely overlooked by the masses, who are prone through the traditional ignorance of a false education, to look upon the problem of health and disease as an inscrutable mystery. Hence the necessity of tearing away this veil of mystery and presenting the subject in its simplicity.

ENCOURAGING FACTS.

It may help the understanding and inspire courage and faith in some reader to emphasize several established facts which throw light upon and confirm this great law of healing and restoration from disease. First: The body in all its parts is continually wasting, and being renewed from the food we eat, the fluid we drink, and the air we breathe. Second: The power which transmutes the elements of nutrition into the living tissues of the body and thus renews it, is the indwelling life, which thereby demonstrates its complete supremacy over the body it thus creates, sustains and repairs, as well as over the materials it uses for this purpose. Third: The prevailing moods and states of the mind and feeling are always impressed upon and affect these processes of re-construction, which processes are much more rapid than is generally supposed. There is good reason for believing that there is a complete change and renewal of all

THE VITAL TISSUES

In the space of a few weeks, possibly in six or seven. Hence while this great process of re-construction is going on within us, the prevailing ideal and convictions of the mind concerning the body, whether of physical imperfection, health or disease, strength or weakness, beauty or deformity, are inevitably impressed upon the nutritive processes and new-forming tissues, and thus form the actual patterns into which these tissues are wrought. Hence also we may have, and actually do have, exactly such bodies as we choose, by the models we entertain in our minds for them.

God's Ideal for us is a perfect one, and the automatic forces of his life in us would work out that Ideal in our bodies if, in our freedom of choice and will we did not interrupt and prevent it, by substituting for his perfect model and way, our own imperfect and deformed ones. Yet in spite of our interference, the original impulse to perfection given by him to the working forces of life, tends ever to improve even upon our own models, so that congenital defects and hereditary bias will be overcome and removed through this process of reconstruction, if we do not too strongly interfere. But if we recognize the Father's perfect Ideal and provision for us, and make these our own in thought, desire and faith, he will by his power that worketh in us, re-construct us into that perfect type, free from every taint and blemish.

These facts make clear and striking our personal responsibility in the matter of health and disease. They also tend to awaken within us the inspiration of a new hope and courage, by putting the key of organic re-construction and perfection in our own hands. It is in our power to recognize God's purpose in us, and by mental co-operation with him in our life, to secure its actualization in personal experience.

It is indeed a most encouraging truth, that while with the mental and moral freedom of men there is the liability, and sometimes the fact of disease, there is on the other hand, the tendency and

PURPOSE OF LIFE

Toward health and perfection of physical organism. This tendency will inevitably work out that result of health, whenever it has the co-operation of the free powers of consciousness and volition. It has the purpose and potency of God in and behind it to this end.

When through ignorance or perversity man has brought disease and weakness upon himself, there yet remains this purpose and potency of God in the life to recover its normal balance of harmony and supremacy, and through this co-operation of the mind to cast out disease in every form, and to restore the man. The promptness and rapidity of the restoration will be in proportion to the exercise and intensity of desire and faith.

This law of mental co-operation with the potency of God in our life for the healing and perfection of the body, gives a solid foundation for the intelligent exercise of faith, and places the control and banishment of disease and pain practically in our power, through a purely mental process, but within certain defined limits. We must breathe plenty of pure air, eat a sufficiency of good food, take a proper amount of rest and sleep alternated with the daily activities of life, observe cleanliness in personal habits, etc. Yet, even in these things the endurance of martyrs under extreme privations, and exposure to the most unhygienic conditions, as well as the experiments of resolute fasters, illustrate the great power of mental supremacy to hold the body against the destructive influence of the most unfavorable conditions, especially when through circumstances beyond control we may be forced to meet them.

In seeking to establish this confidence in and practical control over the healing power of life in our organisms, it should be remembered that while we recognize disease or injuries by the sensation of pain or discomfort they induce, the healing process, like the processes of nutrition, circulation, etc., being silent and without sensation, can be recognized only through the understanding or knowledge of the fact. The

OBJECT OF PAIN

Is not suffering *per se*, but to warn us that something is wrong, that some error has been committed, and to stimulate us to correct the error and right the wrong. Pain, therefore, is a beneficent provision. But for this the useful and indispensable organs of our bodies, as the hands or feet, might be burned or otherwise destroyed, and we be unconscious of the fact till they were wholly gone.

As man is constituted, the least hurt from any cause is instantly telegraphed to the seat of consciousness, and the instinct of self-preservation immediately responds and snatches the exposed member from danger. It is the same with the vital organs and every portion of the body. Suffering comes only from some disturbance or obstruction of the harmonious play of the vital activities, whose only law is health, vigor and general comfort. The discomfort is simply the call to remove the cause of the disturbance, which is always chargeable to some unwise use of personal freedom in the exposure of the body, or indulgence of erroneous habits.

When the error has been corrected to the best of our ability, should suffering continue from complications and secondary causes set in operation by the original disturbance, the healing energy of life is still there, provided for this very emergency, to remove the effects and restore from the fall.

The principle of redemption is eternal, and wrought into the very nature and constitution of things, as the eternal expression of the changeless and quenchless love of the Father for the children of his care and providence. The desire for relief and restoration is the normal and spontaneous prayer of the soul to the overruling and omnipresent Providence of life; while the healing function itself is the divine provision in the life, for the full and complete answer to that prayer when offered in faith through this understanding of the law of demand and supply, and the personal co-operation it involves.

So when the deranged condition is recognized and the cause removed as far as possible, no further recognition of the disease itself nor its sensations, is to be entertained or *mentioned*. We first recognize and name them, to unname and discharge them from our thought and life, but henceforth they are not to be thought of nor spoken of at all. If we have not done all in our power to remove the cause, then we must suffer till this is done. But when once done it is done for all time, and we have no further concern nor business with suffering.

OUR ONLY BUSINESS

Is full and unreserved co-operation with the healing power of life, in the full confidence of its power to cast out the enemy and rescue the body from distress or injury.

Should the suffering arise from inherited disease or congenital defect, the same mode of procedure is required and is equally effectual. The principle of reconstruction, is provided for this emergency also, that the divine Ideal of perfection for man may still be reached in spite of human folly and misdirection, and that their results may be overcome when man himself shall turn from his error and co-operate with the Father to this end. The economy and providence of God would be neither divine nor perfect without this provision.

The redeeming power of God is enthroned in this healing function of life, a divine provision ogainst disease or accident; but in man, personal co-operation by recognition, desire and faith, is required, because endowed with moral freedom of choice and action.

In the recognition, therefore, of this provision of the Father as the basis of our faith, we must not forget the one vital and absolutely essential thing, OUR OWN RESPONSIBILITY. We cannot look at, think of and talk about disease or evil as a positive power in any form, without giving ourselves more or less to it, or giving it power and deepening its influence over us. Therefore this may be laid down as the one vital principle and law of our action in the matter of healing, and of restoration from any evil. After correcting the personal error, divert and turn the recognition, thought and attention wholly from the evil we wish to abolish, concentrating and holding them persistently, and with confident expectancy, upon the redeeming power of God that worketh in us, in the understanding that this very attitude of mind and will secures the result desired.

This is the essential condition of all faith-healing. Whenever we do this we give ourselves a genuine mental treatment. We are not doing this and cannot do it while we continue to watch our sensations and symptoms, and revert in thought and speech to our suffering. So long as we

TALK ABOUT OUR AILMENTS,

We hold them in the mind, and so long as we hold them in the mind we thereby hold them in the body. We must absolutely turn from and *let go of the disease* in thought, if we would have it drop out of the body, and turn our whole attention to the confident realization of the healing power of God in us, if we would co-operate with it and secure the immediate and certain results. This must be done without fear, and in the confident assurance, we repeat, that this very attitude of mind and feeling absolutely secures the result. We should remember that THE DIVINE ECONOMY IS PLEDGED TO THE REDEMPTION OF MAN FROM EVERY EVIL THROUGH HIS OWN CO-OPERATION.

FEAR is the one *demoralizing agent* of the personal life. It lets down the bars and opens the system to the inroads of disease, and invites the very evil that we dread. It creates evil (imaginary), and gives to it its fictitious power. It closes, also, the gates of life, and shuts off the healing action in proportion as the part itself is held under its paralyzing and depressing influence. "Perfect love," which involves perfect confidence and trust, "casteth out fear." FAITH is the *antidote to fear*. It restores and exalts as much as fear demoralizes and depresses. Faith centres us in God and makes the soul invincible.

"Therefore I say unto you, all things whatsoever ye pray and ask for, believe that ye receive them, and *ye shall have them."* Thus in prayer for healing we must recognize and trust the healing power of life already active in the affected part, but quickened and exalted in its action by our earnest desire, and established in supremacy by this very recognition of and trust and confidence in it. Thus we work out our own salvation while it is God that worketh in us, "both to will and to do of his good pleasure."

In attempting to heal either ourselves or others, we must realize the true subordination of the physical to the spiritual, and allow to disease no claim upon us nor power to subdue our thoughts and hold our attention, and thus to bring us into bondage to it through fear; remembering that a divine guest within is only awaiting that same attention and recognition to come forth and cast out the intruder. We must resolutely shut our eyes to and turn our backs upon the disease, and thus put it effectually behind us, while we look to and think only of the healing action even now casting it out and working restoration; keeping this idea distinctly before the mind, wait patiently with a firm expectation of the desired result, and in this attitude rest. Questioning implies doubt. This act is not as difficult as at first appears; persevering effort will accomplish the end desired, and when the art is once acquired, its exercise is comparatively easy. We can take our stand with God for the healing, while in pain as well as when free from it, and by so doing we lose the pain. "Commit thy way unto the Lord, trust also in him and he will bring it to pass."

If there is torpor, weakness, blindness, deafness or paralysis without suffering, still dismiss them from the thought, and concentrate the attention upon the restoring and renewing power of life, and think only of, or strive to imagine and realize the renewed life and vitality, even now being infused into and through the enfeebled structure in response to the prayer of faith, "And ye shall have it." This is an immutable and inevitable law, as announced by the great Teacher and Healer himself; a law so simple and so easily tested by every one for himself, that further statement and emphasis of it should be unnecessary. It is enough to say that any one who intelligently takes hold of and applies this principle will be astonished at the result.

AN IMPORTANT QUESTION ANSWERED.

One question is generally raised: "How can one ignore disease or its power, while suffering, for instance the pangs of gout, neuralgia, inflammatory rheumatism, or the horrors of asthma?" While the body or any portion of it is acutely suffering from disease in any form, we cannot, of course, regard it as sound and free from suffering. But we *can* think of what we would be if free from disease and pain, and therefore what we ought to be and may become, through the application of this law of faith and diverted attention.

We can think of immediate healing and restoration as God's will and provision for us through our co-operation with him in his power in us to this end. Holding in our thought this ideal of what the body and its every part should be, and of God's purpose and provision thereto, we can recognize the healing power of life now active in the process of restoration and healing, working out our own as well as God's ideal of soundness and health. We can recognize and *think* of the healing function of life resisting disease and working to overthrow and cast it out, as truly as we can recognize and think of the disease working against and resisting the healing power of life, even while suffering pain from actual disease.

The disease and the healing power are thus recognized as contending for the mastery, and we must of necessity co-operate with one or the other. Which shall it be?

So long as we fear the disease and recognize its supremacy over our life, we co-operate with the disease and give it that supremacy. And just as surely as we recognize the supremacy of life and its healing potency, and thus throw away all fear of disease, we co-operate with the healing action of life and give it the victory.

The specific influence of fear contracts the vessels, causes congestion, and thus creates and holds disease. Casting out fear by restoring the confidence, relaxes the congested vessels, restores the normal circulation, and thus the health. Remember—there can be no disease where there is no life, *and where there is life there is the healing power always,* and charged with the potency of God, or that supreme energy that moves the world and maintains the balance of creation. Hence, in the nature of the case there can be no possible disease, no stage of disease in man—when not absolutely beyond the fatal point—where the power of life in the diseased structure is not sufficient to rally, throw off the disease, heal and restore the injured parts, and re-establish the health of the entire organism, through the positive and confident recognition of and actual mental co-operation in faith with it to this end.

What one can thus do for himself through this understanding and practical application of the law, he can also do to a greater or less extent for another, through sympathy and mental contact with him. It gives the resolute and fearless mother absolute control over the health of her children and household, because they are practically one with her own life. When one's sympathy is aroused for another in suffering, let him approach the sufferer with that supreme confidence which this understanding gives, realizing the sufferer's life as one with his own and God's, and if he have tact he will awaken and restore the confidence of the sufferer, by which the battle is half won. Let him then recognize the healing power of God in the life of the sufferer, as he has hitherto done in his own case, and by the focalization of desire in faith summon it forth to activity. He will then have given a thorough mental treatment, which if not immediately nor fully successful, will by sufficient repetition become so. (See pp. 59, 80 and 81.)

This method of healing may also be successfully practiced upon the absent by such as have sufficient concentration of mind and purpose, provided the patient be fully taken through sympathy into the life of the operator. The powers of concentration and sympathy—the proper qualifications of a successful mental healer—are readily cultivated and strengthened by this practice. It is a direct means of self-culture in mental supremacy, and for the development of personal power and confidence in one's self, and of faith in the power and supremacy of good—God, for God is omnipresent good.

Fear of disease is thus effectually destroyed, and all recognition of its possible supremacy over the life forever banished from the mind.

The daily practice of this exercise, whether it be upon ourselves or others, will soon render it easy, delightful and successful. It should be practiced by all parents and guardians upon those under their care, not only for their healing when sick, but for their physical, mental and moral improvement. It will develop in him who thus employs it, a

POWER FOR GOOD

Approaching that of the Christ himself.

The application of the principle is unlimited, and its possible power for good when thus developed and employed, is as yet undreamed of by the majority of mankind. It gives to man a buoyant enthusiasm and confidence, because by shutting our eyes to evil as a power, and thinking only of the good, we are "not overcome of evil, but overcome evil with good," and thus become identified and one with it, which is one with God.

The exercise of a genuine faith or confidence and trust identifies the subject in greater or less degree with the object in co-operative sympathy, spirit and purpose. "All things are possible with God," and "All things are possible to him that believeth." Therefore "Have faith in God," and "nothing shall be impossible unto you," because this faith unites and identifies our souls with him in his Spirit and Power.

This understanding of the operation of the healing power of God in the personal life, and of the law and power of faith in calling it forth and co-operating with it to the complete healing and restoration of the body from disease and injury, is one of the most important advances in modern thought, because it takes the "gift of healing" out of the

CATEGORY OF MIRACLES,

And places it where it belongs, among the great normal processes of vitality, all of which stand in a similar relation to the law of mental interference.

It was no doubt a similar understanding of this law to which the prophet referred in the 33d chapter of Job, from the 14th to the 30th verses, in which after a most vivid picture of a long, painful and wasting disease, "the flesh" is represented as "consumed away, that it cannot be seen; and his bones that were not seen, stick out. Yea, his soul draweth near unto the grave, and his life to the destroyer." Then he says, "If there be a messenger with him, an interpreter, one among a thousand to show unto man his uprightness [his true position to this law of healing]: Then he [God] is gracious unto him, and saith, Deliver him from going down to the pit: I have found a ransom. *His flesh shall be fresher than a child's; he shall return to the days of his youth.*" May this simple exposition of a great truth prove to every suffering reader that "messenger" and "interpreter." Then shall there "have been found a ransom" for him, and "his flesh shall be fresher than a child's. He shall return to the days of his youth."

A simple formula, then, for mental healing, whether of ourselves or others, stands thus: First, call to mind and seek to realize the one fundamental truth, that "in God we live, and move, and have our being." The thought that we can exist only in his omnipresent life, will help to this realization. Then recognize, as we must through this understanding, that the healing power of life, or of God in the life, is absolute when fully co-operated with by faith, always greater in the suffering organ or parts than the disease or hurt can possibly be. In this understanding withdraw the attention wholly from the disease or injury and concentrate and hold it with entire confidence upon the healing power, in the expectation of immediate and certain restoration, resolutely denying diseased action any claim upon our attention, or power in or over our life, which becomes perfect in God, when thus recognized by us.

This attitude and position of the mind when actually taken and held, inevitably establishes the full supremacy of the healing power and secures the result: immediate, if in the early stage, pain and diseased action disappearing as if by magic, but more gradual if the disease be of long standing, yet rapid in proportion to the intensity and completeness of concentration and faith. "According to your faith be it unto you," was the confident and emphatic utterance of the Christ.

Different formulations of the principle will help different minds. Here is another, presented by the author's companion. It contains the gist of both the science and art. Other forms will be found in next chapter:

[FORMULA FOR SELF HEALING.—First, realize what man is,—Spirit—Soul—Body.

The Spirit is so much of God within man as is requisite for his illumination, healing and ultimate perfection.

The Soul is the real man ; that combination of faculties and powers which constitute the self-conscious personality.

The Body is the fleshly garment or covering, the external counterpart of the soul, an instrument of service, composed of material suited to earthly conditions, through which the soul may come in contact with and handle gross matter, while acquiring its primary education in the school of the senses.

The Spirit in man is unchangeable and always at-one with God. So much of you is always above the power of disease and sin. So repeat, once, twice, thrice, twenty times if need be, or until you have some appreciation of their significance, these words:

THE SPIRIT IS ALWAYS AT-ONE WITH GOD.

By this means self and sin are put in the back ground, and only God remains. So much of God is yours—yourself.

With this power, God within, command. Banish one by one the sins that beset, physical or moral.

"Let your light so shine before men, that they may see your good works, and glorify your Father which is in heaven;" *i. e.*, Remove the rubbish you have allowed to accumulate. "*Let* your light so shine." You will thus see truth you have never before seen. Keep in mind this power within. Remember it is yours to wield. Its recognition and practical acceptance embrace repentance (turning about) and faith; and open a new life, a new world. Old things pass away and all things become new, physically as well as morally.

God has given each one enough of Himself to control the individual, as thoroughly as He controls the Universe. Through the understanding and realization of this, the entire man becomes at-one with God— body and soul cleansed, healed and restored.

The above is a formula for self-healing. For the healing of others, take them into your life. Make their life one with your own, and proceed the same as for self healing. "Thou shalt love thy neighbor as thyself." E. L. C. D.]

The perfect understanding and ever living consciousness of this great truth in the mind of Jesus, with his deep and abiding sense of the indwelling presence and power of God, and his personal identification of himself with the life of God, enabled him to banish disease at once by his word or touch, and to speak in such

COMMANDING TONE OF AUTHORITY

And truth to the captive sufferer, as to dispel the arch enemy fear, and awaken and turn his attention and confidence in the same direction, and thus to restore him to soundness and health.

It was this clear recognition and realizing sense of the indwelling potency of God in his personal life, and the complete co-operation and identification of himself by faith with it, that made Jesus what occultism calls the "magical" or "miraculous man." "The words that I say to you," he said, "I speak not from myself, but the Father abiding in me doeth his works." "I and the Father are one." He realized that there was but one actual life and power, and that was the life and power of the omnipresent Deity, of which he as an individualized form and personal identity, was an organic embodiment or manifestation—"God manifest in the flesh."

Realizing that he existed and acted only by virtue of the life and power of the Father, since there was no other life and power in which to act, and realizing the absolute supremacy of that life and power, he gave himself in his moral freedom of choice, to know and act only the Father's will, and thus wrought and spake in the Father's name, and with the full consciousness of the divine supremacy of the power he used.

With this understanding of life and its energy, we

can realize how Jesus should accredit to faith such omnipotency. It fully identifies the subject with the object; it identifies the man who has come to a sense of his life in God with that supremacy he recognizes as divine.

"And Jesus answering, saith unto them, Have faith in God. For verily I say unto you, that whosoever shall say unto this mountain, Be thou removed, and be thou cast into the sea; and shall not doubt in his heart, but shall believe that those things which he saith shall come to pass; he shall have whatsoever he saith."

In these remarkable words Jesus gave the true key and secret of that marvelous power which enabled him to convert water into wine, to multiply the substance of a few loaves and fishes into a sufficiency of food for a multitude of thousands, to walk on the water, to quell the tempest, to cast out devils, to cleanse the leper and all manner of disease, to raise the dead, and finally to reanimate his own body after having given it into the hands of his enemies to be put to death. What but the supreme power which this faith gave, enabled him at last to change that same body by a living chemistry infinitely transcending the potency of physical cremation, and pass permanently from the external to the internal, from the physical to the purely spiritual plane of being, in a glorious translation, a triumphant victory of life over death and physical decay?

Admitting the essential truth of the record, these words correspondwith the life and character of the one who uttered them, without which they with similar utterances, would be meaningless; so that if we deny the reality of this exceptional life, we must also ignore the teaching or deny its sanity, and *vice versa*, since the one is of necessity involved in the other.

The same teaching equally affirms and emphasizes the same victorious life and power open to all men, through the development and exercise of this faith, based upon the recognition and understanding of the identity of our life with God, and our inherent ability to thus co-operate with the power of God in us to this end. "Verily, verily, I say unto you, He that believeth on me, the works that I do shall he do also; and greater works than these shall he do; because I go unto the Father." In this the Master claims no exceptional privilege or capacity over his brethren and followers, but plainly declares that the disciple, "when he is perfected shall be as his Master."

If any reliance can be placed upon history, these promises of the Master were realized in Apostolic experience to a marvelous extent, and have been to a greater or less degree with a faithful few in every age from that day to this. The revival of faith in our own day, though associated in the minds of many with the thought of miracle, has already produced such an array of marvels that the principle involved in the teaching of Jesus concerning the power of genuine faith, is sufficiently vindicated to challenge the attention of every thoughtful mind.

The transcendent power of the human soul when awakened by an intelligent faith has not, however, been confined in its development to Christian teaching and experience alone. Every great civilization has had its prodigies of occult lore and mastery, too well authenticated to be wholly discarded as legendary and fictitious.

The simple fact of the existence of the seers, prophets, apostles, and so-called "miraculous men" of history, is sufficient demonstration of the principle involved in this doctrine of healing through mental supremacy, and also of the higher claim of mental and moral exaltation, illumination and personal mastery through spiritual supremacy.

The testing of the principle and law herein presented is so simple, that the words of Jesus in his challenge to the Jews of his time, as they marveled at his teaching, saying, "How knoweth this man letters, having never learned?" apply with equal pertinency to the men of our day in reference to the same teaching. "Jesus answered them and said, My teaching is not mine, but his that sent me. If any man willeth to do his will, he shall know of the teaching, whether it be of God, or whether I speak from myself."

VITALITY, ITS NATURE AND SOURCE.

Vitality being the product of life in organic structures, is simply the measure of life's activities in those structures. Hence a depleted or low state of vitality indicates not so much a deficiency of life, as a deficient activity of the living power, or the energy of life in the vital processes. There can be no actual loss of energy, since what is expended in one direction is always conserved and stored in another direction. Hence, also, energy exists in two forms: first, as latent, stored, or potential energy; second, as liberated and active. This is as true of the specific energy of life as of all other forms of force.

Life is the stored energy or potentiality of God, and vitality is its active manifestation in organic structures. In man, with his free powers of consciousness and volition, the mind is endowed with the inherent capacity for liberating, so to speak, and calling into organic activity this stored energy of life, by the concentration of his mind upon it in desire and faith to this end. So long, therefore, as life holds the citadel in suffering organisms, however inactive or enfeebled it may seem to have become, it has the latent energy to rally and re-assert its supremacy, assuage pain, cast out disease and heal and restore the injured organism, when thus evoked and intelligently co-operated with in faith, by the free powers of the mind concentrated upon it to this end. "A bruised reed shall he not break, and the smoking flax shall he not quench: he shall bring forth judgment unto truth." The smoking flax can be blown into a flame, and the bruised reed renewed by the deposit and appropriation of new material. So with the human body, its waning life may be renewed by the action of desire and faith (the prayer of faith), and its wasted and injured tissues restored by nutrition and re-construction.

That this healing and restoring power exists as a divine potency, latent in the so-called physical life of every man, however low or enfeebled that life may seem to be, and that it may be evoked and called into full activity by a purely mental stimulus from the direct action of the mind itself, is demonstrated beyond question by the numerous facts of immediate and spontaneous recovery of invalids who were actually helpless on beds of fever, or enfeebled to the last degree from lingering, painful and wasting disease, being startled into utter forgetfulness of their weakness and suffering by an earthquake shock, an alarm of fire or other impending calamity. Completely absorbed in the one thought of escape, these invalids, who a few moments before were powerless to help themselves, have risen from their beds in a sudden and marvellous accession of strength, liberated and called into activity by the intensity of the mental excitement, and the concentration or absorption of the attention involved, and performed feats of physical strength and agility impossible to them in their normal condition of health.

These facts have led many thoughtful minds to regard the reserved energy of life as far greater than that which is called into play in the ordinary activities by the unexcited will.

As the fountain of life is with God, its power is simply a question of the ability of the organism to appropriate it. The numerous well-authenticated and continually increasing instances of "Faith cure," "Prayer cure," etc., under nearly every form of religious belief, during the last few years, also attest and illustrate this truth.

The immediate influence of the mind over the vital processes, however, is equally powerful for ill, so that there is a "Mind kill" as well as a "Mind cure." Powerful and intense emotions of joy, as well as of terror, have been sufficient to actually destroy as well as to restore in certain delicate conditions of the organic system. In disease of the heart patients have died under the very act of anointing and prayer for healing, the death being undoubtedly hastened by the mental excitement attending the act. Nevertheless these fatalities but attest the truth of the almost absolute sway of the mental states over the vital processes for good or ill, and illustrate the necessity of a full and correct understanding of this great law.

Minds of ordinary intelligence can be inducted into

this understanding, and taught the practical application of the principle in daily life, to the immediate healing of injuries often severe, and all sudden attacks of disease, and to the cure of chronic ailments and weakness in themselves and others. This has been abundantly demonstrated in the writer's experience in both class and private instruction, so that in view of the great importance of this practical knowledge, all should be encouraged to seek its attainment.

THE MISTAKE OF IGNORANCE.

Through ignorance of this divine energy lodged in his own organism, ready to be evoked and called into activity by mental recognition and active co-operation by faith, man when injured or diseased resorts at once to external agencies supposed to be remedial; whereas if properly enlightened he would realize and understand that the only healing power is in the life and vitality of his own being. He would also understand that this healing power of life is more subject to the direct influence of his own mind than to all other agencies combined, either to quicken and exalt, or to repress and retard its operations. He would know that the understanding and skilful direction of mental influence is the most potent and certain remedial agent possible to employ. He would also understand that next to the influence of the sufferer's own mind over his bodily states, is the direct influence of sympathizing friends; for good or ill, according to their faith or fear.

The processes of life in individuals being subject in greater or less degree to the influence of other minds, in personal contact or sympathy, and especially their influence on the mind of the patient, and through this more potently still upon his body, the understanding and intelligent application of this law enables all to become healers in greater or less degree.

Whether understood or not, the direct and powerful influence on invalids and sensitive people from their immediate associates, is vastly beyond what is generally realized or understood. Even the general state of the public mind, the convictions and impressions that dominate a community—as before stated—affect and mold more or less the life, character and health of the individuals composing it. Only those who have a strongly pronounced personality can wholly resist this influence. Hence when fear and dread of disease and the mental recognition of its power over the life and vitality of man prevail in a community, those of that community who are taken ill, unless enlightened by personal understanding of the supremacy of life and mind over any possible disease, are certain to come into full bondage to its power—power given to it by the mind itself through this ignorance and fear. And when on the other hand a community becomes enlightened on this subject, when a full understanding of this law of the influence of the mind upon and over the vital processes becomes universal, the fear and dread of disease, and with these the power of disease will be destroyed. Each responsible person, then, will have become his own physician and have the power of self-healing. Children, imbeciles, and even the strong, when from severe injuries or any cause rendered unconscious, delirious, or in any way helpless, will be held and restored by the interposition of sympathizing friends.

Nor is the case materially altered whether we regard the functions of life as ordained of God, or as the spontaneous organic deposit of that supreme energy of Nature which upholds the stars in their courses, maintains the balance of harmony in the movements of suns and planets, and operates in all the mechanical and vital processes of the world, and therefore in the specific processes of the organic life of man. The fact and the law remain the same. The constructive, re-constructive, and healing functions of life exist and are spontaneously operative wherever life is manifest in plant, animal or man. And being the organic expression of that supreme energy, the force is of necessity charged with the very potency of the power that moves and controls the world, whether that power be itself governed by a blind necessity or omniscient wisdom and beneficense.

This law of the interaction of mind upon the body, its

necessary influence for good or ill upon the vital processes, and the almost absolute power of faith to quicken, exalt and establish the healing power in supreme activity in any affected portion of the body, remains the same whether we take one view or the other of the supreme energy of Nature and life.

Even the materialist, who cannot realize and therefore does not recognize the existence of a personal Deity active in creation, can accept and enter into this general philosophy and exercise this faith for healing, so long as he recognizes Nature as an organic system animated and governed by a universal principle of life, or a supreme energy that ultimates in life and intelligence, provided he recognizes and understands also this law of the interaction of the mind upon the body. Yet how much more uplifting and inspiring to recognize, in this wonderful bestowment of life and its marvelous functions, the hand of a divine and loving Father, and thus realize ourselves the children of his love and care, heirs to the divine supremacy and beatitudes of being which characterize his nature and existence. How much better to come into the understanding of ourselves as the spiritual beings that we are, in our real nature, endowed with the attributes of our Heavenly Father, and through this understanding assert our inherent spiritual supremacy. It is thus we truly achieve our emancipation from and rise above the limitations of flesh and sense; for the flesh is but a temporary garment of materiality woven into the life, and held by that life around the indestructible form of the spiritual organism for temporary service, while the real man is acquiring an earthly education and discipline in the school of the senses.

While the regenerate life secures the health and perfection of the body as well as the soul, since the body is taken up and held in the perfection of that life, the question of physical health and healing is not a question of morals or spirituality *per se;* for men and women have been exempt from disease and physical disability, who were complete moral and social outlaws; while some of the purest souls who have ever adorned our earth have endured untold physical suffering.

Health is the law and the rule of the animal world, and disease the exception. The same is largely true of the animal man. Hence physical healing in the common life of man, is only a question of the recognition and assertion of mental supremacy over bodily conditions—which any one of ordinary intelligence can learn to exercise, by an understanding of the law herein elucidated—and with this the bestowment of reasonable care on the body.

The question of spiritual illumination and the attainment of the God-consciousness, however, embraces all that is essential in morals and religion. In seeking this attainment, the body must be regarded as the instrument and servant of the soul—not its master.

This achievement of our emancipation from the purely physical sense of life, and the establishment of the spiritual and real sense of indestructible being, effected through the understanding and development of our inherent spiritual nature and supremacy, does not destroy nor injure our physical relationship to and with the external world. On the contrary, it perfects such relationship by subordinating the body and its senses so fully to the higher spiritual nature, that the body itself is held by that conscious supremacy of the soul, while it remains its organic instrument, absolutely above the power of disease from any cause. "They shall take up serpents; and if they drink any deadly thing, it shall not hurt them."

With proper care and physical training, organic health, healing and physical perfection are attainable through mental supremacy; but mental illumination, self-mastery and moral perfection are reached only through spiritual supremacy with proper mental discipline; while the understanding and practical application of the great law of faith and focalized attention are absolutely essential to both.

The recognition and understanding of the fact that the body is but a mere clothing of the indestructible spiritual organism, and as such is designed to be held in complete subordination to and controlled by the power of the conscious ego or *I Am*, will awaken sufficient faith or conscious power to assert this inherent spiritual supremacy, and enable its possessor to achieve personal emancipation from sensuous limitations. With this emancipation he will rise into that realization of spiritual and indestructible being which holds the body and its sensations in full subordination to the soul in its conscious transcendency, and render physical disease impossible forevermore.

The indwelling spirit of God is the inner and divine light in which the faculties of the soul by introversion and inward concentration, may become awake and active and thus take on divine illumination and power. The recognition of this great central truth will awaken the faith needed to give the soul in full and holy consecration to the work of this divine attainment, which, when reached, will be found to embrace all; the perfection of body as well as of soul

Faith is the key which unlocks this

STOREHOUSE OF GOD

In the soul of man, and gives him free access to its inexhaustible treasures of love, wisdom and power. Faith awakens the power to do and to become, and Will appropriates the power thus evoked and expends it in the activities of the personal life. All healthful activity or exercise of the soul's powers in accord with the spirit and purpose for which they were given, tends to their development and perfection. It is "he that willeth to do his will" that "shall know of the teaching," and be enabled to exercise his functions wisely and thus attain perfection in them, even as the "Father in heaven is perfect."

When the gifts of life are used to selfish ends this object is defeated, as the spirit of selfishness is self-limited and self-destructive. The spirit of righteousness on the other hand is self-constructive and limitless as the spirit and purpose of God. Hence, will, exercised in this spirit, will, which seeks to appropriate and apply power to the ends for which it was bestowed, shall bring the personal life and all its functions to the complete realization of its own loftiest ideals. Hence also, the first great injunction of the Master, "Seek *first* the kingdom of God and his righteousness," his righteous ends and purposes, and all needed good "shall be added unto you. " Be not deceived, said the great apostle, "God is not mocked; for whatsoever a man soweth, that shall he also reap. For he that soweth unto his own flesh shall of the flesh reap corruption; but he that soweth unto the Spirit shall of the Spirit reap eternal life."

Faith, exercised in the spirit of love and consecration to God, secures this divine beatitude; while the spirit of selfishness forever defeats its own unholy ambitions and purposes. This spirit of selfishness shuts out of the personal life the choicest blessings which a divine and loving Providence holds in its keeping for *all* the objects of its care; just as fear, anxiety and distrust shut out the healing power of life in diseased and suffering organs and bodies.

This is a universal and inevitable law of life, and embraces the social and national as well as the personal spheres of man. Abundant illustrations of its working have come under the observation of the writer in his experience as a physician.

The physician or healer who most forgets himself in his desire and effort to relieve and help his patients, regardless of the good that may return to him in reputation, increased patronage, or material compensation, will find the more divine and perfect will be his work and its result; while to the full extent in which selfishness becomes the motive and inspiration of his work, will his power for actual service be crippled, and sooner or later wholly lost.

Great natural endowments may enable a selfish soul to prosper for a time, and seemingly refute the universality of the rule here stated; but ultimately the weight of ill-gotten gain will prove a mill-stone around his neck, from which there can be no release, save through an awakened spirit of restitution and ministration.

No man can rise to the perfection of his character and gifts, but through the spirit and purpose that found utterance in the words and deeds of Christ. "The Son of Man came not to be ministered unto, but to minister, and to give his life a ransom for many." Just so far as the healer enters into the spirit which characterized that perfect man and Son of God, and makes it the ruling motive and inspiration of his life and work, will he rise into a corresponding grandeur and nobility of character, and come into possession of the power of the Christly life.

This lesson, however, is not for the healer alone, but for the patient as well. When the Great Teacher uttered that mighty affirmation concerning the power of faith, "Therefore I say unto you, what things soever ye desire, when ye pray believe that ye receive them, and *ye shall have them*," he followed it with these impressive words: "And when ye stand praying, forgive, if ye have aught against any; that your Father also which is in heaven may forgive you your trespasses. But if ye do not forgive, neither will your Father which is in heaven forgive your trespasses."

It is selfish and useless to ask of God or man that which we are unwilling to grant to another, even to a stranger or an enemy; since this spirit reacts upon itself and defeats its own ends. "Whatsoever a man soweth, that shall he also reap."

That spirit of selfishness which seeks the greatest good for the smallest possible return, even without compensation if it can be had, is found to be one of the greatest barriers to both the bestowment and the reception of the blessing. Indeed physicians of all schools have found that those patients who were exceedingly close in the matter of remuneration for service rendered, were the hardest to relieve of their ailments. The spirit that holds self so closely, tends also to hold disease by the same grip; while the generous spirit which desires and seeks to bestow upon the healer a good, equal at least to that which he desires and seeks of him, opens the patient at once to the full benefit which the healing gift is capable of bestowing. "The Greeks held it dangerous to accept gifts from the gods; even at the altar, men must give as well as receive if their relations with the Invisible and the Eternal are to be moral and self-respecting."

If we would one and all come into the blessings of the Christ-life, we must seek and take on the spirit of Christ. "Except a man have the spirit of Christ he is none of his," whatever his profession may be. It is the anointing spirit of the Father in his children; "For he maketh his sun to rise on the evil and on the good, and sendeth rain on the just and on the unjust." "He is kind to the unthankful and the evil."

When the love of God exists in his children and becomes actually manifest in their lives toward each other, it melts and wins the stoniest heart; while the healing power of God which ever flows forth with his love, heals the most obstinate and loathsome diseases.

"As many as are led by the spirit of God, they are the sons of God."

It was in the name and power of this spirit of divine love and ministration, which became incarnate in Jesus and made him the Christ, that men were to "cast out devils," "speak with new tongues;" and if they took up serpents and drank "any deadly thing" it should "not hurt them;" and in which they were to "lay hands on the sick and they" should "recover." It was in and through the same spirit that men were to become endued with power from on high, and to receive those marvelous gifts mentioned by Paul— the gift of wisdom, of knowledge, of faith, of healing, of working of miracles, of prophecy, of divers kinds of tongues, and of the interpretation of tongues.

Let us, then, "have faith in God," and exercise that fidelity to his holy and perfect law of life which a genuine faith implies, the law of charity or love and ministration. Then shall we rise to the highest degree of wisdom, knowledge and perfection of being in the kingdom of life, and realize in the fullest and most literal sense, that grand and blessed promise of the Christ, our great Leader and Spiritual Head, that "Nothing shall be impossible unto" us. May every reader join with the writer in faith and consecration to this end. "Bear ye one another's burdens, and so fulfill the law of Christ."

THE SCHOOL OF THE CHRIST,

OR THE

HIGHER EDUCATION BASED UPON THE SPIRITUAL NATURE AND PSYCHIC POWERS OF MAN.

"GOD IS SPIRIT,"—Intelligence and Wisdom, Love and Goodness, Energy and Creative Power, Omniscient, Omnipresent and Omnipotent. These are the necessary attributes of original, self-existent Being. He is not only the animating life and all-embracing providence of creation, but in a special sense the Father of mankind. This conception and affirmation holds the first and fundamental position in the teaching and Theosophy of the Christ.

Man is the immediate offspring of God, since he is the only self-conscious personal identity and intelligence on our planet, and no other existence prior to man could bestow on him these transcendent endowments. The rational, moral and inspirational powers which distinguish him from the animal creation, are the attributes only of spiritual being. They link man with Divinity and attest his spiritual origin, nature and destiny.

The essential and real man is a spirit; clothed upon with a fleshly garment of refined and flexible material, woven into the life and held around the indestructible form of the spiritual organism, as a physical instrument through which to come in contact with and handle the things of the outer world.

Man is not a physical being or body with an indefinable something called a soul, but a living and spiritual being, with a physical body and its senses as a medium of communication with the physical world, and an instrument of service in acquiring the mastery of that world. Hence all that pertains to man of a physical and sensuous character, is transient in its nature and designed only for temporary service, to be wholly subordinated to and ruled by the higher powers of the internal, spiritual and true man.

As a spiritual being and child of God, man of necessity partakes of the nature and attributes of the Father; yet because he is first a child, that which is actual and manifest in the Father is of necessity but potential and possible to him in his childhood stage, just as the full-grown oak is potential in the acorn and the adult man is a possibility in the child. Nevertheless, because of the inherent

POSSIBILITIES OF GOD-HOOD

In man as the child of Deity, holding potentially his nature and attributes, he must and will under the proper conditions unfold into all the perfection and supremacy of being which characterize the Father.

The human attributes of reason, conscience and faith, are the germs of the Divine Nature implanted in material conditions for their individualization and primary development, and when sufficiently established in organic function on the sensuous plane, are capable of being exercised in and thereby illuminated from the Divine Spirit, and thus take on a divine activity and unfold the real man into the express image and likeness of the Father, a true son or reproduction of God—a God-man. This is the second fundamental concept and affirmation of the Christ in his Theosophy.

God being pure Spirit, his attributes of wisdom, goodness and power could be expressed and made manifest only through a divine economy and government. This necessitates the universe as a field of the divine activities, and makes of it a vast organism, projected from the exhaustless depths of Spiritual Being, and throbbing with the indwelling, energizing principles of the Divine Nature. Hence the conception of the poet,

"All are but parts of one stupendous whole,
Whose body Nature is, and God the Soul."

As the outward universe was a necessity for the external manifestation of the Being of God and the reproduction of Himself in children after his own image and likeness, so the physical body and its senses were a necessity for the individualization of the human spirit and its powers in their differentiation from the divine and universal Spirit, as the offspring of God. Hence the primary development of the human powers on the plane of the external senses was a necessary preparation for their higher evolution on the plane of the internal and spiritual.

The manifestation of God in creation was from within outward, from the Spiritual to the physical; but man being born into and under material conditions, first awakening to consciousness and commencing his career on the plane of the external and physical,

REVERSES THIS ORDER,

And rises as he unfolds inwardly to the final realization of his true being as a spiritaal man and child of God.

The universe, both physical and spiritual, is the birth-place, home, school-room and play-ground for the commencement, development, education and perfection of man as the immediate offspring of Deity. The physical world and the sensuous life are the nursery and primary department of this school, in which the All-Father places his children of the infant classes, for their first rudimentary education and training in the object lessons of this world, through the senses.

This effects the individualization of the human

spirit as a personal identity, and establishes its various powers in organic function and activity. The great primary lesson of life, the recognition of inexorable law, the necessity of personal obedience, and the sense of dependence upon and accountability to a higher power, and so of personal responsibility, is also fully acquired through the discipline of experience in this school of the sensuous life.

The outward world, however, being but the external and temporary manifestation of a corresponding inner world of permanent realities, has served its purpose when it has called forth and individualized the various powers of the spiritual man in their relation to the externals of things. These powers are then prepared to take on their higher psychic activity in their corresponding relation to the internal of things, through which man enters upon the higher department of the school of life, on the plane of the spiritual. "Howbeit that is not first which is spiritual, but that which is natural, then that which is spiritual."

The object of the physical body, as before stated, is the individualization of the spiritual organism and the establishment of its various functions; while the object of the physical senses is to focalize externally the perceptive powers of the mind in their relation to the objects of the outward world as the means of calling forth and exercising the higher mental and moral powers in the study of these objects and their relations.

When this end is accomplished in the establishment of the primary consciousness and sensuous understanding, the perceptive powers of the mind may then in turn become focalized inwardly, by concentrating the attention in desire and confidence to this end.

When the perceptive powers manifest in the five physical organs of sense are thus turned within and focalized upon the purely psychic plane of action, they become one all-inclusive inner sense, through which the mind comes into immediate contact and communication with the internal or soul of things—with their real character, quality and condition. This has very properly been termed the "sixth sense," and also the "psychometric," or true soul-measuring perception.

It should be remembered, that it is not the eyes, ears, and nerves, that see, hear, feel, etc., but the mind that sees, hears, feels, tastes and smells, in and through these physical organs; hence these functions are essentially mental, not physical. The physical organs of sense are but the instruments of the mind's activities on the plane of the external for its primary education and development; but the unfolding powers of the soul were not meant to be confined to the narrow and superficial limits of sense perception.

The external perception being but the outward focalization of the mind's perceptive powers in physical organs, when these powers become in turn focalized inwardly, they combine in unity of action in one all-comprehensive sense of inward perception. But this perception is of the inward quality and condition of things, rather than of the outward form, though the external is readily determined from the character of the internal.

By this unity of action, or unity of the mind's activity on the plane of inward perception or vision, the

POWER OF PERCEPTION

Is enhanced many fold; indeed is made practically perfect. "If thine eye be single thy whole body shall be full of light."

This higher psychic development is open and possible to all men under the proper conditions. Indeed the soul cannot attain the full measure of its normal development without it. Some will say, however, that it is only for the few who are exceptionally organized; that it is not attainable by others in the period of an ordinary life-time. Nevertheless man is organized with direct reference to this experience, which is one of the necessary and legitimate steps in his normal development.

The imperfect and abnormal results of experiment in this direction have grown out of the misconception and misunderstanding of the nature of the development itself, and also of the processes through which it is to be normally attained. In all purely mental processes, the results are largely determined by the dominant ideas at the time of experimentation. "As a man thinketh in his heart, so is he."

We unhesitatingly and positively affirm, from what we have seen in clear spiritual vision, that this higher psychic development is possible to every one whose mental and moral faculties have become fully individualized and established on the plane of the external senses, which it is the chief object of the senses to accomplish.

In the savage and barbaric stages of human growth, the world was not ready for this higher education. The object-teaching of the sensuous life was then a necessity, and the external method the only one either practicable or possible. But when the fulness of time had come, for which the world had been prepared, by the seers and prophets which the ages had produced, the true Spiritual man appeared, introduced the School of the Spirit, and established its interior methods for the higher advanced training of mankind. In the realm of the Spirit this supreme Teacher is still active and at the head of the work of this school, which is thus very properly called "The School of the Christ."

This training of the psychic powers may now be commenced in childhood; and the education of the external man from the first, be subordinated to and co-ordinated with the internal. This has been fully demonstrated in practical experience, some striking illustrations of which are given in the appendix.

"Suffer little children to come unto me," said the Christ, "and forbid them not, for of such is the kingdom of heaven."

The true school of the Christ, with its spiritual method for the higher education and development of man on earth, is not responsible in any way for the monstrous misconceptions and perverted teaching of theology, which, blind to the possibilities of man in this world, is mainly concerned about the heaven and hell, or conditions of another world. The ideal of the Christ for which he taught his disciples to labor and to pray, was, "Thy kingdom come and thy will be done on earth as it is in heaven."

This higher psychic culture is not so much a question of physical susceptibility, as of mental determination. It is true that mind and body are mutually interdependent, and that primarily, physical conditions largely determine mental states; but mind is designed and destined for the mastery, and so in turn may and can determine absolutely physical conditions.

The primary object of physical sensation is to awaken, develop and focalize the attention, and thereby awaken, individualize and call into activity the perceptive powers of the mind in their separate and divided activity, through the several physical organs of sense, and through perception, to call into action the still higher mental and moral powers in their relation to the objects of the outward world to which the attention has been called; in other words, to awaken and compel thought and establish understanding. But when from this spontaneous reaction of the mind upon sensation, the power of attention is developed and the perceptive powers fairly focalized in and through the organs of sense, by which the higher powers of thought and understanding are established, the attention may in turn be controlled by volition. It is then concentrated upon any object externally or internally at will, by which the perception is also turned and focalized in the same direction; and thought and understanding correspondingly awakened and established in reference thereto.

All action on the primary plane of sensation, is from necessity, spontaneous; but on the higher plane of mentality or of thought and volition, when these are fully established, it becomes a matter of determination and choice. It is true that habit finally renders chosen and selected paths automatic and spontaneous; but even these in turn may be broken up and changed by an effort of choice and will.

So while the activities of mind and soul are spontaneous on the plane of the sensuous life, and in a large degree like the activities of the animal, an enforced necessity, on the higher planes of mind and spirit sense becomes subordinated to soul, and sense-perception to inward vision, and the higher judgment and volition become the determining power of both sensation and mental as well as physical action.

Man is not only a circumstance, but a centerstance as well. At first a creature of circumstances he holds potentially within himself a power which sooner or later becomes awakened, and springing forth, enables him to rise above circumstances and create and direct them to suit himself. This is the

SUBLIME DESTINY

Awaiting all men through the achievement of man himself, the strong helping the weak.

The school of the Christ opens its doors to the humble as well as the great, and converts the strong into willing, loving helpers of the weak. In this school, all distinction of caste and rank is lost in the spirit of Brotherhood and the recognition of equality of rights and privileges.

External vision is spontaneously opened by the stimulus of the impinging environment, and the attention and perception thereby awakened and focalized; but internal vision and perception are opened only by focalizing the attention upon the object of desire, by direct volition. The psychic vibrations of focalized desire upon the inner medium of communication—the spiritual ether—creates the light in which the object of desire is perceived; hence the clearness of the vision depends upon the completeness of the inward focalization.

Thus the process of developing the psychic powers of the sixth sense, is the reverse of that on the plane of the external and sensuous. On the internal plane man sees, hears, feels, tastes and smells only that to which his attention is directed, and upon which his perceptive powers are focalized; while on the external his attention is spontaneously awakened and focalized by and upon what he first sees, hears, feels, etc.

Sensation first awakens attention and calls forth perception, thought and volition; but when these are fully developed, they in turn may direct perception and control sensation. It then becomes simply a matter of choice and volition, or desire and faith, since what a man really desires to do and believes he can, that he will do.

It is not denied but this psychic development is and will be more readily attained by some than others, yet we re-affirm that it is

POSSIBLE TO ALL,

Through the earnest effort which comes of real desire and faith. "All things are possible to him that believeth." This is the emphatic teaching of the Christ, and the concordant teaching of all truly inspired seers and teachers.

Is it because the nature of this attainment and of

the higher education it involves are misunderstood or misconceived, that so few really desire them? "Who hath believed our report?" asked the prophet. When the call to this higher education is made, do they not all with one consent begin to make excuse? The attractions and demands of the sensuous life outweigh with the many, those of the spiritual. "Where thy treasure is there will thy heart be also."

As the primary consciousness of the external man is awakened and established by mental and moral contact and communication with the outward world through the senses, so the higher spiritual consciousness and understanding are awakened and established by mental and moral contact and communication with the inner world through this inward focalization of attention and perception.

When these are turned to the plane of the sixth or psychometric sense, communication is had only with the internal conditions of personalities and things. But when turned in sufficient desire and faith upon the inmost realm of the Divine and Impersonal, the kingdom of God, the deeper spiritual and seventh or

TRUE GOD-SENSE,

Is opened unto him, which is found to embrace all the rest; since the entire man, outward as well as inward is included in the spirit and its vision, as all beings, things and qualities are included in God.

So long as the human consciousness and the mental and moral activities are confined to the sphere of the external senses, man will be governed by the law of the animal life under which he was born—the law of self and self-seeking. But when he is born into the true spiritual consciousness, the Divine Spirit witnessing with his spirit that he is a child of God, and if a child, then heir—heir of God and joint heir with Christ,—he comes under the law of the spiritual life, the law of impartial love and ministration.

The birth of all men into the physical world, or the first awakening of consciousness in the body, is of necessity on the plane of the external through physical sensation, and under the law of the animal life—physical generation. So the awakening of the spiritual consciousness on the plane of the internal and spiritual, through the inmost or God-sense, constitutes a second birth under the law of the spiritual life—a regeneration from the Spirit.

This, then, is the third fundamental and positive affirmation of the true Christian Theosophy, "Ye must be born again." "Except a man be born anew (from above), he cannot see the kingkom of God." "That which is born of the flesh is flesh; and that which is born of the Spirit is spirit." " Howbeit that is not first which is spiritual, but that which is natural" [pertaining to outward nature], "then that which is spiritual. The first man is of the earth, earthy; the second man is of heaven. As is the earthy such also are they that are earthy; and as is the heavenly, such are they also who are heavenly. As we have borne the image of the earthy, we shall also bear the the image of the heavenly." "The law was a schoolmaster to bring us to Christ," and Christ by his method—the internal and spiritual—brings us to the Father. "And no man cometh unto the Father but by" him, or the method instituted by him. No other way is possible.

The school of Christ is the

ROYAL GATEWAY

To divine wisdom and supremacy. This anointed Teacher is indeed "the light of the world," and they who follow him "shall not walk in darkness, but shall have the light of life." He truly says, "I am the door; by me if any man enter in he shall be saved, and go in and out and find pasture." And again, "If ye continue in my words, then shall ye be my disciples indeed; and ye shall know the truth, and the truth shall make you free." He was a living example and illustration of "The Way, the Truth and the Life" for all men, and no man can follow that example without coming to the Father, nor can any man come to the Father without following him in that example.

The spiritual senses and the inspirational power they confer on man as a source of enlightenment and means of unfolding and bringing to perfection all the powers of the personal life, as much transcend the external senses and methods of education and development, as the soul transcends the body. The cultivation of the inner psychic powers and the processes of their development and activity, are as normal and legitimate also, as are those on the plane of the external.

The deepest research and highest attainment of external science, only bring the more forcibly to bear the painful consciousness of the sensuous limitations; and the aspiring soul the more deeply yearns to break through these narrow confines of physical sense, and find some more direct access to the arcana of knowledge and wisdom. Such access truly awaits man through spiritual sense and inspiration. The philosopher's stone and the elixir of immortal youth were no vain dreams of mediæval sciolists. They exist and will be found by man when he shall cease his vain seeking through the physical, and turns to the spirit within.

As the outward universe or the external departments of the Macrocosm are but the projection outwardly from the internal and inmost, which is pure Spirit, the spirit in itself embraces all. Man being a microcosm or re-production in miniature of the Macrocosm, has within himself the elements and substance of all that is. As the inmost of his being is pure Spirit, it embraces in its exhaustless depths all that he can possibly yearn for and aspire to, as in and through it he is made one with the Divine, from which all things proceed.

The development of the external powers and the study and mastery of external science, are a necessity to the primary education and discipline of the soul's faculties on the sensuous plane, and when pursued with the proper motive can result only in good. The same is true of the cultivation and development of the psychic powers and the mastery of occult science on the plane of the internal or sixth sense.

When occult science is studied for and applied to the advancement of the race and the improvement of man, it is as normal and legitimate a sphere of activity and experience as the corresponding study and application of physical science. But this also has its limitations, and like the knowledge of physical science may be perverted and made the instrument of evil as well as of good. The sphere of the sixth or psychometric sense, being the inner life of personalities and things, the perception of their character, condition, etc., is still the sphere of secondary causes, and under the discipline of inexorable law.

The deepest yearning of the human soul, however, is for absolute freedom and supremacy, and these await man, as the child of the divine Paternity, when he shall seek them in the right direction and true spirit. This is "the glorious liberty of the children of God."

This freedom can be realized only on the plane of

the Spirit, the inmost and highest sphere of human activity and experience, in which being is perfect, and so above all possibility of perverted motive or activity. Being at-one with God, all selfish and isolated interests are forgotten, and the individual interests become merged into and one with the whole, and the universal good the only basis of personal good.

In this realm of the Divine, personal considerations and preferences are impossible, because it is the realm of the impersonal and absolute. Those who attain this condition of being, become a law unto themselves; since every possible desire of the heart is one with the universal, and so one with the supreme law of life.

Until this condition and plane of life is attained, man needs and will have the discipline of law and penalty. Until he rises above all

PERSONAL CONSIDERATIONS

In the presence of universal needs, and thus becomes one with the supreme law of universal love and impartial justice, he is unfit for the possession of unlimited knowledge and absolute power.

When this condition of being is reached, and man becomes at-one with universal law, his life is one spontaneous expression of goodness and truth, love and wisdom, which carries with it all power of mastery. There being no need of law for him, all law in any external sense becomes a dead letter unto him. Though existing in law and one with it, he is yet above law, "and cannot sin because he is born of God."

Studying man in the light of the life and teaching of the Christ, and the corroborative experience and testimony of all inspired souls, and of those also who, whether worthily or unworthily, have sought to fathom and master the realm of the occult and invisible, we find clearly defined and illustrated this three-fold nature of man. Consequently we have to recognize the three distinct spheres or planes of conscious being, activity and experience open to him; each being separated from the other by discreet degrees, rising one above and within the other, from the outward and physical to the inmost and divine.

Each sphere of conscious activity in man the microcosm, relates him directly to the corresponding sphere of the Macrocosm, and thus establishes his three-fold relationship to it, the external, internal, and inmost; the purely physical, the occult or mid realm, and the purely spiritual or divine.

The primary education, development and activity of man, is of necessity on the external plane and within the sphere of the sensuous life. Physical science, art, literature, trade, commerce, government, the daily industries and all that pertains to the external life of mankind, are embraced within and the legitimate products of this sphere. It is not only the right, but the duty of man to make the most of all these, and to bring them and that portion of his nature which they represent, to perfection. But as he has a three-fold nature and the external is but the lowest and primary, this cannot be made perfect without the corresponding development and activity of the other and higher portions of his being, with which it is related and must be co-ordinated.

All the silent forces and secret processes operative in the physical world, being invisible, belong to and are included in the realm of the occult. Hence the perfection of physical science and the full mastery of the outward world are impossible without the corresponding development and mastery of the occult, and for this, the development of seership and all the higher psychic activities are a necessity. So when the perceptive powers of the mind are turned within and become focalized in the one all-comprehensive psychometric sense, or inward perception of the secret processes, man enters upon the higher education for which the psychic powers are needed and were given.

Entering upon the inner and higher plane of the psychic activities, he passes beyond the vestibule of nature, to which physical science is limited, to pursue, in her inner courts those higher studies which the All-Father has provided for the culture and training of his children. It is, therefore, not only the right but the duty of man to enter upon and pursue these studies also; and thus to cultivate and perfect the higher psychic powers with which divine wisdom and goodness have endowed him. He is recreant to his high trust if he does not.

The materialist may deny the existence of these higher psychic powers and the possibilities they involve; and religionists may lift up their hands in holy horror at the "profane" attempt to pry into the "inscrutable mysteries" of nature; nevertheless these higher powers exist, and have been developed and exercised in greater or less degree by thousands. Their existence, furthermore, is the

EXPRESS COMMAND

Of the giver to use them, and behold, what a field he has provided for their activity in the yet unexplored regions of the infinite.

Our great Exemplar and spiritual Leader, assures us that "There is nothing covered that shall not be revealed; neither hid that shall not be known." With his example before us, who controlled the tempest and the waves, walked upon the water, multiplied the loaves and fishes, healed the sick, cleansed the lepers and raised the dead, by the exercise of a psychic power, and promised that his faithful disciples should do the same, we need not hesitate to claim the study and mastery of occult science to be as legitimate to man, and its processes as normal, as are those of physical science; while its power to exalt mankind and improve the world, is vastly greater.

The acquisition of knowledge and the attainment of power on the plane of both the physical and occult sciences may be, it is true, and unless the right spirit is first attained, are liable to be, turned to private and selfish ends, instead of the universal or general good.

The greater the gift and the higher the attainment, the greater the evil when perverted. But when the true spiritual life is first sought, and the law of the Spirit becomes the motive and inspiration of every effort, then man may develop with safety all his powers, and in the higher freedom and power of the Spirit, acquire with ease the knowledge and mastery of both the occult and physical worlds, and make them the better servants of mankind for the mastery.

When man enters into and operates from the inmost and highest plane of his being, his mind becomes illuminated from the omniscient wisdom, his moral sense becomes inspired from the divine goodness, and his faith becomes the channel or expression of divine power; that power which speaks and it is done, which commands and it stands fast. Man then becomes practically one with the Father, and thus sees, speaks, and acts in and from the divine wisdom, goodness and power. He is then enabled to see, speak and act from the throne of being, and wield power from thence; but from that plane he will wield it only for the general good; since such find their own good only in blessing others.

This was the actual life of the Christ, and the method of its realization. "Seek ye *first* the kingdom of God and his righteousness, and all these things shall be added unto you." The kingdom of God is the kingdom of Wisdom, Goodness and Power, the kingdom of the Spirit, whose law is righteousness. It crowns its subjects with the Christly life, and endows them with

SPIRITUAL GIFTS,

Among which is the gift of healing, the Christ power, which is immediate and absolute in its working. O, seeker after power to heal and bless, "seek ye first the kingdom of God and his righteousness," and ye shall have it. "Have faith *in* God," not in something about God,— "and nothing shall be impossible unto you."

As the so-called physical senses are but the external, divided and limited expression of the one all-inclusive inner sixth and mental sense, they are really included in it, and the outer five and the inner sixth sense, are in turn included in the still deeper and higher activities of the seventh and divine sense of the Spirit. The higher of necessity includes the lower, and the inner includes the outer.

Thus the external senses require the co-ordinating activity of the deeper and more comprehensive penetration of the inner psychometric sense, to render mental perception of the truth of anything accurate and just. But, with this, when the perception of the external appearance and the internal character, quality and condition of things is perfect, it is yet only perception, not necessarily understanding. The most complete knowledge of the external and internal qualities of things, does not of itself constitute or imply wisdom.

The power that reads the meaning of facts and correctly interprets and applies their significance, is higher and deeper than is their perception. This is the function of the Spirit in the faculties of mind and sense. Spirit is the only illuminating and interpreting power.

The object of normal introversion for the inward focalization of mental perception, is not, therefore, to wholly suspend the action of the five external senses for the development and exercise of the internal and sixth sense, but to so unfold the power and activity of the inner sense, that it shall act in conjunction with the external, and give the inward perception of the character and history of all things which become the special objects of external attention and perception. Thus the external senses are enhanced and perfected by the awakening and co-operation of the internal psychometric power and penetration.

The independent exercise of the sixth sense is

required only when the object of observation and study lies beyond the sphere and limits of the external senses.

The normal process of introversion for the cultivation and perfection of the psychometric power, upon which all the higher psychic activities are based, does not, we repeat, involve or require the abnormal conditions of somnambulism or trance. The principle on which the result is based lies wholly in the

CONTROL OF THE ATTENTION

By will and determination.

On the external plane as previously explained, the attention is spontaneously awakened, directed and focalized by physical sensation. This concentration of attention awakens and focalizes the perceptive tive powers on the object of attention. The perception of the object of attention, in turn awakens and calls forth thought about the object, and thought awakens some degree of understanding concerning it.

So it will be seen, that physical sensation *spontaneously* enforces attention, and this in turn awakens perception, and this again compels thought, and thought judgment; each process of necessity opening inward, approaching nearer and nearer the fountain of spirit within, and receiving the light of its original intelligence. By this process the human mind has been gradually unfolded from the savage to the civilized condition, in the slow advance of the ages, and is now practically repeated in all the mental activities of every day experience. But when we come to this higher plane of the psychic and spiritual, above the sphere of physical sensation, the awakening and direction of the attention is wholly a matter of desire and will, or choice and determination—direct volition.

On the external plane the impressions from external objects through physical sensation, awaken and

ENFORCE ATTENTION,

And this in turn awakens perception; but on the plane of the internal the mind perceives only that to which the attention is voluntarily directed, and this we repeat is *wholly a matter of choice and volition.*

When the attention is fully concentrated in desire and faith upon any legitimate object or subject of perception on the internal plane, that perception or vision is as spontaneously and necessarily awakened and focalized, as on the plane of the external senses; and the full development of the internal perception in any direction, awakens and calls forth corresponding thought in that direction, which opens a high degree of understanding of the same.

In this state of inward concentration, all these processes partake in a greater or less degree of intuition; as a fuller influence of the spirit is felt and its light called forth in greater degree by this inward, than by the external process. But when the full and perfect light of the spirit is recognized, and this process of introversion and inward concentration is brought to bear in this understanding, and the desire for the illumination and teaching of the spirit is focalized in confidence upon the object or subject of attention, the perception under the enlightening power of the spirit becomes the clear vision of truth, thought becomes intuition, and understanding inspired wisdom.

When the mind and heart have been fully awakened and trained on the plane of the internal, through these processes, all the external powers are overruled and guided by the internal or psychic activities, and these in turn by the spiritual and divine. The mind in all its activities, on the plane of the external or internal, is then illuminated and governed by spontaneous wisdom, the heart enlightened and inspired by supreme goodness, and the whole life crowned with kingly power. The man is then at-one with himself, and so with God; and the plane of the Christ life is reached.

No intelligent and practical effort will be put forth to attain this divine realization, however, until the divine nature or pure spirit is recognized as the inmost life and illuminating power of the soul, and the soul itself is recognized as the organic personality, the real and spiritual man; and the body its organic instrument of service to be wholly subordinated to and ruled by the soul. The mind is the focalized intelligence of the soul; and when fully illuminated by the spirit becomes the focalized intelligence of the spirit.

We have already shown that the inward vision perceives only those things to which the attention is voluntarily directed. This is an important fact and law of mind which must not be lost sight of, especially in seeking the development of its purely psychic activities on the plane of the internal and spiritual. We must therefore remember that while the consciousness of God in his omniscience embraces all things at once, the consciousness of the spiritually illuminated man, is omniscient only in a single direction, at once. But on whatever object, subject, place or thing, the fully illuminated mind is centered, in that single direction it is practically omniscient, omnipresent and omnipotent.

The light of the outward world is caused by the vibrations of the solar ray on or in the surrounding atmosphere of the globe, or from the radiation of some artificial incandescence. In this light all objects are seen on the plane of external perception.

On the inner plane of psychic perception, the light in which objects are seen, is produced by the vibrations of mental activity upon the spiritual ether or internal atmosphere, already described, as the medium of internal communication between mind and mind, and the inward activities of all beings and things. It is the direct medium of thought transference, and of psychometric perception and impression.

The inward focalization of desire and attention, in confidence upon any object, produces the light in which the object itself is seen. But on the plane of the spiritual, the light in which any object or subject is seen, is the light of pure intelligence and goodness. It is the pure vision of truth and righteousness. It is the light of omniscient wisdom and absolute goodness,

THE VISION OF GOD,

In which no limit or mistake of perception, unjust or imperfect discrimination is possible. But it should be remembered that while God in his omniscience always sees and knows all things perfectly, the human mind can see and know only one thing *perfectly* at once. "If thine eye be single thy whole body shall be full of light."

The human spirit is the specialization of the Universal Spirit, expressed through organs of special sense and function; hence, however perfect this organic expression may become, it must of necessity be in the direction of the special function in and through which it is expressed.

The development of the spiritual vision, therefore, does not involve or imply the suspension, suppression, or absorption of any power or function of the external man by the spirit; but rather, the full coming forth and embodiment of the spirit in the organic powers and functions of the external man, by which they are brought to their highest perfection of activity and use, and the external becomes one with the internal and true man.

Remembering the three-fold nature of man and the three corresponding distinct planes of his possible mental activity and experience, and remembering further, that on the internal plane he can see only those things to which his attention is specifically directed, it will be understood that if his attention embraces only the psychic activities of the sphere of the sixth sense, his experience will be held to the limitations of this sphere, however these may transcend those of the external. Hence if he would have the unlimited freedom and infallible vision of the spirit, he must direct his attention in desire and faith *wholly* upon the spirit.

The key to this exalted experience of spiritual illumination and power, was fully indicated and illustrated in the teaching and experience of George Fox and the early Friends. The history of that movement in the day of its power, is a treasury of suggestive illustration of priceless value to every seeker after the higher wisdom, next in importance to that of the Christ and Apostolic experience, and of especial value to us, because so near our own time and of unquestioned fact.

Had they not been trammeled by the blinding bias

of tradition, which centuries of misconception and perverted teaching had fastened upon the religious thinking of the world, they would have restored the fulness and power of the Apostolic life and experience to the world.

Ignorant of the nature of man and his divine possibilities in this world, and biased by the dominant absurd impression that the operations of the spirit on and in man here, were only to save him to the heaven and from the hell of another world, they limited their attention and effort to a purely religious experience; which, however, in their case was honestly made to embrace the entire conduct and relations of life. Their distorted views of the next world and the relations of this life to that, tended to cast a sombre hue over the present, and prevented a full rounded development of their whole being.

Under these conditions some degree of fanaticism and absurdity of conduct were inevitable. Still, in spite of these drawbacks, they had the most remarkable demonstrations of the reality of inward spiritual illumination, leading and power, which the world has seen since the Apostles went to their rest. Other centuries have not been wanting in similar spiritual awakenings and leadings.

The secret of the remarkable spiritual experience and power of the early Friends, lay in their full recognition of the inner spiritual light,

THE CERTAIN POSSIBILITY

Of all men being directly illuminated, taught and led by the spirit within, and the absolute necessity of silencing the activities of the outward man, and looking and listening to the divine light and voice within, and speaking and acting only in and from the immediate inspiration they were sure to receive. "Mind the light," "Do not go before you are sent," and similar injunctions were the common exhortations of their inspired leaders.

Out of this central principle of their inspirations and experiences, grew their form of silent worship; and the mighty openings and movings of the Spirit among the silent waiters and inward listeners, was often greatest when no word was spoken or any outward service engaged in. Large gatherings would sometimes thus be simultaneously moved to deep moods and waves of melting, weeping tenderness and love, and strangers even, witnessing for the first time these silent, awe-inspiring scenes, were often stricken with a solemn sense of a Divine Presence, and, moved to deepest contrition of soul, would seek and find that peace and reconciliation of heart and life found only in "the washing of regeneration and renewing of the Holy Spirit."

Many going to these strange meetings to laugh or disturb, would remain to pray and cast in their lot with the humble but maligned and persecuted worshippers.

When moved to address the meeting they would often speak with such directness and power to the condition of those present, and sometimes to particular individuals, that the secrets of many hearts were revealed, the proud humbled, and the weak and struggling strengthened and encouraged.

No one can read with unbiased mind, the authoritative record of that mighty movement, without recognizing in their experience a practical demonstration of the reality and power of the Spirit in the life of man, and unmistakable confirmation and illustration of the principle of illumination, set forth in this book.

In the days which followed the Apostles, the setting up of external and arbitrary authority and ceremonial observance, closed the gates of inspiration and shut their followers up to an outward and lifeless form. So it was with the followers of these modern prophets of a better day; and they who held the key to what might have been the

MIGHTIEST UPLIFTING

And advancing movement the world has known, have dwindled to the most insignificant of the religious bodies of our time.

The three-fold nature of man, the sensuous and external, the higher psychic and internal, and the inmost and purely spiritual, when recognized, indicate the true law and method of growth, and the only pathway and means of human perfection.

The lower must be subordinated to, co-ordinated with, and ruled by the higher.

External sense, or perception, needs the co-operative illumination of psychometric penetration, and the understanding needs the interpreting power or illumination of the Spirit, without which neither perception nor understanding can be perfect.

To attain this full co-ordination of the three-fold nature, the higher illuminating and guiding the lower in wisdom and goodness, truth and righteousness, the psychometric sense and the inward illuminating power of the Spirit must be recognized as belonging to all; and so brought forth to take their true position in the personal life of each. The only process through which this can be normally and perfectly accomplished, is by the awakening and cultivation of the higher without the suspension, but by the overruling of the lower.

Every one who fully recognizes the inner light and power of the Spirit, and by introversion turns his attention and mental gaze inward and upward in desire and faith, to that divine centre of his being, will so surely receive a corresponding influx of light and power into all the dependent and subordinate departments of his nature. This influx will also as surely illuminate the mind, enlighten the moral sense, chasten the affections and desires, subdue the animal and the lusts of the flesh, heal the body and bring the whole being into polarity with the spiritual nature, and thus into oneness and harmony with itself, and so with the Divine.

The spirit is always at-one with God, and when the outward and fleshly life is brought into harmony with and under the control of the spirit, it is thereby brought into unity and fellowship with God, and can be brought into the divine unity and fellowship in no other way.

We have said that the spirit in man is so much of God in him, and therefore always at-one with God. So when man recognizes this and lays hold of the spirit within, in thought and desire, as the inmost and highest element of his own being, he lays hold on God. God speaks to man and ministers unto him directly in and through the spirit that is in him; and through this immediate and vital inspiration and ministration of the Father only, can man as his child unfold and realize the power of personal mastery.

As spirit is the inmost and essential life of all men and things, all men, by the gift of choice and volition, are endowed with power to co-operate with God in and through this indwelling spirit, in the development and perfection of their own being. But they cannot do this without seeking at the same time to advance the true interests of all other beings. This is the law of the spirit, and the unity and harmony of man with himself, with God and with his fellow man,

CAN BE REALIZED

In no other way. The first duty, therefore, as well as privilege of man, is to seek this co-operation with God in his life, by listening to and walking in the light of the spirit that the Father has given him. This will teach him all things essential to his own, and the well-being of others; guide him into all truth, and endow him with power to perform and finish the work given him by the Father to do.

There can be no integral education without this recognition and cultivation of the three-fold nature, the spiritual holding the supremacy. Happily, this may be commenced at the first dawning of the sense of responsibility.

The earlier in life this integral education is begun, the better for the individual as well as for society and the world; for man can never be at his best even in the external, without the co-ordinated activity and influence of the internal and spiritual; since the external was designed only as an instrument for the outward activities and manifestation of the internal; and this was meant to be and may become perfect.

The three-fold nature of man was designed for a unity of action and expression by the co-ordination of the lower and external with the higher and internal.

But this is impossible without the recognition of the existence and rightful supremacy of the spiritual nature, and the necessity of its development and activity in the personal life from the age of discretion. This is

THE ONLY BASIS

Of the perfect education and harmonious development of man.

We may define the external man as that consciousness of being which is derived from the activity of the rational and moral powers on the plane of the senses, in their relation to the external world, and under the law of the animal life. The internal man may in like manner be defined as that consciousness of being which is derived from the activity of the same powers on the internal plane of intuition and divine inspiration, under the law of the spiritual life.

When both of these natures have their full normal and legitimate development and activity, the external and lower will be spontaneously subordinated to and ruled by the internal and higher. The equilibrium and harmony of the personal life will then be supreme and perfect, and perversion of function, disease and discord, whether physical or moral, will be impossible.

When, however, the external is developed greatly in excess of the internal, the law of the animal life, which is selfishness, dominates the man, and if the spiritual nature be not entirely suppressed, there will be constant warfare from the protest of the spirit against the perverted activities of the flesh. Hence, when the cultivation of the spiritual nature has been so long neglected as to practically lose its power and influence over the personal life—unless the rational and moral faculties are well developed—the man is liable, under any seductive influence from the outward world that touches peculiarly his animal nature, to fall a victim to its lusts and be brought into complete bondage to its power.

The unrestrained indulgence of the appetites, propensities and impulses of the animal nature, is perfectly normal and legitimate to the brute creation, the animal being organized with direct reference to this law; but utterly demoralizing and destructive on the plane of the human.

Man and his physical powers were organized with specific reference to the activity of his rational and moral nature on the higher plane of the human, under the inspiration and law of the spiritual life. The true work of man on earth is, therefore,

THE SUBJUGATION

Of the outward world; beginning with the physical and animal in his own economy, and bringing all things finally under his dominion and control. "And God said, let us make man in our own image and after our likeness, and let them have dominion over the fish of the sea, and over the fowl of the air, and over the cattle, and over all the earth, and over every living thing that moveth upon the earth."

The physical body and its organs of sense are but the organic instruments of the strictly human powers, in this work of subjugation and attainment. The animal nature and functions were given to provide for and sustain the body, and the spiritual nature which connects man with the divine, to hold the supremacy over all, by which he has power to enter into his kingdom as a son of God.

Until man has acquired this mastery of himself—the kingdom of his own personal life—how is he to grapple with, subdue and bring under his control the forces and conditions of the external world? Absolute self-mastery is possible only through spiritual supremacy, and self-mastery is the only key to universal mastery.

Thus the human body was given as an instrument for the divine activities of the human soul under spiritual inspiration and guidance, while the animal in man was given to serve the body under the control of the spiritual nature. So long as this condition of normal relationship and activity is maintained, nothing but good results; as the activities of the animal functions in their true sphere of use in the human economy, are indispensable and of the most beneficent service to man. Without them the necessities of the body would be forgotten and neglected in the pursuit of truth and virtue, knowledge and wisdom.

Then let the animal in man be cherished and honored, and while held to its subordinate sphere, let it be trained to loyal and useful service, that the physical body may be preserved in health; and life on the plane of the physical be prolonged, until man shall have completed his work in this world, and be fully ripe for his entrance upon higher scenes, for which such experience is a needful preparation.

Since all development of intelligence, and all power of mastery over the outward world must come from the spirit within, the sooner the mind is awakened to the consciousness of this fact, and to a knowledge of the law of mental co-operation with spiritual inspiration, the sooner will it enter upon the path of enlightened progress in the true integral education and perfection of its powers.

The first step in this education, is the liberation of the mind from its sole dependence upon external sense impressions and perceptions, for its knowledge of things. This is effected by the awakening of its activities upon the interior and higher plane of the sixth or psychometric sense, in the full recognition of the still deeper illuminating and interpreting power of the Spirit.

Thus only can the potentialities of all the faculties become fully unfolded and brought to their highest degree of organic perfection, and through this higher attainment, the outer world correctly interpreted and fully mastered.

Since it is not the senses, but the mind that perceives, etc., through the senses, and determines the nature and quality of the things of the outward world with which it thus comes in contact, and since all intelligence proceeds from the spirit within, the mental power to correctly interpret and understand the outward world, depends upon the degree of inward illumination the mind has attained; and this points to the only true source of mental enlightenment.

External perception reaches only the external and sensuous qualities of things, and the appearances thus presented, do not always correspond with the reality for which they stand. Hence the need there is of a corresponding internal and more penetrative vision, to enable the mind to "judge not according to appearance, but to judge righteous judgment," as the Master enjoined.

That this inner power of psychometric perception exists latent in all men, is

FULLY DEMONSTRATED

By its development and activity in the few. So long, however, as man does not know that he possesses this higher psychic power of internal perception, he will not, of course, turn his attention to its cultivation and development.

Were these higher psychic and spiritual powers of the soul universally recognized and cultivated with the external and sensuous, from childhood, as the legitimate and normal education of man, an equilibrium of the mental and spiritual forces would be established in all, as in the childhood of Jesus; the spiritual holding its rightful supremacy.

The reverse of this being the rule, the vast majority of mankind grow up and remain in bondage to the limitations of the sensuous life and understanding.

In order, therefore, to awaken and call forth the long suppressed and dormant higher powers of the soul, and thus restore the lost balance of the inward and outward life, special attention must now be given to their cultivation and development.

Until this unity within the man is established, there is no basis for the unity of the individual with the race in a brotherhood, or with God as the Father and spiritual life of all.

"A house divided against itself cannot stand." Hence this division and want of harmony or true balance in the development of the external and internal powers, is unquestionably the real source of all the diseases, discords and antagonisms that afflict the individual and the social life of man.

In the story of Eden, which so fitly symbolizes the innocence of childhood, the partaking of the forbidden fruit—whereby came the knowledge of good and evil—

plainly meant that yielding to the demands of the animal and sensuous nature against the protest of the spirit, which destroys the just balance between them.

This giving the preponderance to the development of the seusuous, and the corresponding suppression and dwarfing of the spiritual side of man's life, constitutes what is called "The Fall;" and to restore the equipoise and enthrone the spiritual in its rightful supremacy, is

THE PROVINCE OF REDEMPTION;

The work of the higher education in the School of the Christ.

Add to the external man the inward activity of the higher psychic powers, and to these the full illumination and guidance of the spirit, he would be unerringly led in all matters of thought and conduct. "And thine ears," said the prophet, "shall hear a word behind thee, saying This is the way, walk ye in it, when ye turn to the right hand and when ye turn to the left." This is the true "voice of the Lord God walking in the garden" of the soul.

The animal nature in man being lifted up into conjunction with the human, and taking on something of its higher capacity, became "more subtle than any beast of. the field which the Lord God had made," and constitutes the beguiling serpent. This animal nature knowing nothing of truth and right, and speaking in and to the sensuous life, disputes the warning voice of the spirit, and denies the dangers it predicts, seeing good only in indulgence. This is the real devil referred to by Jesus as "a murderer from the beginning because there is no truth in him; he is a liar and the father of lies."

The animal in man, however, is true to the law of its own life on the plane of the brute creation, where the animal body is organized with direct reference to this unrestrained indulgence; but in the human economy its activities are to be restricted to the demands of that higher economy.

On the plane of the animal creation, the inward and the outward life correspond and are practically one. The individual animal is in harmony with himself and his environments. The strong and ferocious have no goadings of conscience for tearing and feasting on the weaker as their prey, because they have acted in obedience to the law of their life; but man, having a conscience, and accountable to a moral law, must be true to himself and act in obedience to this higher law of his own life, through which his highest well-being can alone be realized. He must by the cultivation of the higher and spiritual, acquire the mastery of the animal, which was given to provide for the necessities of the body, not to use it as an

INSTRUMENT OF INDULGENCE.

Each animal obeys the law of its own being; and as

a result is led by an almost unerring instinct. This instinct of the animal, prefigures the nobler intuition and divine inspiration of man, when he too shall come into unity and harmony with himself, and "that which is without becomes as that which is within," and the two now dissevered natures shall become as one. When the lion and the lamb in man shall lie down together, and a young child—the life of innocence—shall lead them. When man being at-one with himself, shall be at-one also with his brother man and with God the Father over and in all.

Method and Specific Processes

OF THE HIGHER EDUCATION.

"Social life is a tumult, in which mankind is entangled. If one, however, will find a fixed point, and not allow himself to be carried away, he may observe the course of things as they pass by him, judge them and weigh them. Such an one lives in freedom and learns that which no instruction can teach him. What passes without is explained and interpreted by the spirit within. But so long as man has only eyes and ears for things external, the inner faculty takes no cognizance of them. All should proceed from within. There lie many hidden mysteries in nature and in man of which we know nothing, because our eyes and ears are wholly engrossed with external things, and because the sounds from without drown the voice from within. O, beloved! wondrous is the life of the inner world by which we live and have our being; and whence flows our consolation and our all. But alas! it awakens no wonder in us. We should be happy if we would listen to the soft whispers of the Spirit, and were not deafened to its murmurs by the mill-wheel of the world."

The key to this

SPIRITUAL SUPREMACY AND ILLUMINATION

Is the union of the external with the internal man,

reached through the inward focalization of the attention in desire and faith upon the divine light and power of the Spirit.

Man can come into conscious unity of being with God only through his inmost and spiritual nature; that is by the co-ordination of the external with the internal, spiritual and true man, which it should never be forgotten, is always at-one with the Father. The recognition and thought of this truth, — that one part of us, and the essential part, is always right and perfect,—is itself a great stimulus and help to the attainment of this unity.

The realization of this internal unity of the lower with the higher and true self and with God, gives the

SPIRITUAL CONSCIOUSNESS,

Or the consciousness of being independent of physical sensation.

The complete co-ordination of the external with the internal man, fully subordinates physical sensation to the higher and permanent sense of spiritual and indestructible being, or the real sense of life in God, and gives the soul complete mastery over the bodily sensations and the functions of the animal life.

The divine beatitude of this state of being must be experienced to be known; it can never be told, save in the inspired language of Scripture, as "the peace of God which passeth all understanding."

Many individuals have had moments of this spiritual consciousness, beatitude, and the attendant illumination, when under some peculiar condition the spiritual has gained a temporary ascendency. These moments of spiritual exaltation are ever remembered as the divinest experiences of life.

In these moments of quickening and exaltation, one flash of intuition has given more real insight than could have been acquired by months of intense study in the same direction, on the external and purely intellectual plane. The

YOUTHFUL JESUS

Among the learned Rabbis in the temple with an understanding vastly beyond his years, was a good example of normal intuition and inspiration, though his full illumination did not come until his public consecration through John's baptism at Jordan, when "the heavens were opened unto him, and the Spirit descended and *abode* upon him." The external was made permanently one with the internal and inmost, and the higher spiritual nature and life descended to abide and become one with and manifest in all the powers and functions of the lower and subordinate nature. The outward and the inward nature became one luminous and divine man.

All who have had fragmentary experiences of this kind, can readily understand what wisdom and power such a condition, if permanent, would confer on its possessor. Such will not wonder at the exceptional life and marvelous attainment of the young and externally uneducated carpenter of Nazareth, after this spiritual supremacy and illumination became the permanent condition of his life.

Seership and all the psychic powers of the sixth sense were evidently fully developed and active in him, brought forth by his spiritual illumination. His perception of distant objects independent of outward vision, and hearing conversation beyond the range and independent of outward hearing, were demonstrated at the calling of Nathaniel by Phillip at the fig tree. His power also to discern the thoughts and read the past and present of those he met, was continually manifest; but in a specific and striking manner with the woman at the well of Samaria.

These powers of psychic vision, hearing, etc., are, however, but the most primary developments of those higher gifts conferred by the spiritual nature, as illustrated in the wisdom and divine supremacy of Jesus. The understanding of the great problems of life and destiny opened to the soul, and the power this understanding gives, for the mastery of the outward world, and over the conditions of life and death, and especially for the mastery of self and the attainment of moral perfection, and a

GODLIKE NATURE,

Are the ultimate blessings conferred by, and to be specially sought for, in this higher education, or the development and co-ordination of the three-fold nature of man. The functions of each, though separate and distinct one from the other, are correlated and become a unity of action when fully co-ordinated.

It is the function of the external senses, or of the mind in and through them, when these activities are accurately trained, to perceive and acquire specific knowledge of the external qualities, relations and condition of things, and thus be enabled to intelligently appropriate and apply them. This, as before remarked, is the legitimate sphere of physical science, art, trade, commerce, the daily and necessary industries, and all that pertains to the outward man. These functions upon which so much depends in the primary education and development of man, cannot be ignored nor neglected with impunity.

It is the function of the inner sixth or psychometric sense, or of the mind's activity on this plane, to perceive and acquire specific knowledge of the corresponding internal qualities, relations and condition of personalities and things, and thus come in contact with and impress itself upon them.

The development of the psychic powers of this sense, or the awakening of the mind's activity on this plane, gives that

NORMAL SEERSHIP,

By which distant persons and objects to which the attention is directed, are distinctly seen, conversation heard when special attention is directed thereto, and any desired subject or specific form of knowledge, as history, science, art or philosophy, directly apprehended, understood and appropriated without the aid of external means or contact; illustrations of which will be found in the Appendix. The development of these psychic powers, and the mastery of occult science acquired only through their development and normal exercise, are a necessity—as a complement to external science—for the full education and training of the mind for the mastery of the outward world and the completion of the work which the All-Father has given man to do here.

The function of the inmost, seventh and true spiritual or God-sense, or of the mind's activities upon the plane of the purely spiritual and divine, is the perception, apprehension, understanding of and affiliation or union with universal principles, absolute truth, impartial justice, impersonal being, the realization of supreme wisdom, goodness and power, to govern and control in every direction, and on every plane.

The focalization of the mind in the specific development of its activities on either one of these planes of the soul's life, requires the special concentration of attention and desire in that one direction, in full expectation and confidence of realizing the result aimed at. Repeated efforts may be necessary, but success is certain through perseverence.

"All miracles," says Eliphas Levy, "are promised to faith; but what is faith except the audacity of a will which does not falter in the darkness, and which advances towards the light in all trials, and overcomes all obstacles? To accomplish anything we must believe in our ability to accomplish, and this faith must be at once translated into action. Faith has

NO TENTATIVE EFFORT;

It begins in the certainty of finishing, and works calmly on as though it had omnipotence at its disposal, and eternity before it."

On the lower and outward plane as we have seen, the attention is enforced by the external environment through sensation, so that thought and desire are spontaneously awakened in relation to the things of the external world.

On the internal plane of the psychic activities, and of spiritual illumination and supremacy, the order of development is reversed and becomes wholly a matter of choice and volition. Desire is awakened only by thought in these directions, and the attention voluntarily directed and held by choice and will through faith.

METHOD AND SPECIFIC PROCESSES.

Perfect results are impossible except through entire devotion to a single object at once, as this suspends undue activity in other directions, and focalizes the full working power upon the work in hand.

When through special effort and discipline the mind has become fairly focalized, and its activities developed upon either one, and each of the internal and higher planes, that is, of the psychic or psychometric plane, and of the inmost spiritual and divine, it is then capable of centering itself and its activities by a moment's undivided attention and concentration, upon either plane at will; and for the time become sufficiently oblivious to everything else to enable it to accomplish the object of desire.

When the inward concentration reaches the degree of *absolute* oblivion to everything but its own condition, it becomes a state of complete entrancement. If the plane of the sixth sense only is reached, it is simply what has been called the magnetic or mesmeric trance; a state of artificial somnambulism or statuvolism; if the higher plane of the spiritual, it is the deeper *ecstatic* trance, both of which are abnormal and incompatible with the harmonious development and healthful activity of the mind's powers.

The complete unconsciousness of the trance to everything but the one condition, is unnecessary to the unfolding of the mind's powers on either the psychic or the spiritual plane. All that is required is the subordination of the external activities to the internal, until they are completely overruled by them. Their entire suspension, we repeat, is unnecessary.

When the higher powers are sufficiently unfolded and established in their rightful supremacy, by the practice of normal introversion and inward concentration, without the entire suppression of the lower, they acquire such a

PERMANENT MASTERY

That external influences, impressions and sensations, have no longer power to prevent their free and full activity. The lower in their normal action become spontaneously co-ordinated with the higher, because activity in their subordinate sphere is a necessity for a full-balanced and normal mental operation.

In the first efforts at focalizing the mind's activities upon either the psychic or spiritual plane, the whole attention must be given to the processes involved, and persevered in until the specific result aimed at is reached. This may require in some cases repeated efforts; but when once fairly accomplished, the focalization may ever after be effected in a moment, and often instantaneously.

But from first to last there is no occasion for entrancement, or entire suppression of the external sensibilities; and no danger of this result, when the mind has been properly instructed and understands the law of normal introversion.

Recognizing this three-fold nature and the three distinct planes of the mind's activities, it will readily be seen that the exclusive cultivation of its powers on either plane, will give a distorted and imperfect development. Neither plane of human activity can be ignored or neglected with impunity.

There can be no integral and harmonious development of man without the full share of each portion of his being in the processes of education, for which full attention must be given to each in proportion to its relative importance, and this is readily determined by the character and position of each in the economy of our being.

There can be no harmonious education, we repeat, nor perfect mental action, without the full development and co-ordination of all the soul's powers; and true co-ordination is impossible without the full proportionate development, activity and supremacy of the higher.

The inmost, central and spiritual nature being the

TRUE CO-ORDINATING

And controlling power, should therefore first be brought forth to take its rightful throne of supremacy, as under its harmonizing and co-ordinating influence, all the powers of the outer and inner man, or sensuous and psychic, may be cultivated to their highest degree without danger of excess or perversion. Hence the method and instruction of the Master, "seek ye *first* the kingdom of God"—the spiritual plane of life—and under its law of righteousness "all these things shall be added unto you."

The intuitions of the spiritual nature will prove an infallible guide in the cultivation and development of all the subordinate psychic and sensuous powers. As these are unfolded under the guiding influence of the spiritual, the mental and moral powers take on its illumination, and the co-ordination becomes complete; the animal and the physical are thus brought under entire subjection to the mental and moral, and these to the spiritual and divine. Man becoming one with himself is one with God, and so one with all that belongs to the kingdom of God.

The three planes of the mind's activity have also their corresponding physiological planes, or nerve centres of physical relationship. The cerebrum, or large brain, is the physical seat of its activities, in relation to sensation and the outward world. It is the co-ordinating centre of bodily sensation, and the impressions derived from the external world through the five physical senses. The activities of the mind that dwells in and is conscious only of the sensuous life, are confined in their physiological seat of action to this brain.

In sleep and somnambulism, natural or artificial, the

METHOD AND SPECIFIC PROCESSES.

cerebrum becomes quiescent, and sensation correspondingly shut off. When the sleep or hypnotic trance is perfect, sensation is entirely suspended. The energy, nervous or mental, manifest in the waking activities of the cerebrum, have retreated to the cerebellum, which is the co-ordinating centre of the involuntary powers and organic functions, whose normal and perpetual activities are without sensation.

When the mind is awakened to activity on the internal plane, as in somnambulism and the mesmeric trance, the cerebellum is the seat of its physiological action, and it comes into more immediate and direct relation with the automatic functions of the involuntary life which never sleep nor rest.

This is one reason for the

INSTANTANEOUS

And almost absolute power of mental impressions from the psychic plane, over the vital processes. And being disconnected from the centres of sensation, the mind is enabled to pursue its higher psychic activities undisturbed by them.

The mesmeric and hypnotic trance or sleep as they are called, serve to close up the avenues of sense by putting the large brain to sleep and centering its active forces upon the *cerebellum* or small brain, which is the physiological centre of all the psychic activities of the sixth or inner sense.

In the ecstatic or deeper spiritual trance, the activity of both the *cerebrum* and *cerebellum*, or large and small brains, are to a grea degree suspended, and the active forces of both become centered upon the *medulla oblongata*, which with the *solar plexus*, hold the balance of vital action and prevent an entire suspension of the organic functions.

In the ecstatic or spiritual trance, when fully induced, the soul becomes so transported by its comparative freedom from all mundane restraints, and by its beatific sense of spiritual being and heavenly communion, that its rapture is reflected upon the body which in a degree becomes transfigured, and the countenance luminous with a heavenly radiance.

Experience has demonstrated that every condition that is of practical value in either artificial somnambulism or spiritual trance, in the liberation and development of the higher psychic and spiritual activities of the soul, may be established as a permanent development, by a gradual unfolding of them through the process of normal introversion, without the entire suspension of normal activity in either the front or back brain, but in conjunction with them.

As the inward and higher activities are awakened and unfolded by specific cultivation, the external and lower become subordinated to them, and when the full development of both the psychic and spiritual powers is reached, a complete and

PERMANENT CO-ORDINATION

Of the three planes is also effected, and each one exerts its due influence in all the activities of the personal life.

The following graphic and luminous description of the great nerve centres and their relation to the mind and the corresponding planes of its activities, from the pen of Dr. W. F. Evans, so forcibly and clearly illustrate the doctrine we have endeavored to set forth in these pages, that we venture to quote it. It may be well also to remark that Dr. Evans writes from practical experience, having demonstrated the general truth of the doctrine in his own person. He says:

"There are three degrees or planes of mental life, like the three stories of a palace, or, more correctly, like three concentric circles or spheres, each within the other. The doctrine of the degrees of the mind is imaged in the cerebral system. There are in reality three brains. We have first the *cerebrum*, the large brain. * * * * Then we have the *cerebellum*, or little brain, about one-eighth part of the former in size. * * * * * Though smaller in size it has far more vitality. For these three brains are like the mysterious books of the Sybil—as they decrease in quantity, they increase in value. Next we have the primitive brain, the *medulla oblongata*. It is that which is first formed in the fetus, and the other portions of the cerebral system proceed from it in order. * * * * To one whose inner vision is unveiled, there dart from it in every direction millions of rays of a pure light into every part of the system. It is much smaller than the cerebellum, but a myriad times more sensitive and vital. These three distinct brains, as we have reason to believe, are correspondences and organs of the three degrees of the mind. Either may act by itself, or our mental activity, our memory and consciousness, and perceptivity, may use either as its organ. In our normal state, and our waking hours, we use the cerebrum as the instrument of our thoughts and volitions. This in sleep becomes quiescent, as we have had reason to notice in cases of fracture of the skull, where a portion of the cranium has been removed. Its pulsations cease and all is still as the tomb. Its vital force has retreated backward and downward to the cerebellum. On the dividing line between sleeping and waking, the mysterious dreamland, the mental powers become greatly exalted and quickened, so that the experiences and perceptions of hours, and even weeks and months, are crowded into moments. The mind breaks loose from its material thraldom, the limitations of time, place, and sense, and asserts its innate freedom. It sees without the external eye, and to distances almost unlimited. It perceives distant objects, persons and things, something as we see the image of an absent friend in the mind, only with more objective clearness, and they do not appear to be in the mind, but external to it, like the scenery around us in our every-day life. There are those who can enter this state at will. It has become, in fact, their normal condition. We have experimented much with it, putting it to severe tests, a thousand miles away, and have found it as reliable as our ordinary vision. The power of thus suspending the action of the cerebrum, possessed by a scientific person, is of great value in the diagnosis of disease. It is a condition of the highest wakefulness, though physiologically it is a state of sleep, and has been denominated somnambulism. It may exist when the

METHOD AND SPECIFIC PROCESSES. 261

external senses are not oblivious to the objects surrounding us. It is a waking up from their usually dormant state of the undeveloped powers of our inner life. Like the apocalyptic angel, it breaks the seals of the closed book of nature, and unrolls the parchment on which are written characters that our usual vision cannot read, and the wonders of an inner world pass in panoramic review. The veil of sense, ordinarily opaque, becomes transparent, and through it the interior man looks out upon the universe. It is a state of *illustration*, or interior illumination, which may be permanent, normal, and attended with no loss of consciousness as to our surroundings. It is governed by fixed laws, which may be the subject of education, but is none the less a gift of God for this. Blessed is the man to whom it has been given, and who consecrates it, with all his activities, to the good of universal being.

"In the trance" [ecstatic], "both the cerebrum and cerebellum are quiescent (when it is with the individual subject an *abnormal* state), and their vital force has passed to the primitive brain, the *medulla oblongata*. The mind is awakened to the most intense degree of activity and power of which it is susceptible, in the present stage of our existence. Usually, but not necessarily, there is a loss of consciousness of the outward world. The pulse sometimes becomes nearly or quite imperceptible. The movement of the lungs is tacit, and the spiritual body only breathes. But these are not necessary concomitants of this interior state, for all the degrees of the mind may be consciously active at the same time. Persons may be developed normally into this almost angelic range of the soul's powers and activities. In this degree of the inner life the heavens are opened, the separating veil is rent if not removed, the curtain is rolled up, the invisible appears in sight, and the soul is transported in its vision to the perception of the solid and enduring *realities* of a world veiled in darkness to our common sight. In this degree of the unfoldment of the soul's life, man possesses the properties and powers of a spirit. * * * * * Hidden imponderable forces, to a certain extent, come under his control, and he may appear to a sensuous world as a Thaumaturgus, or wonder-worker, and like a partially developed Messiah, he heals all manner of sickness and disease among the people. Such a mind has blossomed into angelic proportions.

"The next step beyond is what men have called death. In every step and degree of progress towards it, the mental powers become more and more exalted, and their range of action extended. Viewed in this scientific light, death is seen to be only transition to a higher life. It cannot be a punishment for our sins, but a necessary step and normal process in human development. Having finished the work committed to our hands, and accomplished our appointed use here in the plan of Providence, when our friends shall call us dead, we shall have only languished into life."

Recognizing the three planes of the mind's activities, and the three corresponding physical or nervous centres from which it acts, the phenomena of somnambulism and trance lose much of their mystery.

Take the functions of the cerebrum and the cerebellum: the cerebrum or large brain is the co-ordinating centre of all the bodily sensations, voluntary activities and impressions, derived from the outer world through sensation. The cerebellum or small brain is the co-ordinating centre of all the involuntary activities of the organic life, and these activities are without sensation.

The large brain is the seat and organ of the mind's activities in their relation to the outer world, in which sensation plays so important a part. The back, or small brain, is the seat and organ of the mind's activities in its purely psychic functions, independent of physical sensation. When, therefore, the mind withdraws from the external plane of observation and activity, and centres itself in its perception and activity upon the internal, it simply retreats from the front to the back brain, and, withdrawing its activity from the one, centres it upom the other. The result is, the large brain or centre of sensation becomes quiescent, and when this transfer is complete, the mind is wholly disconnected from sensation, and so from the outer world through sensation.

Being free from the diverting influence of physical sense, the mind is free to give itself wholly to anything to which the attention is directed. It is a state of

INWARD CONCENTRATION.

If the attention is directed to the body, it is enabled to impress itself,—through the immediate connection of the cerebellum with the vital organs,—with all this power of concentration upon the vital processes, and produce immediate and even instantaneous results, impossible from its centre of action in the cerebrum. It then has supreme power either to create or expel diseased action, and suspend or produce any sensation desired, whether of pleasure or pain.

From this interior plane above sensation, it is also free to impress itself with this same power of concentration upon another, and being free from sensation, is free from all fear induced by sensation, and so enabled to give itself in perfect faith to the healing or the accomplishing of any good desired.

It is this higher sense of freedom from physical limitation, that enables the mind to enter so fully into the untrammeled exercise of its higher psychic powers in the study and mastery of the occult world. But to attain this condition of inner concentration and freedom in a normal manner, without losing the consciousness of the outer world and the immediate surroundings, the transfer of this centre of action must be made without the entire suspension of sensation and cerebral action. Unless this is done there can be no co-ordination of the outer with the inner counsciousness and activity, and the true and normal object of the transfer and inner development is unattained.

While the primary object of life on earth is education and discipline, in the very attainment of these ends man is to grapple with and master the conditions of the world, and turn it into a world of beauty and a garden of delight. He is not, therefore, to retire from the world in order to unfold and exercise his higher powers, but bring these inner powers forth in co-operation with the external for the attainment of this mastery. "God sent not his Son into the world to condemn the world, but that the world through him might be saved."

The isolated development of the mind's powers on either plane, however perfect that development might be, would

DEFEAT THE ENDS

For which they were bestowed. Neither class of powers or plane of activity, can subserve their purpose in the education and perfection of man only as they are brought to their normal development and activity in full co-ordination one with the other.

The lower need not and should not be entirely suspended for the development and exercise of the higher, else co-ordination of the different planes would be impossible. The lower, however, are to be subordinated to and overruled by the higher, as this is the law of their co-ordination; and because this is the law, it is all that is essential to secure the result, which when secured renders it both normal and permanent.

In this higher development and co-ordination of the soul's powers there are two fundamental conditions of absolute importance, which must not be lost sight of; first: the five external senses are to be subordinated to, co-ordinated with, and overruled by, the inner psychometric sense; second: the animal nature and the law of the selfish life is to be subordinated to, co-ordinated with, and governed by, the spiritual nature and the higher law of the spiritual life, which is the law of unselfish love and impartial ministration. The attainment of the latter first, gives power to secure the former with ease and certainty, co-ordinates the whole under the law of the perfect life, opens the spiritual understanding, and secures divine illumination of the mind on all the planes of its activity.

In the chapter on healing, the law of mental co-operation with divine power, was given as diverted attention; on the ground that withdrawing attention from pain and diseased action, suspends them to the degree to which the attention is diverted; and that the concentration of attention upon the healing power and process in confident expectation of its immediate realization, correspondingly quickens the healing action and secures the result.

As the cerebrum is the seat and centre of physical sensation, and also of the mind's activity in the sphere of sensation, while the mind is held to this centre of its activity, it will be difficult and perhaps impossible for the majority of persons to wholly divert their attention from actual suffering, and hold it on a process that is without sensation; hence

THE IMPERFECT RESULT

In so many attempts at Mental and Faith healing. But when the mind has acquired the art of transferring its centre of action from the seat of sensation in the

METHOD AND SPECIFIC PROCESSES.

front brain to the back brain, beyond the reach of sensation, it is not only free from the diverting power of pain, but is brought into immediate conjunction with the vital processes, and so in a position to throw the whole force of its concentrated action into and upon the healing process.

To secure this result, we again affirm it is not necessary to entirely suspend the action of the front brain, but simply to overrule it by the higher and more interior action of the back brain, which enables the mind to assert its ascendency and control over both sensation and disease. The same is true of the exercise of the psychometric penetration, inner vision, occult power and all the higher psychic activities of the sixth sense.

The presence and direction of one who is familiar with the processes and conditions of this psychic education and development, is a great advantage; yet it is not an imperative necessity. If the student carefully studies the exposition we have given, until he has familiarized his mind with the princeples involved, then faithfully follows the instructions which we will make as plain and specific as our command of language will permit, there is no reason why he should not be entirely successful.

Experiment has demonstrated that even the unconscious trance can be self-induced by those who have been fully instructed in the law and process, more readily even than under the supposed necessary manipulations of another.

Dr. Fahnestock, one of the most successful operators in our own country, in inducing the clairvoint vision, in the trance, or what he called "statuvolism or artificial somnambulism," demonstrated, as he believed, that this state was always self-induced; that the manipulations so much resorted to and depended upon by magnetists, served only to establish expectant attention, when the subject passed into the condition he was expecting, through his faith in the process employed.

Dr. Fahnestock, after this discovery, never resorted to manipulation nor any of the mesmeric processes, but taught the art of self-induction into the statuvolic condition to large numbers; some of whom had tried the mesmeric process in vain. His experiments were confined wholly to self-healing, and the development of the inner sight, hearing, etc.

Those he taught were enabled to enter this condition at will, and often in an instant; and thus become at once as oblivious to persons and things around them—unless their attention was specially directed to them—as though they were in another world. They became equally oblivious to every bodily sensation, even though in acute suffering at the time of passing into this condition.

Before returning to the normal wakeful state, if

METHOD AND SPECIFIC PROCESSES. 269

attention was directed to the suffering or diseased condition with which any portion of the body was affected when awake, by resolving while in this state of inward concentration, that the parts should be healed and suffer no more, that resolution

WAS SUFFICIENT

To effect the result, and on returning to the normal condition, which they could accomplish at will, that portion was kept in the insensible condition until fully restored, which was always in a very short time, and often immediate. Severe fevers were thus broken up, and the full healthful action of the system restored in a single transition of this kind.

While his students thus learned to heal themselves and control sensation, to banish all unpleasant memories and strengthen weak ones, etc., the majority of them were trained in the exercise of their psychic powers of inner-sight, hearing, etc., of distant objects, persons and places, and some of these experiments were, indeed, very remarkable.

He did not carry or push these developments beyond the plane of the sixth sense, however, and if he was familiar with the deeper spiritual state, or with the doctrine of the higher spiritual plane of the mind's activities, it does not appear from his book. His method of inducing "statuvolism" will be given in his own words, with some illustrations of his success, in the Appendix.

Had he realized that all the practical results he secured through artificial somnambulism, could have been equally and fully secured without the entire suspension of external consciousness, he would have accomplished much more than he did.

His belief that the trance was *always* self-induced, even when various other processes were employed, was and is still shared by many of the most prominent and advanced experimenters, both in this country and in Europe.

Whether this be always true or not, the fact that all the desirable results can be and are secured by self-induction and without the suspension of external consciousness, has been fully demonstrated by experiment.

Let this fact once become fully and generally recognized, and the further fact that the highest or spiritual plane of mental action can be reached by all who desire it,—and without the trance,—and that through the spiritual condition self-mastery is fully attained, and the rapid and perfect unfolding of all the soul's powers made easy and certain, the door of immediate and

UNIVERSAL EMANCIPATION

And improvement is opened to the world, and whosoever will may enter.

Few experimenters have realized or even recognized the practicability of attaining and applying the higher spiritual condition to the immediate improvement and illumination of the mental and psychic powers in their normal and practical activity on the outer and inner, or physical and psychic planes.

The partial and imperfect development of spirituality in the religious teaching and experience of the world—largely due to the cramping and narrowing influence of a dogmatic and materalistic theology and the emotional diversion of an impractical sentimentalism—has blinded the world to the real power of spirit.

The banishment of creed and dogma, and full immersion into the spiritual life, of which the water immersion of John the Baptist was the outward and prophetic symbol, would reverse all this.

The spirit being perfect and always at-one with God, when it has its full and perfect sway over the external man, the powers of the external will of necessity be brought to perfection. But so long as creed and dogma, or intellectual opinion—the letter of a book, or standards of external authority—are held above the immediate inspiration and guidance of the spirit within, the great dearth of spirituality or the life and power of the Spirit must continue in the religious world.

While the unfolding and discipline of the mind's powers on both the external or sensuous, and the internal or psychic plane, have each their own specific laws and processes, there can be no perfect development and activity of these powers, only as they are subordinated to, co-ordinated with, and governed and illuminated by the spiritual.

This nature being co-ordinated with and governed by the Divine Spirit, when it is the ruling and guiding power of the personal life, brings the whole man under the

IMMEDIATE INSPIRATION

Of omniscient wisdom, infinite goodness and absolute power.

The Psalmist in one of his seasons of spiritual exaltation and prophetic inspiration, voiced the divine promise of spiritual illumination and guidance in these encouraging words: "I will instruct thee and teach thee in the way which thou shalt go: I will guide thee with mine eye." The spirit which is *in* man, as the essential life and foundation of his being, is the specialization of God in him, and the only channel and direct expression of God's word of instruction or impartation to his consciousness and understanding. Being a portion of the Divine Spirit in man, or that point of contact where the Divine Omniscience touches human intelligence, it is the eye of God, the eye of omniscience with which He will guide the one who turns to it and walks in its light. The spiritual part of man is so much of God in him to instruct him and teach him in the way that he shall go. It is the divine or

OMNISCIENT EYE

To guide him. So surely as any man focalizes his attention in desire and faith upon it, just so surely does he focalize the divine omniscience into and upon his own soul.

Both the possibility and the practicability of the full realization of this Divine Ideal by all men who sufficiently desire it, was demonstrated by our great Exemplar in his own experience before the world, and who thus became the "Elder Brother" of his race, and "The Way, the Truth and the Life" for all men. From the divine altitude of his experience and inspired wisdom, he assured us that the same experience was open to, and within the reach of all; the great and the humble alike; that whoever believed in him as an example for themselves, should do the work that he had done, and even greater.

"Ye shall receive power when the Holy Spirit is come upon you, and ye shall be my witnesses," were among the last words which he spake to his disciples as he was about to pass from their outward vision, through a glorious translation. These same disciples in and through whom this transfiguring power of the Spirit was to become manifest, were selected from among the unlettered and humble fishermen of Galilee, as if for the express purpose of showing what his gospel could and would do for all men, however humble in position and attainment, on the plane of the external life.

The subsequent history shows how fully and divinely the promise was fulfilled and realized in Apostolic experience, and the religious history of the world gives abundant confirmation to the divine certitude of the promise, in the corroborative experience of all men, to the full extent of their genuine faith in the promise, and the corresponding fidelity to the conditions of its realization.

To keep a clear understanding of what is meant by the Holy Spirit coming upon men, let us revert again to the signification of the word Holy, which is "whole, entire, complete." By the Holy Spirit then is meant the whole Spirit, or that which is wholly spiritual.

Keeping in mind the three-fold nature of man, classified by St. Paul as body, soul and spirit, when the consciousness which is begotten of the mutual relation and activity of soul and body is awakened to the recognition of the higher and deeper, or inmost realm of the spiritual, and the attention is fully turned in desire and faith upon it, the whole external man becomes, by this uplifting prayer of faith, merged into and united with the spirit, and they twain become as one.

Thus when the whole thought and desire of the man rises to the plane of the spiritual, the highest and inmost realm of his own being, he comes under the law and power of the spiritual life, and the

HOLY SPIRIT,

Or that which is wholly spiritual, has come upon him. The "seventh seal" of the book of life is opened; the seventh or deepest and inmost sense of his being which opens "the heavens unto him," or the realm of the heavenly and divine, is awakened and established, by which he is continually under its influence, and is enabled at any moment to centre his thought and consciousness upon it, as through the opening of the sixth sense he is enabled to centre himself upon the psychic plane in thought and activity.

These blessed words of the Christ, therefore, imply that when this condition of conscious life was reached by his followers through fidelity to his instruction, they would reproduce essentially his life and experience in themselves. How else could they be witnesses for him, in the fulfillment of his oft-repeated promises to them, and to the full truth of his teaching before the world?

Fidelity to his instructions was to bring his followers into an experimental knowledge of the truth of his great doctrine of human possibility, and the realization of its emancipating power in personal experience. "If ye continue in my words," "ye shall know the truth, and the truth shall make you free."

We cannot be true disciples of this supreme Teacher and Leader, without personnally following his example. The record of that example is so plain and simple, the "wayfaring man though a fool need not err therein."

With the prescience of the great mission of his life pressing upon his mind, he was ready "to fulfill all righteousness," in the completion of the last outward rite of the old covenant dispensation, which he was about to put forever behind him, as he entered into the fulness of the new, and passed beyond the letter into the spirit. In "coming out of the water"—the external—and turning his back upon the old, "he prayed, and *as he prayed*, the heavens were opened unto him, and the Spirit descended and abode upon him."

Here was the uplifting prayer of entire consecration to the spirit and its full leading in the life, which opened the heavens unto him and brought the full influence and power of the Spirit permanently into all the activities of his daily life, and will do the same for every one who truly and faithfully follows his teaching and example. The Day of Pentecost stands as a notable demonstration of this truth, and the reproduction of Apostolic experience in all who truly follow their example, is its perpetual corroboration.

After this immersion into the spiritual life, Jesus was led by the spirit into the wilderness to be tempted of the adversary. He needed, at that great crisis, to be in a solitary place alone with God; in the completion and ratification of this New Covenant with the Father, which he was to fully realize and extend to the children of men. Every temptation of the old man to rebel against the law of the Spirit and return to the enticing pleasures of sense, was to be overcome, and the fleshly life be brought into full and permanent reconciliation to the law and leading of the spiritual life.

This is the first work of the Spirit in the life of all who come under its influence and power. But how few stand the test of the trial, and come out as our great Leader and Exemplar did, with every power of the external man brought into complete and permanent reconciliation and oneness with the inward and spiritual nature, and so with the Father in true and loyal sonship. This constitutes the

NEW COVENANT

Of God with men as his children; a covenant which requires man's full committal. When he gives himself fully to the leading of his own spiritual nature, he commits himself to the law of God in his life, and becomes the filial and obedient son of the All-wise and beneficent Father. He enters into the NEW COVENANT.

How many of us who have been lifted up to the Mount of heavenly vision and communion, and permitted to feed on heavenly manna, or partake of the bread and wine of the kingdom, when the hour of trial came for the testing of loyalty and obedience to the law of that life, like the Israelites in the wilderness, have turned longingly to the flesh pots of Egypt; or were content to patch up a compromise, clinging to fleshly desires, while still holding feebly to our spiritual leader.

The temptations which came to Jesus were those of the spirit of self, or of the selfish life; a prompting to use the new found power to the ends of personal desire and ambition. On returning to take up the active duties of life after a prolonged fast, during a season of spiritual absorption and communion in which the demands of the flesh were forgotten, "he was an hungered." Then said the flesh, "If thou be the Son of God, command that these stones be made bread." A simple and natural suggestion from the physical point of view. A normal hunger and a legitimate demand for nourishment. Nothing wrong of itself in the exercise of extraordinary power for the supply of the immediate bodily necessities, when shut off from the ordinary means. "It is written" said the Spirit, "Man shall not live by bread alone but by every word which proceedeth out of the mouth of God."

In the open vision of the Spirit, Jesus had seen that all life was one; and in that unity every demand of the universal life was a word proceeding from the mouth of God. It was to be his meat to do his Fathers will, who had sent him to break unto mankind the true bread of life. He was to find his life in giving it for others.

Here was a temptation to use the newly conferred power to supply his own personal necessities, before he had used it in ministering to others, and thus place self before the brethren; but the power that could convert stones into bread, could sustain the body until such time as he could share with his brethren.

Then came the larger plausible temptation of working out for his race the realization of the Jewish traditional ideal of the Messianic Mission. Surely he could wield this divinely conferred power in liberating his people from the galling yoke of Roman sway, "restore the kingdom to Israel," and, sitting upon the throne of his father David, extend the sceptre of his dominion over the kingdoms of the world; making the glory of them contribute to the supreme exaltation of the chosen people of God.

How gladly would the Jews have accepted such a Messiah. There was nothing in the history of God's providential dealings with this people through his inspired leaders of the past, against such a hope and procedure. But in the open vision of the spirit he had seen that

THE TRUE ISRAEL

To be redeemed from the dominance of the enemy was the spiritual nature of man everywhere. That the kingdom to be set up was the supremacy of the spirit in which all men were to become kings and priests unto God, sons and daughters of the Lord Almighty.

Then came the last temptation of the outward life; surely in the working out of his great mission, he could perform signs and wonders as an evidence that he was the favored of God, his appointed Messiah and Leader.

Here were the demands of the flesh, ambitions of the worldly spirit, and personal pride, each presenting its plausible claims in a form not in itself specifically wrong or evil, but legitimate to the natural or external life. In the light of the Spirit, however, in which no personal claims or preferences are possible, whose law is the universal good, and impartial ministration, to have yielded would have compromised his gift, violated his vow of consecration and despoiled him of his Messiahship.

He might still have wrought marvelous works as others had done before and have done since, who have attained some degree of psychic power—sought, may be, at first with honorable motives—but when attained, could not resist the temptation to turn it to the ends of self-glory and personal aggrandizement.

The cultivation and development of the psychic powers are, we repeat, as simple a matter as the cultivation and development of the physical powers; and may be entered into by any one with certainty of success, who will faithfully observe the conditions of this culture. But when these higher attainments are turned to selfish and personal ends, it is a prostitution of noble gifts to ignoble purposes, for which they were not bestowed, and such perversion will in the end bring

TERRIBLE RETRIBUTION.

"He that exalteth himself shall be abased." The higher the self-exaltation through perversion of noble powers, the deeper the fall and ultimate debasement certain to ensue.

In entering upon the higher life of spiritual supremacy, the temptation will come to every one to form a compromise instead of a union between the old man and the new; and the majority of those who have had a genuine spiritual experience, are thus trapped, and become handicapped for life to a crippled religious warfare, sometimes the saint in the ascendency, but oftener the sinner.

There is no safety, or life of exultant victory, except in the complete reconciliation or at-one-ment of the external with the internal; the law of the Spirit becoming the supreme law of the personal life, which makes all life and all interests one; in which the recognition and love of neighbor is one with the recognition and love of self.

When this victory over self is achieved, through the at-one-ment of man in the Spirit, the "power of the

Spirit" becomes in his hands the key to all achievement and victory. "Ye shall have power" when the whole spirit "is come upon you, and ye shall be my witnesses." The whole man becomes a unit of activity on the highest plane of his being, in which he becomes the resistless and "magical man;" but he is this only for the good of his kind. All personal considerations and preferences become merged into the general and universal good.

When in that crucial hour, our great Exemplar and Leader had put all self and personal considerations beneath his feet, and his whole being became permanently one under the law of the spiritual life, "He returned in the POWER OF THE SPIRIT into Galilee, preaching the gospel of the kingdom of God." "And they were astonished at his teaching, for his word was with power."

Here is the one supreme example for us all. The true power, the true victory, and the true life with the simple and only steps to their realization, are clearly revealed and fully illustrated.

All men are spontaneously moved more or less with desire for power and achievement. On the plane of the sensuous life it is external emolument, wealth, position and power of mastery, for personal ends. On the plane of the spiritual, attainment of wisdom and power for the advancement of universal well-being, becomes the inspiring motive. "He that is greatest among you, let him become servant of all."

The attributes of Spirit, when embodied and organically expressed, are Wisdom, Goodness, Power. When the subordinate nature of man is co-ordinated and made one with his higher and spiritual nature, these attributes become the crowning glory of his life. The full development of the power and perfection of the personal life is possible only through the co-ordination of all the powers of his being in a unity of action; and this is impossible except through the full subordination of the lower to the higher.

This co-ordination and integral development of all the powers in unity of action, which gives such power of achievement, are as readily commenced and carried forward from childhood and youth as in adult life; and indeed much more so, as there is less to overcome.

By this co-ordination and unity of the outward and inward life in childhood, or youth, power of achievement and success in all legitimate efforts, are secured to the humblest capacity, and a true motive and inspiration supplied.

"Where thy treasure is, there will thy heart be also," and where the heart is there will be the motive and the effort. Let these then be made right from the start. If the imperishable and incorruptible treasures of love and wisdom, knowledge and power, the power of all mastery which wisdom and goodness alone bestow, be the dominant desire of the heart, they will be freely given. "Ye shall seek me and find me, when ye shall search for me with all your heart." As Spirit is

IMPERSONAL BEING,

When man in his individual capacity comes into at-one-ment with the spiritual life, he lives no longer for self, but for the general good. Hence to enter into the true spiritual condition and realize the supremacy of the Spirit and its illuminating and saving power, the spirit of self and all personal considerations and motives must be laid down and left forever behind.

The one desire to be led and governed by the Spirit, through which the will and purpose of the Father can alone be fully known and obeyed, must become the supreme motive of the soul. There must be an entire and unreserved consecration to the Spirit, the will to do only the Father's will. As our great Leader and Captain said of himself, "It is my meat to do the will of him that sent me, and to finish his work."

All men have this same work to finish through co-operation with the Father in the working out of their individual and social destiny; and this co-operation with the Father is possible only through obedience to the law of the spirit which he has given us. "He that willeth to do His will shall know of the teaching." This *must* become the ruling motive, if we would enter into the illumination and power, and achieve the victory of the Christ life, and thus become witnesses for him.

The following specific process of introversion for transferring the seat of the mind's activities from the front to the back brain, without suspending external consciousness, and developing the higher psychic powers, will be found simple and reliable; and if intelligently and persistently applied, certain in its results.

The first step is the complete inward focalization of the three leading senses, viz: sight, hearing and feeling. To acquire this art will be found easier for some than for others; but perseverance will bring success to all.

First select a quiet, retired and comfortable place, free from intrusion and outward disturbances, and sit or recline in an easy position, with complete relaxation of the muscular system. Dismiss all care and anxiety, close the eyes, shut out as far as possible the outward world, and, collecting the thoughts, throw or project the mind to some distant place or person that you would like to visit, and that has sufficient interest to hold your attention during the experiment.

The secret of success in this process is the control and concentration of the attention. For this reason, a favorite and familiar place or person should be chosen for the experiment. The revival in memory of some past scene or experience of absorbing interest, is a good exercise.

When this attitude is taken and the place or person is focalized in thought, concentrate and fasten, or hold the attention calmly but firmly upon the same, and imagine yourself spiritually there. Now *try to see* the person or place that you are mentally visiting, and everything concerning them that you wish to see. Form a complete mental picture of the same, and study or observe it minutely until the mind has become absorbed in the contemplation.

This may seem to be the work of your own fancy or imagination, but no matter. It is of no consequence whatever, at first, whether what you see be a true vision, or a picture of the imagination; so long as the attention becomes absorbed in it and you can for the moment forget your surroundings and sensations in the contemplation. It serves to focalize the attention inwardly and this is the first object of the sitting.

The object of thus mentally visiting a distant place or person, is to get the mind

OFF FROM SELF

And the immediate sensations and surroundings; and this can be done only by focalizing the attention and holding it upon something else of sufficient interest, until these are forgotten. Remember the law of mind, that the attention cannot be concentrated in one direc-

METHOD AND SPECIFIC PROCESSES. 287

tion without its suspension in all others. This exercise develops the power of directing, holding and controlling the attention at will. When this art is acquired, the first great step in this development of psychic power is taken.

To form a mental picture of some distant object and hold the attention upon it in the effort to see the reality for which it stands, serves to secure the inward focalization of the sense of sight; and this in time will develop the real inner vision. When this inner vision is fully awakened, it will soon be easy to distinguish between the pictures of imagination and objects of real vision.

The rapidity and perfection of this development of the inner sight, will depend upon the degree of concentration and absorption in the process. As with the attention, so with each of the senses; they cannot be directed fully in one direction or upon one object, without suspending their activity in other directions; and contrawise, suspension in one direction aids their activity in another. So withdrawing the attention from the outward plane of observation, and focalizing the three leading senses, sight, hearing and feeling, inwardly upon any object of interest to which the attention is directed, that is, by seeking to mentally see, hear and feel the object, serves to suspend the external action of these senses, and correspondingly awaken them upon the internal and psychic plane.

Repeated effort will in a short time fully focalize, develop and establish the senses in this inward action, without the entire suspension of their hold upon the external.

When this is effected, a moment's concentration of attention, will be sufficient at any time to bring the internal action into complete supremacy over the external, and enable the mind to suspend physical sensation at will, or to exchange suffering for comfort.

The first effort should be with sight, as this is the leading sense, then hearing and feeling; but with the transfer of sight from the external to the internal and the full development of the inner vision, the other senses are usually spontaneously transferred with it. When this is not the case, the same process applied to each will soon effect the desired result.

The first object of this effort is to bring the bodily sensations and conditions under complete mental control, and this is accomplished by the inward focalization of the three leading senses—sight, hearing and feeling.

When the mind is enabled to transfer the activity of these senses from the physical to the mental plane at will, it may then shut off all diverting and disturbing influences from the outward plane, and establish perfect conditions for the development and training of the higher psychic powers.

In acquiring this art of introversion and the development of the psychic powers, there are two things to be especially guarded against; first: revery, which is neither genuine meditation nor true abstraction; but a diffusive mind wandering, which is fatal both to intellectual development and the psychic vision. It is the opposite of clear thinking and mental concentration. Second: somnolence or sleepiness, to which many will find themselves liable. If this occur from weariness, postpone the experiment until rested. If not, then rouse yourself at every recurrence of the drowsiness, and proceed with the effort, resolved to reach the inward focalization without the loss of consciousness. This all can do who really will it. Without this precaution, some will fall into the hypnotic sleep, and unless one, who is present for the purpose, speak to them, and awaken mental action in the somnambulic condition, they will awaken after a longer or shorter sleep, without knowing that they have been in the somnambulic state at all. Sleep thus induced, however, is remarkably refreshing and restorative. It is said that Gen. Butler, John Kelly and other men noted for their extraordinary power for work and endurance, had from early life the faculty of throwing off all care, even in their busiest hours, falling asleep at once, and waking on the exact minute determined upon before going to sleep, perfectly refreshed and renewed. The majority of people could acquire this art by following the hint here given.

As the external senses, or the mind's action in and through them, are thus focalized inwardly, their external action is for the time correspondingly suspended, the front brain rendered quiescent, and the mind's activity centered upon the back brain. This being effected without the abnormal condition of trance or somnambulism, the development and exercise of psychometry, normal seership, mental healing and all the occult powers of the sixth sense, in

THE WAKING STATE

Are rendered comparatively easy and practicable. The inward focalization of sight, gives the inner vision; of hearing, the inner hearing; and of feeling, the inner sympathetic or psychometric sense.

This transfer of sensation and activity from the physical to the psychic plane, secures the perfect conditions, also, for the unfolding of the higher gifts of the Spirit, through the opening of the deeper and true spiritual or seventh sense, as it is a state of great inward concentration and corresponding stillness of the outward man.

We are fully assured that this art of introversion may be acquired by every one who is sufficiently individualized and unfolded to appreciate and desire it.

In the state of diverted attention and inward concentration thus readily induced, the mind becomes supreme over the body, and the will to suspend sensation in any part, is sufficient to produce the result, which remains until revoked by the will in the same condition, subsequently induced. Self-healing then becomes a simple matter of the will.

The mental healing of others, also, is vastly more prompt and certain from this psychic plane of inward concentration, than is possible from the ordinary plane of mental action. But when in this state of concentration the attention is turned in thought and desire upon the divine fountain of Spirit within, the whole being becomes flooded with spiritual light and power, a wisdom and energy that is heavenly and divine. Then power to heal by word and touch is absolute; because the act is wrought in God.

The casting out of devils and reforming the vicious, the reclaiming of drunkards and restoration of the insane to soberness and reason, giving strength to the weak and courage to the lowly and disheartened, and working "not after the law of a carnal commandment but after the power of an endless life," for the universal emancipation, enlightenment and uplifting of mankind, become the easy and true work of life.

Man then becomes one in spirit and purpose with the divine, and is led, governed and crowned with wisdom, sympathy and power. It is the Christ or God-anointed life; the true at-one-ment of man with God, the human with the Divine, Christianity as Christ taught and lived it.

Spirituality the Only Basis

OF A

TRUE NORMAL AND PERFECT LIFE.

Man can do and be his best only by the exercise of his best powers, or as he puts forth effort from the highest plane of being. To seek to centralize himself upon this plane should, therefore, be the first business of life; then the legitimate result or realization of every laudable ambition is within his reach. The development and perfection of all his powers, the complete mastery of self and attainment of personal supremacy in the kingdom of life, are his. "Seek *first* the kingdom of God," which means "spiritual power on earth," and all these things will be easily attained.

Let no one for a moment indulge the thought that spirituality calls for the life of a "recluse," "asceticism," "mortification of the flesh," or any abnormal condition whatsoever.

SPIRITUALITY

Is the only real naturalism or true rationalism possible to man.

Materialism and sensuality, are as abnormal and distorting to true manhood, as the opposite extremes of an austere fanaticism or a morbid sentimentalism, which too often pass for religion and true piety.

God is Spirit, and the most natural Being in existence. All the joyous life of nature breaking forth in the beauty and fragrance of the flower, the song and charm of bird, and the spontaneous exuberance and delight of animal activity, are but the manifestations of his omnipresent cheer and perpetual inspiration in the life of his creation. When man comes into unity with God through unity with the spirit that is in himself, he too will be as spontaneously happy and exuberant as is the life of flower or bird.

The self-denial which spirituality demands, is not the destruction of the flesh or its functions, but their subordination to and co-ordination with the spiritual nature. This insures temperance, chastity and the healthful and vigorous activity and hearty enjoyment of every function of soul and body, each in its own legitimate sphere, time and place. "To everything there is a season, and a time to every purpose under the heaven." "Render to Cæsar the things that are Cæsar's, and to God the things that are God's."

As in physical healing we have only to recognize the healing power of God in the life,—which is always one with His life,—and turning from all thought of disease, unite with that power in desire and faith, to secure the immediate healing of the body, so in spiritual illumination and guidance, we have only to recognize the light of God in our spirit—which is always one with Him—and withdrawing from the external unite with the spirit through desire and faith, to secure its immediate illumination and teaching.

The remarkable success of the two French noblemen, in the spiritual development and education of their families, given in the Appendix, was due to their recognition of the spirit and its rightful supremacy in the personal life, and thus making that the basis of all their efforts. In our specific instruction for the development and training of the psychic powers, it is presumed that the student who has followed us thus far, has come to recognize and choose this only true basis as his own. When this is done there can be no question of his success, and the achievement of a victorious life.

If in the first effort in focalizing the attention upon some absent and familiar friend or place, the student fails to form a clear mental picture of them, or is unable to hold the attention ten or fifteen minutes, try another, and if necessary, still another; but make a thorough trial of each.

With some whose power of concentration is weak, the tendency will be to fly from one object to another, before a fair trial is made of either. This only serves to confirm a bad habit; the very thing that must first be overcome.

If one falls back and says, "My power of concentration is too weak for me to succeed in this effort, there's no use in my trying," he exercises faith, of necessity; but more faith in the power of a bad habit than in the deeper power of his soul to overcome it. This attitude is destructive to success in anything. The object of this book is to awaken in all, the recognition of the infinite possibilities of man, and to inspire all faint hearted and doubting souls to arouse themselves to a determination to become co-workers with God in the achievement of a destiny and career worthy his children.

No one with a fair degree of resolution need fail even in this. Turn at once from all thoughts or recognition of inability in this direction, and think only of success and its certainty through proper effort; then "gird up the loins of your mind" with the resolution and determination to realize it, remembering that "God helps those who help themselves."

In the first efforts, friends and familiar places are chosen as the objects of mental visitation, because it is easier to concentrate and hold the attention on things of personal interest. It is impossible to thus mentally visit a distant person or place and form a clear mental picture of the same, and become so absorbed in the act as to forget for the time one's immediate sensations and surroundings, without the mind becoming focalized inwardly, and thus enabled to bring out the inner sight, hearing and feeling.

When this is done, the mind can then turn its attention to the body and

EFFECT ANY CHANGE

In its sensations and conditions desired. Do not be satisfied until the inner vision is opened and established. If the inner hearing is not spontaneously opened with the inner sight, give the whole attention to it, till this also is established. *Try* to hear whatever there is to hear in connection with what you see. Speak silently in mind to your friend and he will answer you truthfully. His real thought becomes—though unconsciously to him—vocalized to your inner hearing in response to your mind thus concentrated upon his.

This may not come at once, but persevering effort will bring it. The same is true of feeling. Seek to enter into the feelings of your friend, both mentally and physically, and you will soon be astonished at the revelations this will open to you. This will develop the psychometric power to perceive, enter into, and realize the character, states and conditions of all persons and things to which the attention is inwardly directed. Sight, hearing, feeling, taste and smell can all be exercised mentally, through inward focalization, upon any object to which the attention is thus directed, but only one of these at a time, as the whole attention is required for each; though the transition from one to the other is so quick as to be practically one operation.

When the inner sight, hearing and feeling are fairly developed in relation to distant objects, places and persons, they should be exercised upon things in the immediate vicinity, where they can be readily tested. The seer should be able to tell what persons in an adjoining room or house are doing, saying or thinking; should be able to designate the title of a book with eyes closed or bandaged; and after some training, to read the contents of a book.

When the sight and other senses are sufficiently specialized and trusty in their action, from exercise in various ways, the psychometric power may be applied to the systematic education of the mind and the acquisition of any kind of knowledge desired.

The progressive exercises employed so successfully by Bertolacci, given in the Appendix, will furnish helpful and valuable suggestions for the earlier development and training of the psychic powers of the sixth sense, as well as for the higher phases of study, healing, etc.

There are three important conditions that should not be forgotten in the development and exercise of the psychic powers; as complete results are impossible without them. These are, first: the centering of the mind's activity upon either one of the inner planes at any time, requires the UNDIVIDED ATTENTION for the time, in the act of introversion, as well as for its first attainment. Second: the perception of any object, or seeking for any form of knowledge, or any specific exercise, as of healing, etc., also requires the whole attention for the time and in the act. Third: that in the psychometric examination of any object, subject or person, the attention needs to be especially directed to the separate features to be noted, and where the different senses, as of taste, smell, hearing, etc., are to be brought into internal or psychic action, only one at a time can be exercised; and the attention must be specifically directed to its action, as on the psychic plane the mind acts only in a single direction at once, and if the attention is undivided, the whole mental force is thrown in that direction. For this reason the mind acts with such marvelous freedom, quickness and power, on this plane, when the attention is fully concentrated in any one direction.

It should be remembered, also, that while on the outward plane the attention is attracted and enforced by contact with objects through sensation,—sound, odor, taste, touch or sight,—on the psychic plane the attention must be

DIRECTED BY VOLITION

To the object, before the sight, hearing, feeling, taste

or smell can be awakened to them. This is a very important law of psychic action which must not be lost sight of, as imperfect results will invariably be found to depend upon the ignorance of, or inattention to it.

Trained psychometrists and seers, with a clear understanding of the work they have to do, voluntarily turn their own attention in every direction required; but neophites generally need to have their attention called or turned in special directions, to secure a full examination in any given case.

If these conditions are remembered and observed, the best results may be expected and realized.

In the psychic state of inward concentration, the mind is brought into sympathetic contact with every object or subject to which the attention is directed, and enabled to enter into and perceive its prevailing conditions, qualities and characteristics, time, space and material barriers being no obstruction.

The secret of success, which needs to be reiterated over and again, until it cannot be forgotten, is, CONTROL OF THE ATTENTION by volition or will. No progress is possible without it; and with it success is certain. The attention must be fully withdrawn from the external and sensuous plane of observation, and concentrated inwardly in desire and faith upon a specific object or subject, to the exclusion of everything else. This confident desire, which is the prayer of faith, focalizes the inward light upon the subject of inward observation, when all that is essential to be known concerning it will be fully and specifically opened to the mind.

The seeker after psychic development may rest assured that to the extent to which the thought, desire and attention are withdrawn from all else and focalized in concentration upon any specific object in full recognition of the inner light, to that extent will the object be revealed. When the whole attention becomes absorbed in the act, the result will be perfect. This is a law of mind in its relation to Spirit,—which embosoms all intelligence,—as surely as it is a law that in its contact with the outer world through the senses, it should perceive the externals of things.

This law of inward illumination was revealed in that luminous saying of the Christ, so often quoted by us, and which will bear many repetitions: "If thine eye be single thy whole body" [being] "shall be full of light. But if thine eye be evil" [divided attention and desire] "thy whole body shall be full of darkness; and if the light that is in thee be darkness," [shut out from thought and recognition], "how great is that darkness."

When this art of inwardly concentrating and uniting the mind with the spirit is mastered, the initiate has taken his first step in true christian adeptship. He has then the ability not only to focalize the inner light upon all matters of legitimate inquiry and knowledge, but in the sincere desire to bless another, he may come at once into unobstructed spiritual presence and contact with the object of his desire, and focalize upon him the quickening, illuminating, comforting and healing power of the Spirit, and pray him, so to speak, into the realization of the desired blessing.

Let two or more unite truly in the spirit for such a work, and the power will become absolute. The most marvelous and

UNDREAMED-OF POSSIBILITIES

Await this united action in the spirit. This all-important principle of united spiritual action should not be forgotten, either in carrying forward the true work of the spiritual Adept, or in efforts after the attainment of adeptship, associative effort being much more effective and rapid in results. United effort in any direction succeeds where individual effort often fails. There is not only an increase of power from the union of numbers, but there is a stimulus and inspiration from the association which quickens and enhances the specific effort and power of each. It is better, therefore, that two or more earnest souls should unite in the spirit of brotherhood and mutual helpfulness, in these efforts of psychic culture and attainment of spiritual gifts.

Had the disciples on the day of Pentecost been each by himself in separate and isolated prayer, that mighty awakening and influx of spiritual life and power might not have taken place. They had been specifically instructed by the Master in this united and associated effort, and implicitly followed that instruction by meeting "with ONE ACCORD, in ONE PLACE." "Again I say unto you, That if two of you shall agree on earth" [in the body] as touching anything ye shall ask, it shall be done for them of my Father which is in heaven. For where two or three are gathered together in my name, there am I in the midst of them."

When two or more truly unite in seeking this attainment of "spiritual power on earth," they practically become one soul of communion, and are united in that spirit which constitutes the unity of the Godhead, the "Holy Spirit," which makes all "perfect in One."

In this unity of spirit among themselves, they come into unity with God, with Christ and the whole Brotherhood of the Spirit in God; and the Power of God as manifest in the Christ, becomes at once manifest to and in each according to the measure of his faith and consecration.

The full power and inspiration of the Spirit opened to any group through this united seeking, becomes the immediate and permanent possession of each, as he is true and loyal to his leading.

Let every seeker after spiritual attainment find others to unite with him in earnest effort to this end, and having fixed upon the time and place of meeting, hold them sacred to this purpose, allowing nothing to inter-

SPIRITUALITY THE ONLY BASIS. 303

fore therewith. This done the conditions of success are established. The Quaker method of silent waiting upon the spirit within will bring the blessing.

The true spiritual Adept has not only the ability to attain unto all useful and legitimate knowledge of men and things, but to become a direct co-worker with his fellow-men and divine Providence, in bringing the world of mankind to perfection through this immediate inward or spiritual action upon them.

Immediate and instantaneous healing is always effected—whether consciously or unconsciously—from this spiritual plane of mental action, whether in the healer's own body or upon another.

As one flash of spiritual intuition reveals more real truth to the mind than months of hard intellectual effort secures, so one full unobstructed touch of this divine energy of Spirit, will effect more healing action than weeks or months of mental treatment from the mere intellectual plane, or where this introversion is partial and incomplete.

Where the inward concentration of the healer—in spiritual contact with the patient—is perfect, he with his patient, being absorbed in the one thought, desire and expectation of healing (the united prayer of faith), the divine touch is secured and the healing is inevitable.

In this state of inward concentration and mental unity with the spirit, which when once fairly established, can at any time be induced in a few seconds at will, the

POWER OF THE SOUL

Over the body is made absolutely supreme.

As men come into unity of life and action on this plane, they become practically one soul of communion and fellowship, and not only one supreme power of resistance against the encroachments of evil in any form, but one resistless power of ministration to emancipate, heal and bless all who turn to and co-operate with them to this end.

The understanding of this supreme law of mind and spirit, brings out the divine helpfulness of that unqualified assurance of the Master quoted above: "Again I say unto you, that if two of you shall *agree*," etc. This law thus graphically presented by the Master, in the tremendous sweep of its power, is like all the divinely established laws of being, immutable and universal in its bearing and application. It implies that the real union of two, in one act of divine ministration, become one in God, and thus the channel or focalization of divine power in the accomplishment of the end sought.

And still further, these words of the Christ imply that two or more cannot thus unite in spirit to carry on his work, without coming into direct personal contact and union with him, and so with all the vast and mighty fellowship of souls who dwell in unity or oneness with his perfect life in God.

The carnal mind, or mind on the external plane, can know absolutely nothing of the divine realization of this experience, and of the power it is destined to bring into human life when large numbers of men in the body shall thus become a unit in the spirit, and so one with the Father, and with the Christ and that august Brotherhood of souls who have risen to the blissful level of his life in God.

Men in the body, coming into the unity of the spirit, become specific channels of divine ministration and the focalization of divine power in the outward world, and the larger the number of the earthly with the heavenly, the mightier becomes the focalization of heavenly power and ministry.

This is the principle as well as the solution of all marvelous answers to prayer for the healing and moral reformation of men and women with which the religious history of the world abounds.

United prayer when the inward concentration and unity of the spirit is complete, is absolute in its influence; not only over men as individuals, but over large movements and combinations of men, the direction of events, and in wonderful degree even over the elements, forces and conditions of the physical world. Storms have been abated and rains induced through the concentration of power in united prayer. The violence of pestilence has been wonderfully subdued and sometimes the pestilence itself wholly stayed by this means alone. Some striking illustrations of the control of both storm and pestilence in this manner, are related by Pres. Mahan, formerly of Oberlin College. The growth of vegetation has been accelerated also, to a marvelous degree by this concentration of supreme energy in prayer, an instance of which is given by Bertolacci, in Appendix.

Who that believes in the Divine Existence and Providence, questions for a moment the ability of God to exert an immediate and direct control over all these things? Why, then, should we question the ability of his children in united action, under his inspiration and guidance, to approach to something of his omnipotence? Indeed, in conferring moral freedom on man as his child, and placing him at the head of his creation in this lower world, God has left it for man to thus become a co-worker with him in the completion of his work on this planet; and man is recreant to his trust if he do not rise to the occasion and with the Father's help manfully and loyally meet and fill the opportunity. He can neither see the opportunity nor appreciate its high privileges and responsibilities, while he is content to remain absorbed in the petty ambitions, beguiling allurements and ignoble purposes of the sensuous and selfish life.

When this principle of human co-operation with the divine is fully understood and applied,

THE SUPREMACY OF MAN

Over nature through united action on the plane of the spiritual, will be complete. And when large numbers or groups of consecrated souls have entered this unity and oneness of life in the Spirit, they have through unity in and between themselves, come into corresponding unity and oneness of life in God, so that each individual is enabled to dwell, walk and act, not only in the actual combined power of the group to which he belongs, but with Jesus he can practically say, "The Father abiding in me doeth his work."

This assurance is most clearly given in that emphatic utterance of the Christ, "Verily, verily I say unto you, He that believeth on me, the works that I do shall he do also, and greater than these shall he do, because I go unto the Father." He stood absolutely alone at that time, the only truly begotten Son of God. No other living soul was one with him in the possession and exercise of this spiritual life in the body. His disciples had not yet awakened to the full realization of the spirituality of his teaching. While he remained bodily present with them, they looked too much to the external man. He saw, and told them that it was expedient for them that he should go away, that they might turn within and find the true comforter and teacher, and so come into oneness with him in this life and power of the spirit—the only way in which unity with him is possible.

On the threshold of his departure from the earthly life, foreseeing the consternation and demoralization that would come to his disciples when he should fall into the hands of his enemies and suffer martyrdom, he said to them, "Behold the hour cometh, yea, is come, that ye shall be scattered every man to his own, and leave me alone; and yet I am not alone, because the Father is with me." He saw, also, that through his death and resurrection they would at last awaken to the truth, and through their faith in him and his promise, would seek and enter into the divine life of the Spirit, and thus receive power and be witnesses for him; and to secure this result in the earth and before men, he cheerfully gave his life for them.

"And greater than these shall he do because I go unto the Father." He stood alone in the focalization of divine power in the world, but saw that through his death and departure from the world, numbers would be brought into oneness of this spiritual life in the body, and become a still greater focalization of divine power in the world, and thus perform even greater works than he had done. This is the principle these words involve, and when fully understood and applied by men, through genuine faith in him, will unquestionably bring the full realization of his divine promise into their actual experience.

All life is One by virtue of the omnipresent indwelling Spirit of God, which is the essence of all life. Each individual, therefore, whether conscious of the fact or not, is a vital part and individual expression of "one stupendous whole." He has but to enter into the spirit of his own being to realize his oneness with all life and all being, and hence the marvelous power to work for and in another that comes to every one who dwells in and works from the plane of the spirit.

Right here must be emphasized again one important law never to be forgotten, that man can enter into and exercise absolute power, that power which speaks and it is done, which commands and it stands fast, only in and through the divine plane of his being, in and through the spirit which is in him, by which he becomes one with divine power. He cannot come into this unity with the inward spirit and divine power, without losing all selfish motives and personal considerations, and so all desire to possess and employ it, save to wise and beneficent ends and purposes. Until this motive rules the soul, he is not prepared for, and therefore cannot possess and wield it. Herein is established forever the only conditions upon which absolute power is to be attained and employed.

WHEN SUPREME POWER

Is sought for itself alone, independent of truth or right,

the very motive will forever defeat the effort. But in proportion as truth and righteousness are loved and sought for their own sakes, regardless of the power for power's sake, which their possession confers, does man become clothed with the power of the divine which he thus takes on.

The supreme desire for the personal exemplification of truth and right, rather than the display of power, by Jesus in the hour of his great temptation, gained that glorious victory over self, and enthroned him in the divine supremacy of personal life which followed. He would not use the divine energy with which he was endowed to supply in a miraculous manner the demands of his personal necessities, yet did not hesitate to use it in behalf of suffering men when occasion required. He arose from sleep to rebuke and quell the storm at sea for the safety of his disciples, healed and fed the needy multitude by a seeming miracle in the desert place, and even converted water into wine to promote the festivities of a wedding feast where he was an invited guest.

The manifestation of the spirit, like the sunbeam which symbolizes it, is three-fold. Light, the surface ray, corresponds to intelligence and wisdom; heat, the inner ray, corresponds to love and goodness; and the chemical or inmost vivifying ray to the creative, sustaining and transforming energy of Spirit, the divine inmost of all life. Hence the knowledge of truth, though essential, is not in itself enough. Love and goodness, or the Spirit of righteousness, are deeper than knowledge, and must be reached before the true power of a son of God can be realized. Truth and righteousness are the only avenues or channels through which divine power can flow; the only conditions under which it can be expressed or made manifest.

It will be seen that the processes through which spiritual illumination and occult power are attained, are but an extension, and further application of the principle involved in physical healing, as unfolded and illustrated under that head. This, briefly stated, was, that by diverting the attention and thought from the pain, injury or disease, and concentrating them with confidence on the healing power of God in the life, in the understanding that this mental co-operation invariably secures the result, was certain to secure it.

In the matter of physical healing, when the mind is divided by fear and doubt, fear of the disease and doubt of the healing power, to that degree will there be an interruption of the healing process.

The power of volition could not be conferred on man without involving him in personal responsibility for the choice he makes, and the bearing also of the consequences of his choice and action. Hence the law so fully emphasized by Jesus, and so often referred to in this book, "Verily I say unto you, Whatsoever ye shall bind on earth shall be bound in heaven; and whatsoever ye shall loose on earth shall be loosed in heaven." Thus, whatever limit man sets by his own thought to the divine activity in his personal life, whether for physical healing or spiritual enlightenment, he of necessity binds God to that limit in these processes. So in like manner to the full extent which he recognizes the potency of God in his life, or which better expresses it, that he has no life but God's, and co-operates with him through confidence and trust for the healing and perfection of body and soul, he binds

ALMIGHTY POWER

To the accomplishment of this result.

The power is of God; but the choice, demand and limit, are with man. God as an unchangable, because perfect Being, in the very act of bestowing the gift of freedom upon his children, not only binds them to the personal responsibility of their own free choice and act, but binds himself to the full result of that choice, whether it lead to destruction or salvation. Hence if man binds disease in his flesh by thought and fear of it, and limits the action of the healing power by doubt, to that extent he holds the disease and prevents the healing power from casting it out, which it would do spontaneously if not interrupted and interfered with by the limits imposed from the action of fear under his freedom of choice and volition. But if he put away the fear of disease by the recognition in thought that the life *he has* is one with the life of God, and thus connects *him* with the divine perfection of Being, and, throwing away all fear and thought of disease, unites with the divine in perfect confidence and trust for the realization of that perfection in himself, the power will be correspondingly manifest in the immediate healing of whatever disease or injury there may be. It is the realization of unity with divine power, and the appropriation of supreme good, physical or spiritual, which the infinite wisdom and goodness of the All-Father has provided for his children, through their own co-operation, which fear and doubt prevent, and confidence and trust secure.

There is and can be but one life, and that is the all-pervading life of God. In him we live and have our being. The mental recognition and realization of this great truth, that the life we have is not only one with, but is *the life of God* in us, destroys all fear and doubt—fear of disease and doubt of the healing power—and brings the realization of healing and health to the body.

To secure this realization, sit down quietly by yourself, and enter into the understanding that however much you may have been or are diseased or debilitated, the life that still remains is perfect; because it is one with the life of God. Then by laying hold in thought of this life, and casting both the disease and the fear of it out of mind, you have taken hold of the power of

God, and in thought becoming one with it, you are renewed and made whole in body.

To assist in securing this realization, repeat thoughtfully and reverently these words, until your whole thought and attention are focalized in their deep significance, THE LIFE I HAVE IS THE LIFE OF GOD IN ME, and the realization of this makes me every whit whole. The complete focalization of thought and attention in this truth, to the forgetting of everything else—which the intelligent and earnest repetition of these words secures,—brings its realization in the immediate healing and restoration of the body.

The healing of others is effected in the same manner. Sit down, whether your patient be present or absent, and focalize your attention in the thought that all life is ONE; therefore his life is one with yours, and both are one with God's. Then turn from all thought or recognition of disease, and thinking only of the health this perfect life insures, repeat these words until you realize the power of this truth for him: OUR LIFE IS ONE IN GOD, and the realization of this truth makes us every whit whole. This realization, in the full sense of the oneness of his life with yours, emancipates his mind and secures the healing and restoration.

A small bay whose waters are one with the mighty ocean and are kept alive and pure by the perpetual ebb and flow of the tides, illustrates the oneness of the life of man with the life of God. The life of man is the specialization of the life of God, in matter; and just as the inlet of the bay may become clogged with earthy deposit, and prevent the full circulation of the water, so fear and doubt close up the inlet of this life of God in us, whose ever moving energies are necessary to keep our measure full and our life perpetually renewed in health and vigor. This unity through thought and faith, of our life with God, opens this inlet, and permits His living energies to flow in and out, and makes us one with Him.

This is also a simple and effectual exercise either for an individual or a group seeking spiritual illumination; associative action of a group in perfect concord being more immediate and certain in result. Let such come together "with one accord in one place;" a retired "upper room" is preferable, shut away as far as may be from the noise and bustle of the outer world, and set apart and consecrated to this purpose. The reading of inspired writings and the singing of spiritual hymns for their uniting and harmonizing influence, is a good opening exercise for ten or fifteen minutes; but the waiting upon the Spirit for illumination and guidance should be in *silence* and perfect quiet.

Close the eyes and withdraw all thought from the sensuous and physical plane; then unite the mind with the spirit, by turning the attention inward and focalizing it upon the spiritual centre of your own being, realizing that this is so much of God in you, and that "He is light and in him is no darkness at all;" and that unity of your mind with the spirit in yourself, unites you wholly with Him, and brings the "Holy Spirit," that which is wholly spiritual upon you, for the time.

The focalization of the attention in desire and faith upon the spirit within, until the thought and understanding become absorbed in the realization of its illuminating nature and power—if prepared to yield yourself to its every impulse and leading—will bring the revelation of God to your soul, and that illumination which "will guide you into all truth and teach you all things" needful for your well being.

Remember that desire is the only true prayer, and that all desire for good, focalized in faith or expectation of receiving it, is the prayer of faith which secures the blessing.

To assist this act of introversion and inward focalization, let the entire group repeat silently, each to his own soul, these words: OUR SPIRITS ARE ONE IN GOD and WITH CHRIST IN THE GREAT BROTHERHOOD OF SPIRIT; and the realization of this truth brings the power of this divine fellowship and communion into our life and makes us one in it. Not a careless, but a thoughtful repetition of these words serves to focalize the mind in this truth, and thus bring its realization in experience.

Man cannot concentrate his undivided attention in desire and faith upon any legitimate object, with corresponding effort, without its practical realization in experience; whether it be the healing of the body, the illumination of the mind, the attainment of some needful information, or a blessing upon another in body, spirit or estate.

The union of two or three in such prayer and effort, correspondingly enhances the result. This is a law based upon the very nature and necessity of things. God and his universe are

PLEDGED TO THE FULFILLMENT

Of every legitimate desire and good possible for man to seek, when sought in conformity with the law of its realization.

All true prayer is answered, therefore, not by any violation of the physical or moral order, but by divine provision and appointment in and through that order, established in the eternal necessity of the Father's Being.

How important then that this understanding should become universal; that through such enlightenment man may work out his own salvation in obedience to Apostolic injunction, while it is God that worketh in him, "both to will and to do of his good pleasure."

As the inner sight—Clairvoyance—and the inner hearing—Clairaudience—have by some been called the sixth and seventh senses, it seems necessary to correct this mistake by calling attention again to the distinguishing characteristics of the true sixth and seventh senses, and especially of the latter; that all confusion of thought on the subject may be cleared away.

This is the more needful also, in view of the widespread psychic phenomena of modern spiritism; lest in this confusion of thought, the order of development outlined in the preceding pages be confounded with the different phases of "mediumship," "spirit control," etc.

Mediumship, it should be observed, is not the result of, nor in any sense dependent upon the development of moral character, or of spirituality in the medium. It is the result of an unusual degree of physiological and psychological susceptibility to impressions from without, coupled, as a rule, with an imperfect personality and feeble will, or power of moral resistance.

Clairvoyance is the internal focalization of external vision; clairaudience of external hearing. Each and all of the five senses may be focalized inwardly and become active on the psychic plane of the sixth sense, and thus included in this sense. Mediumship, as we shall presently show, is a perversion of some of the activities of the sixth sense.

All the psychic powers of this sense, as previously shown, may be developed and exercised to a high degree, without direct spiritual illumination from the opening of the seventh sense, just as the mental and physical powers may be cultivated to a high degree on the sensuous plane. Yet we must remember that neither the outward nor the inward phase of mentality can be brought to perfection, without the full influence, illumination and guidance of the spiritual nature. Were mediumship either admissible or desirable, the only safety in its cultivation would be in first calling forth the spiritual nature. But this would prevent mediumship, and remove all occasion for its supposed desirableness. The whole problem of

IMMORTALITY AND SPIRITUAL DESTINY

Is solved in the open vision of the Spirit; all life becoming one unbroken fellowship and communion.

Admitting without argument all that spiritism claims as fact, the "medium" is simply an instrument in the hands of other personalities, who may be higher or lower than himself in the scale of moral character and spiritual enlightenment. Even when there is admitted inspiration without direct or full personal control of the medium, it is at best but the influx of intelligence from other personalities; not the opening of his own soul to the light within and the immediate illumination from the Divine.

These controlling or inspiring intelligences may be either high or low in the scale of morals and true spirituality. Hence, allowing the full claim of "mediumship," there is, to say the least, quite as much likelihood of personal demoralization, as of elevation from it on the part of the "medium;" since the peculiar susceptibility which opens him to the influence of the high, must of necessity equally subject him to the liability of influence from the low.

After about forty years of spiritism in its modern phase, it turns out that there is to be found quite as decided practical atheism, irreligion and rank materialism of thought, in as out of its ranks. Hence it is left for aspiring souls to draw their own conclusions as to the source and character of the inspiration that makes possible this result.

No objection or argument is here raised against either the fact or possibility of the supposed communication with the departed through mediumship, but admitting the claim, the objection still rests against the abnormal character of mediumship and its demoralizing effect upon the medium. Communication with the departed under normal conditions should be elevating in its influence, and in no case any more demoralizing than communication with friends in the body. But when this is gained at the expense of the individuality of the medium, the yielding up of his organism to the control of another's will, becoming a mere automaton for the manifestation of another personality, and often the total suspension of his own consciousness, it is an outrage upon the sacred gift of individuality and personal freedom, and a violation of the law of personal responsibility. It is against this spoliation of the sacred gift and the violation of the holy law of individuality and personal responsibility, that this protest is raised.

Every human being was unquestionably designed to attain personal mastery over all his environments through the development and perfection of his own intelligence and personality; never to become a mere instrument or automaton for the expression of the will or intelligence of other personalities; whether high or low, in or out of the body.

True clairvoyance or normal seership is not mediumship; neither is its development and exercise, or that of any other of the psychic powers of the sixth sense, in any way dependent upon the influence of "spirits," or the personal influence of any one.

While help, stimulus and inspiration to successful personal effort come always from union with others in true associative action and work of any kind, and especially in psychic and spiritual development, yet the unfolding of the powers of each, must be from within; the opening up and organic expression of the divine from the inmost of each soul, not from anything taken on from without. A true growth and permanent development can come in no other way.

All the psychic powers necessary to human well-being, are of necessity lodged in every human soul, and through the proper cultivation may receive their full normal development and co-ordinated activity. The "discerning of spirits" is one of the functions of the psychometric sense under spiritual illumination, and psychometry is the primary and fundamental expression of the sixth sense.

We repeat again for the encouragement of every reader, that the five physical senses are but the external expression of this all-inclusive sixth and inner sense; and that the psychometric power may be awakened in everyone who is sufficiently individualized and unfolded to appreciate and desire it. When this truth becomes generally known, this will become a part, and the fundamental part of universal education.

Dr. J. R. Buchanan, of our own country, was the first to recognize, name and practically as well as scientifically study and develop this sense, in its deeper and occult range of activities; and has probably done more to pave the way for that higher education which the discovery and understanding of these powers are now opening to the world, than any other individual of our century. Though ignored by the scientific authorities and schoolmen of his day, his work and genius will receive due recognition and appreciation by another generation.

The personalities of those who have cast off the material body, are as truly within the reach of the unfolded psychometric perception and communion, as when in the body. It is the soul and its spiritual organism, not the body, which constitutes the man, and through the development of the psychic powers he may establish a mental telegraphy with the inner realm of the soul-world and its peoples, whenever such special communication is desirable and wise.

It is by the more practical application to the daily needs of men, of this unfolded inner sense, that disease is correctly diagnosed and prescribed for, that the Mental Healer is enabled to come into sympathy with, speak to, and take hold of the real condition of his patient, and thus successfully treat or heal him. It is through this power also that the teacher can effectually reach the condition and bring forth the innate powers of his pupil. Through it the preacher is enabled to perceive and speak to the condition of his hearers, and thus enhance his power for good many-fold. Through it the scientist will be enabled the more effectually to penetrate the secret labyrinths of nature, and bring forth to the light of day her hidden truths and mysterious processes, and also to lay hold the more completely of her occult forces and subject them to his service. "For there is nothing covered that shall not be revealed; and hid that shall not be known." It is through the perfection of this sense that man shall

BECOME PERFECT IN KNOWLEDGE,

And in that power of mastery which true knowledge only gives.

The true seventh sense we have termed the God-sense, because it is that higher and deeper sense of God, or of life in Him which lifts the man out of himself, and above the absorbing sense of *personality* and of *things*, into the sphere of the absolute and universal. The full awakening of this sense, is the opening of the Divine inmost of man to his personal consciousness, and gives him that sense of identity of nature with God, which makes him one with the infinite or All of things. It inducts man into the sphere of the Divine, Impersonal and Eternal, so that the consciousness of being in and one with the Father is his. In this unity of consciousness with God, it is no presumption for man to say, "before Abraham was,"—behind and above all personality—"I Am."

It is only through this spiritual sense of being as the immediate offspring of God, partaking of his nature and attributes, that man can realize his ONENESS with the Father; the highest possible plane of human consciousness and experience as a child of the Eternal.

It was on this plane and in this sense of being that

JESUS DWELT,

As is evident from many of his recorded affirmations concerning himself. "The words that I say unto you I speak not from myself; but the Father abiding in me doeth His works." "Believe me that I am in the Father and the Father in me." "I and the Father are one."

Yet while making this claim for himself, he assures his followers that through faith in him, as the God-anointed Example, Leader and Teacher, a faith that leads them to follow him in this full and holy consecration to the Father's will and the leading of His Spirit, they should do the works that he had done, and greater even than he had manifested.

There are undreamed-of powers in every human soul awaiting development through the unfolding and activity of these inner senses. The opening and activity of the sixth sense awakens all the practical working powers of the soul in the sphere of invention, art, science, and whenever intuition, seership and inspiration can apply to the mastery of the outward world. Yet it is through the seventh sense only that the practical omniscience of spiritual illumination, and that higher condition of intelligent activity is reached, by which absolute dominion over the outward world can be achieved, and the so-called miracles of Jesus reproduced in modern life. Man can acquire absolute dominion over all that is without and beneath him, only by unity in spirit and will with the divine that is within and above him.

The healing power, clairvoyant vision, psychometric penetration and all the powers of the sixth sense (including mediumship), may be developed and successfully exercised without a corresponding degree of spirituality, which comes only with and through the opening of the seventh sense, and the unfolding of the God-consciousness. The reason of this is, that the activities of the sixth sense and the powers based upon it, are confined to the sphere of personalities and things.

Even when the psychometric sense and clairvoyant vision extend to the personalities and things of the world of spirits, it is still within the sphere of an objective world and secondary causes, and does not involve spirituality *per se*.

The home of the departed, though invisible to physical sense, is, in fact, as objective to the organic senses of its inhabitants, as is the physical world to our external senses. Hence, as man in his real organic personality with his mental and psychic powers, is precisely the same in the body as out of the body, and also out of the body as in it, the scenery and persons of the soul-world are as legitimate objects of perception and study, by the unfolded and illuminated psychic powers, as is the soul of things in this world. When man is properly unfolded and qualified for this study under normal conditions, he will find an open door of access to it.

The lower circles of the soul world peopled by those who have not yet awakened to any degree of spiritual life, are held to the sphere of sense. Each soul on leaving the body gravitates to the society and circle of those whose development corresponds with his own;

the law of elective affinity ruling in that world as gravitation rules in the material.

Those who have entered into the spiritual life in this world, have become already members of the Holy Brotherhood, and dwelling in unity and fellowship with them here, enter at once on their departure from earth, into the full life of that inmost sphere, the kingdom of God, that "third heaven," into which Paul was intromitted through entrancement, and heard and witnessed scenes and things which no earthly language, or symbols could portray.

This inner heaven of light and blessedness, can be entered only by preparation through spiritual enlightenment and purification. It is "the pure in heart" only, that "shall see God." Contact and communication with the unspiritualized circles of the soul world may be had through the proper training of the psychometric power; but real communication with the spiritual heavens can be had only by this same power being lifted up to that plane through spiritual illumination.

Presence and absence on the psychic and spiritual planes, are not measured by space distances, but by states of sympathy or antagonism. To think of a friend on the internal plane, is to be present with him; whether he be on earth or in the highest heaven. No power can shut off from the spiritually unfolded soul this high communion and fellowship. Did not the disciples hold direct personal communion with the risen Jesus? So may all his true disciples to the end of time. What has been done may be done under like conditions forever. But this communion is possible only on the same plane of the spiritual life upon which the apostles enjoyed it.

Through the unfolding of spiritual life in the soul, we come into living unity and unbroken fellowship with the entire Brotherhood of the Spirit on earth and in the heavens, whose life and aims are one; living to serve and work out the emancipation and spiritual enlightenment of the race, both on earth and in the lower spheres of the soul-world—"spirits in prison."

In this exposition of the laws and conditions of psychic and spiritual development, we could not be just to the subject nor to our readers, without giving

THIS WORD OF WARNING,

And disclosing to the seeker after the higher wisdom and experience, the specific danger that lies in the pathway from the outer to the inner life. This danger comes from the development and exercise of the psychic powers of the sixth sense, without the corresponding unfolding and guiding power of the seventh. It is the danger of the perversion of the psychometric impressibility to the abnormal conditions of mediumship, and the unnatural control of the personality

SPIRITUALITY THE ONLY BASIS. 329

by the intrusive wills of disembodied spirits of the "mid-region."

Through this impressibility of the sixth sense, we are affected by and in turn enabled to act upon and affect whomsoever and whatsoever we are in psychometric *rapport* or mental sympathy and contact with. It is through the power to act directly upon those with whom we are in psychometric sympathy, that mental telegraphy is possible, and that true mental healing is effected. But when we yield ourselves to the conditions into which we thus mentally enter, and fail to maintain our individuality and power to react upon them, we are liable to become subject to them and lose our own self-control.

Without this precaution, there is liability of taking on the diseased conditions of the sick, instead of healing them; and should our contact be with spirits of the "mid-region," who are ever active and moving within the sphere of our earth, we are liable to come under their influence and control, instead of holding the mastery of our own organism, and of their influence in its relation to us, and so lose all power to benefit them, or to safely communicate with them.

Once become a medium and subject to the "control of spirits," observation shows that it is next to impossible to break away and become fully emancipated from their controlling influence and intrusive interference while in the body.

While thus held the subject of these occult influences, and the intrusive wills of other personalities, the medium is prevented from rising to that higher condition of divine communion and fellowship to which the opening and development of the true spiritual, or God-sense, lifts and inducts man.

If the unfolding and activity of the higher powers of the seventh sense, —direct Spiritual Intuition under divine Inspiration,—is first sought, there will be perfect safety in the cultivation and highest possible development and activity of all the psychic powers of the sixth sense. They will then become focalized and illuminated for practical service in the mastery of the outward world and the personal environments, under divine inspiration and guidance.

By this wise course the human will becomes united with and reinforced by the Divine Will, which fortifies the soul against any possible intrusion of or disturbance from foreign wills, or any external influence whatsoever, whether occult or mundane.

Before man can, by the exercise of a power developed within himself, suspend or overrule the forces of the physical world, so as to walk upon the water, control the tempest, cleanse the leper, and instantaneously heal otherwise incurable maladies, and finally to dematerialize his own body so as to pass without dissolution, in a glorious translation and final victory of personal life over death and physical decay, to his true and permanent home in the spiritual heavens, he must come to that personal realization of unity with God in the Spirit, attained only through the opening and supremacy of the seventh sense, the deepest sphere of his being. This supreme realization of personal unity with God on the plane of the spiritual and divine, enables man to speak and act in the name and power of God, and thus to approach nature from the high

THRONE OF BEING,

And control her forces at first hand.

When this plane of consciousness and the experience of divine communion and fellowship which it gives, is permanently reached, all the psychic powers unfolded on the plane of the sixth sense are lifted up to the plane of the spiritual, in spontaneous Intuition and mastery, and thus brought to absolute perfection in the supreme light and power of the Spirit.

This transcendent attainment, however, is impossible without the entire and unreserved consecration of all the powers of the personal life to the Spirit and its leading, the absolute abandonment in thought and desire of all external and personal considerations, and becoming absorbed in the supreme desire to know God and to execute His will alone. "If any man willeth to do his will he shall know of the teaching." "Ye shall seek me and find me, when ye shall search for me with all your heart."

From what has been said, the danger of yielding to the influence and control of spirits of whatever claim, will be seen, as well as the absurdity of so doing. All the psychic powers that might be developed through mediumship, and the influence or control of spirits, exist latent in the organism of the medium, and may be cultivated and brought to perfection by the proper psychometric training under divine guidance and illumination, which by consecration and prayer are within reach of the humblest. The normal seership thus attained, on both the psychic and spiritual planes, permits a form of spiritual intercourse to which there can be no objection; since the spiritual attainment of the seer would of itself open to him communion with the heavenly or divine order of intelligences, and give him power also to enlighten and help the benighted ones of the "mid-region," or the lower orders, should he come in contact or communication with them.

The manifest object of every personal existence is the unfolding and perfection of his own individuality, in full recognition of the corresponding freedom and responsibility of every other personality, conferred on man as a sacred trust, to be individually and socially cherished and guarded. Any enforcement of arbitrary control by one will, or combination of wills, over the will and personality of a single individual, to the prevention of the full development of his personal powers, in harmony with the corresponding rights of others, is pure despotism, whether individual or social; and as such, an open violation of the divine law.

God never arbitrarily coerces the will of one of his children. Having endowed them with moral freedom, He leaves them perfect liberty of choice, whether they seek to co-operate with Him in working out the perfection of their being, or refuse his guidance and seek to do it in their own strength and wisdom.

As the All-Father will not coerce or arbitrarily control the will or personality of one of his children, neither will any spirit, in or out of the body, who is in unity with His Spirit, seek to coerce and control the will and organism of another. Any spirit, therefore, who attempts this, whatever may be his claims to intelligence, wisdom or goodness, cannot in truth be an angel or messenger of God. This principle discloses the

IMMORAL CHARACTER

Of mediumship, under spirit control, and forever brands it as an imposition, perversion, and an unholy violation of a sacred gift and trust.

The ministry of angels, who have come to minister unto and strengthen men in the struggle of life, "All ministering spirits sent forth to minister for them who shall be heirs of salvation," are in the divine order, and as such, are the chosen instruments of the Father in the manifestation of His special providence to the children of men. The Hebrew and Christian Scriptures are filled with the record of such special providences at the hands of heavenly messengers. The very law and prophecies of the Old Testament as affirmed by the inspired Stephen, were given "by the disposition of angels." The same inspired authority assures us that it was "an angel of the Lord" that spake in the name of God to Moses from out the burning bush.

We are told by the Evangelists that "angels ministered unto" Jesus in his hour of mortal struggle, and "strengthened him." They came not to do his work for him, nor to use him as "an instrument" for their own, but to encourage, sustain and strengthen him for the work and mastery the Father had given *him* to perform. Jesus himself assured his followers that he could through prayer to his Father in heaven, summon to his aid, if needed, "more than twelve legions of angels." When we remember the work that one angel wrought for the rescue of Peter from prison and the Roman guard, in response to the prayers of his brethren, we can readily imagine somewhat of the mighty power attending the more than twelve legions of angels that may be summoned to the aid of a faithful and consecrated soul like Jesus, through prayer to God. And if this strong Son of God needed the help of angelic ministration, who of all the sons of men may not need and claim it?

Nevertheless, he who best knew, both from experience and insight, the needs and capacities of men, as well as the law and conditions of realization, bids us "seek first the kingdom of God" within, "and all these things shall be added" unto us. Let us close with the description which that illuminated

CHRISTIAN HIEROPHANT,

St. Paul, has left us of the "Gifts" conferred on men by that One Divine and Eternal Spirit—a portion of which is in every man—through the consecration of man to it: "Concerning Spiritual Gifts, brethren, I would not have you ignorant." * * * * "Now there are diversities of gifts, but the same Spirit. And there are diversities of ministrations, and the same Lord. And there are diversities of workings, but the same God, who worketh all things in all. But to each one is given the manifestation of the Spirit to profit withal. For to one is given through the Spirit the word of wisdom; and to another the word of knowledge, according to the same Spirit; to another faith, in the same Spirit; and to another gifts of healings, in the one Spirit; and to another workings of miracles; and to another prophecy; and to another discernings of spirits; to another divers kinds of tongues; and to another the interpretation of tongues: but all these worketh the one and the same Spirit, dividing to each one severally even as he will." "But desire earnestly the greater gifts. And a still more excellent way shew I unto you."

"If I speak with the tongues of men and of angels, but have not love, I am become sounding brass, or a clanging cymbal. And if I have the gift of prophecy, and know all mysteries and all knowledge; and if I have all faith, so as to remove mountains, but have not love, I am nothing. And if I bestow all my goods to feed the poor, and if I give my body to be burned, but have not love, it profiteth me nothing. Love suffereth long, and is kind; love envieth not; love vaunteth not itself, is not puffed up, doth not behave itself unseemly, seeketh not its own, is not provoked, taketh not account of evil; rejoiceth not in unrighteousness, but rejoiceth with the truth: beareth all things, believeth all things, hopeth all things, endureth all things. Love never faileth: but whether there be prophecies, they shall be done away; whether there be tongues, they shall cease; whether there be knowledge, it shall be done away. For we know in part, and we prophesy in part; but when that which is perfect is come, that which is in part shall be done away. When I was a child, I spake as a child, I felt as a child, I thought as a child: now that I am become a man, I have put away childish things. For now we see in a mirror, darkly; but then face to face: now I know in part; but then shall I know even as also I have been known. But now abideth faith, hope, love, these three; and the greatest of these is love."

APPENDIX I.

Having quoted briefly from the "Nature and Aims of Theosophy," for the purpose of contrasting our claim for The Theosophy of the Christ with that of the older Theosophy of the East, it seems but just that we should add an Appendix for the fuller presentation of the claim made by the author, in his earnest and candid appeal to the intelligence of our age, that it may be fairly represented. In reference to the Eastern Brotherhood and their treasured wisdom, described in our quotation, he says:

"It will at once be asked, how have these Brothers been able to keep their very existence so long a secret?

"I answer, that the Law of Silence was ever the first to be observed, and that according to their statement their safety has often consisted in that the people refused to believe such an existence possible. Read the account given by Abbe Huc, for which he was unfrocked by his ecclesiastical superiors, and his still more startling statements outside his published works. Or in more ancient times read the account that Apollonius of Tyana gives of his visit to these Brothers, though it is evident on every page, that he conceals far more than he reveals. Again, read the account in that old work, '*Hermippus Redivivus*' of these 'Sons of Light.' Coming down to more recent times, read the account that travelers, and even missionaries, give of the wonders performed by half-naked traveling Fakirs, a faint echo of the transcendent powers and lofty genius of the Holy men of the Himavat, the existence of whom the Fakirs would declare, could they be induced to speak.

"In spite of evidence to be derived from many sources, some no doubt will content themselves with denying the whole thing as simply incredible, an old woman's fable, and go on repeating, 'We do not know,' or 'We do not care.' Those, however, and they are many, who have read Mr. Linnett's Occult World and Esoteric Buddhism, and the later work by Two Chelas; Man, Fragments of Forgotten History, ought to supplement them with those rare jewels, The Idyll of the White Lotus, and Light on the Path: and if by this time they are not interested enough to inquire whether this is all true, and if there is more from the same source they may as well defer the matter till the next incarnation.

"Soon after the appearance of Isis Unveiled, the head-quarters of the Theosophical Society removed from New York city, first to Bombay, and subsequently to Adgar, in the Madras presidency, India, where they permanently remain. Branch societies are scattered all over India and Ceylon, as well as most civilized countries of the globe. The Theosophical Society is the medium, through which the Brothers have undertaken to present to the world their long-cherished doctrines, in such form as the world is found ready to receive, and in such measure as the times require, practical, not merely intellectual, Universal Brotherhood being the one condition of affiliation insisted on, while the terms of more intimate relations with the Brothers themselves, or Chelaship, are clearly set forth, for, to use their own words, they say, 'We refuse no one.'

"Upon the organization of one of the Branch Societies in India, it was thought by some of the members, that it would be a good thing to organize on a different basis from the rest, and to have certain educated Englishmen connected therewith, taken in hand by the Brothers, and drilled in practical occultism, taught, in fact, the secret wisdom which had been so jealously guarded for centuries, and so constitute a Theosophical Hierarchy. One is not likely to misunderstand the answer returned by one of the Brothers to this suggestion. I quote a portion of the unpublished letter:

"'The world in general and Christendom especially, left for two thousand years to the *regime* of a personal God, as well as to its political and social systems based on that idea, has now proved a failure.

"'If the Theosophist says we have nothing to do with all this, the lower classes and inferior races, those of India, for instance, in the conception of the British, cannot concern us, and must manage as they can, what becomes of our fine professions of benevolence, philanthropy, reform, etc.? Are these professions a mockery; and if a mockery, can ours be the true path? Shall we devote ourselves to teaching a few Europeans fed on the fat of the land, many of them loaded with the gifts of blind fortune, the *rationale* of bell-ringing, cup-growing, and astral body formation, and leave the teeming millions of the ignorant, the poor and the despised, the lowly and oppressed, to take care of themselves, and their hereafter, the best they know how? NEVER! perish rather Theosophical Society with both its hapless founders, than that we should permit it to become no better than an academy of magic, and a hall of occultism; and it is we, the humble disciples of these perfect Lamas, who are expected to allow the Theosophical Society to drop its noblest title, 'The *Brotherhood of Humanity*,' to become a school of philosophy. Let us understand each other. He who does not feel competent enough to grasp the noble idea sufficiently to work for it, need not undertake a task too heavy for him. But there is hardly a theosophist in the whole society unable to effectually help it, by correcting the erroneous impression of outsiders, if not by actually propagating himself this idea. Oh, for the noble and unselfish men to help us effectually in India, in that divine task! All our knowledge, past and present, would not be sufficient to repay him. The true religion and philosophy offers the solution of every problem. That the world is in such a bad condition morally, is conclusive evidence that none of its religions and philosophies, those of the civilized races less than any other, have ever possessed the truth. The right and logical explanation of the subject of the problems of the great dual principles, 'right and wrong,' 'good and evil,' 'liberty and despotism,' 'pain and pleasure,' 'egotism and altruism,' are as impossible now as they were 1881 years ago. They are as far from the solution as they were; but to these there must be somewhere a consistent solution, and if our doctrines will show their competence to offer it, then the world will be the first to confess it. That must be the true philosophy, the true light, the true religion, which gives truth, and nothing but the truth.'

"It will thus be seen what are the principles and aims of these exalted Brothers, in relation to the masses of mankind, and that they are no respectors of persons. It may be asked, why have these transcendent truths been so long withheld from the world? To this it may be answered, that they who possess and comprehend them, are likely to know also the times and seasons when they can make headway in the world, and to announce them prematurely, would be to lose them and destroy their custodians, if they had not power to provide against such a catastrophe. It is a cardinal principle in occultism, that by a knowledge of, and conformity to the laws of nature, the Adept is able to accomplish that which to the ignorant seems miraculous. Says a wise occultist, 'The wicked obey the law through fear; the wise keep the law through knowledge.'

"Political freedom and the advancement of science have on the one hand, made the promulgation of these doctrines possible, while the crumblings of creeds, and the materialism of the age, have rendered them necessary to the well-being of the human race.

"Again it may be said, that the Secret Doctrine has never been without witnesses in the world, and though these witnesses, like the doctrine itself, have been surrounded by mystery, and have written or spoken in a language unintelligible to the profane, yet have they ever been open to all who have knocked in the right way. These mysteries have cropped out in many forms, though never for ages so plainly as now, FOR THEIR TIME HAS COME.

"These Holy Brothers of the Himavat, deeming the time propitious, offer to the world, for the first time in many centuries, just so much of their treasured wisdom as it shows itself willing and capable of receiving. To this promulgation, it has already been shown, one only condition is attached, viz.: that the neophite shall work with the Brothers for the elevation and liberation of the whole human race, without regard to color, sex, creed or nationality; to all such the doors now are wide open, and to none others, though the sublime philosophy is published to the world. This basis of universal brotherhood, however, involves more than it is at first supposed. It involves the idea of what Bohme calls the 'Becoming Man,' *i. e.*, that man shall not merely give intellectual assent to the propositions, but that he shall *become* that

APPENDIX I.

which he professes, and, sinking self, exercise universal philanthropy and love of man. 'DEEDS,' say they, 'ARE WHAT WE WANT; FINE SPEECHES COUNT FOR NAUGHT.' * * * *

"In the way of the progress of this great work, stand not only the creeds of Christendom, but those of the whole world, each claiming a patent of authority direct from the Most High; each striving now, as for ages, to tear down all others, that it may build up its own, in which insane effort, it has been truly said, more blood has been spilt, more lives sacrificed, than by war, famine and pestilence combined; in short, MOLOCH! THE SCOURGE OF THE HUMAN RACE. * * *

"The *father of lies*, is also the father of creeds, and not He who made of one blood all the nations of the earth. The time is not distant when we must choose between our creeds and the Brotherhood of man, for they are antagonistic to the last degree; and that faith which is to remove mountains, was never yet involved in the mumbling of creeds, else had the earth long ago become a dead level. Modern science has yet to learn the height and grandeur to which human beings may attain on this earth, as the focalized result of the dual law of evolution and involution; and professed believers in Christ have also to learn the truth of the assertion, 'these signs shall follow them that believe.' The days of miracle have, indeed passed, for those of law and enlightenment are at hand, enlightenment through obedience to law, the higher law of love and Universal Brotherhood. Had but a tithe of the wealth squandered in the propagation of creeds in foreign lands where better creeds prevail, been spent in uniting the human race under this higher law, the millennium would long ago have dawned. Theosophy has this one central idea, the Brotherhood of man. Among its devoted followers are Jews, Catholics, Protestants, Buddhists, Brahmanists, Mohammedans, Parsees, people of every race, clime and color. All that is asked, is that each sect shal go back to the fountain head of its own religion, assured that when they have removed the accretions of time, the innovations of greed and selfishness, the false interpretations of ignorance, they will find beneath it all, the pure *Wisdom Religion*, the Divine Sophia of Jacob Bohme, the Divine Beatrice of

Dante, the Pure Gold of the alchemists, the White Rose of the Rosicrucians, the Virgin of the World of Hermes Trismegistus, the Virgin Isis, the Virgin Mother of the Christ of all the ages that are, that have been, that shall be; forever pure and virgin, yet forever bringing forth; mother, wife, sister, and daughter of Osiris; the gentle, loving, tender Woman-side of the Life-giver of the Universe; the better-half of every man of woman born, through which alone at-one-ment of the human race is possible, through which alone the God which is One can ever become all in all, THEO-SOPHIA."—(*The Nature and Aim of Theosophy, by J. D. BUCK, Cincinnati.*

APPENDIX II.

Since the practical development and successful application of the method and processes set forth in "Introduction to the Theosophy of the Christ," and "The Way, the Truth and the Life," to the higher psychic education and training of classes, a book giving a remarkable corroborative experience has providentially fallen into the writer's hands.

This book—now out of print—published by Emily Faithful, in London, 1864, was written by William Robert Bertolacci, of France, in which the author records the most remarkable development of spiritual gifts and occult power in his own family circle, and their unique and specific application to the complete education of his children, by processes original with himself.

These remarkable and successful experiments are such a striking illustration as well as confirmation of both the doctrine and method developed and practiced by the writer, that he feels he will do his readers a favor by giving them liberal extracts from this book.

These experiments began in 1853, in the early days of Spiritism in France. Bertolacci became impressed at the very beginning of the singular and startling manifestations, witnessed by himself, that while communication with the departed might be permissible under proper conditions, yet to seek this as an end was a perversion of the power thus manifest, and would lead to ultimate disaster. It seemed to him a providential indication of the dawning of that era of Scripture prophecy in which the Spirit of God was to be poured out upon all flesh, and the sons and daughters of men were to have visions, and prophecy, etc. Hence, instead of seeking exclusively for communion with the souls of the so-called dead, they should seek first direct communion with, and guidance from the GREAT OVER-SOUL. Acting upon this conviction, he sought this high communion and guidance from the first.

His first communication with the invisible but intelligent Power, was through the rappings, then the direct writing through the planchette. . Through the latter he received the specific instructions for conducting the experiments which followed and resulted in the remarkable experiences recorded. These, with some views and suggestions of his, we give in his own words, as follows:

THE WISDOM OF THE PHENOMENA SPEAKING FOR ITSELF.

I have said [in the Introduction] that new phases of the great Spiritual Phenomena of these times have been developed, during the last eleven years, within my own family circle.

By them we have been made to comprehend—for it has been most undeniably proved to us—that (notwithstanding there is good and bad in this as well as in everything else in creation), in the sign here sent on earth, while it is the latest, are to be found the seeds of the greatest gift that man has received from Providence, since his first fall from his divine origin.

We have been told many things by the intellectual agent operating in these manifestations, and have in many cases verified the truth of its teachings.

I. That it is a latent power belonging to *Man;* but as it is of a higher order of things than all that our temporal reason is based upon, and has received its greatest development from, it cannot be accounted for nor understood by our *minds*, such as they have been formed by the corrupt education of the past ages.

II. That this power or faculty can, not only be developed and transmitted, but ought by all who obtain it, to be thus turned to useful purposes and to the benefit of our fallen fellow-creatures.

That it is like the diamond which, given to man in the rough state, requires to be cut and polished by his hand to show forth its perfections; like the iron deposited, for man's use, in the crust of the earth, which may be turned by him into implements of husbandry or weapons of war; like many metals so essential to the progress of industry in machinery, to our welfare in divers ways through manifold chemical processes, yet how fatal, as poisons, if misused.

III. That according to the spirit in which we receive these manifestations, they will be developed among us.

If we receive them as a mere amusement, as a toy, they will for a time astonish our minds and amuse our childishness; but they will follow the fate of all toys and foolish pleasures. * * * *

If we allow ourselves to be frightened into the persuasion that they are entirely the "WORKINGS OF SATAN," they will, in some cases, overthrow our reason, impair the faculties of our minds; and in many, deteriorate our health, and affect our happiness.

If we attribute them *exclusively* to the intervention of the souls of the departed, and the "Spirits" of other worlds, we thereby refuse to acknowledge the secret workings of our own inward man, and as it were disinherit our souls from all participation in such things as are passing on the surface of this globe, where we were originally placed to be the "*Image of the Living God,*" and "*Lords of the Creation;*" and then, with regard to all that is beyond those animal functions and material operations which we can account for, we become fearful and hopeless, in a state of superstition and fatalism.

If we seek for the *causes* of these phenomena in the physical or material side of nature, * * * * and in the presumptiousness of our own wisdom, we invent an imaginary substance and add it to the chain of matter, as a new link, under the name of an "*imponderable fluid,*" we therefore fall into a fresh labyrinth of useless theories and technicalities, alike racking to the brain and sowing desolation and contest in the heart.

IV. But if we receive these signs as "*the grains of Mustard Seed,*" if the parable of the *Kingdom of Heaven,*—in other words as the forerunner of the *gift of spiritual power*—to be fostered and cultivated by us with veneration, in a spirit of Faith, Hope and Charity, we may then expect to find developed, through these providential means, in our own hearts, that "*Spirit of Light and Truth*" which has been promised us as our "CONSOLER" for those "*latter times*" when the "*Spirit of God*" *is to be poured out* "*upon all flesh*," and by the strength of which we shall be qualified to "*place our hands on the heads of our children*," that "*our sons and daughters may prophecy.*"

For it is written that "*every one shall be rewarded according unto his faith.*"

Our Saviour told us that "*unto whosoever believeth all things are possible*," that if we believed in Him and followed His precepts, not only should we be enabled to repeat the miracles performed by Him, "*but still greater works than these shall we do.*" Now those who call themselves Christians have no right to contest the promises made by Jesus, a great number of times, during His earthly career: promises which are particularly specified at the end of the Gospel according to St. Mark, St. John xiv: 11, 17, etc., and corroborated by numerous subsequent facts related in the "Acts of the Apostles."

V. We have also been told by this invisible agency that its principle is that of the life of all things—the hidden force by which all things exist—that it is impossible for any one thing or being, or for any number of things or beings, to explain or comprehend it in a material point of view, as *by it* all things are explained, and *in it* all things are comprehended. That it is the basis of all religions, the origin of every science, and the promoter of philosophy. That the Bible is a register of its acts, the book that shows its power and teaches to respect, venerate, and fear it. And that the Gospel is the key to its use, in love, joy and confidence, in order to obtain, on the one part, life eternal, or the living, indestructible consciousness of our intellectual being as *man* in God through Christ, the living principle of Charity, and through the *Man Jesus* made perfect in the temporal by the action of his own *free will*, in perfect harmony with that decree of Divine Providence, by which He was the predestined Messiah; and on the other part, to attain, in the temporal, our regeneration as men. That, having received within our hearts, "the gift of the Holy Spirit," we shall become "*the living tabernacle of the Lord,*" "*the temple of God on earth,*" and in that state be invested with divine power, enjoying "*the glorious liberty of the children of God.*" * * * *

Now as the vegetable reign succeeded to the mineral one, which was followed by the animal reign, so *must* the spiritual reign eventualy grow out of the highest order of the animal creation. That which distinguishes man and establishes his claim to the first place in God's creation, is the progressive character of his intellectual faculties. The human intellect, like every principle, is two-fold in its operations—it is rational and inspirational. The former appertaining to the temporal, or material order, is developed by the acquirement and appliances of physical science.

Man, in devoting himself exclusively to the rational development of his intellectual being, has become the kingdom divided against itself: thence his fallen state. Now, as man by his nature is *the progressive being,* his intellectual faculties cannot stand still, they *must* move either forwards or backwards, they *must* either ascend or descend. That which moves forwards or backwards, the rational or mundane intellect, has advanced because he has cultivated it, but as he has neglected the inspirational or divine science, he has fallen below the animal creation in regard to instinct, which is the mark of divine Providence, the manifestation of God's presence, in the beast; but which in man—from the principle of progression of which he is the living type—ascends to the faculty of divine Revelation or perfect Wisdom, when duly cultivated. That is the Spirit of Light and Truth,—the Consoler which is to teach us all things; and the earthly fruit of that Wisdom is the spiritual power of man over all flesh, or the direct action of His will upon all things created. * * * * It is that state of redemption *in* CHRIST unto which Mankind was destined to rise, and is *consequently* of a higher order than that in which he was first created; "*the first man Adam was made a living Soul, the last Adam is a quickening Spirit.*" * * * *

Among the teachings we have received in the inspired writings given to us by the Spirit of our communions, has been the following: "God is not an *extraneous*, individual, isolated Being, but the internal, collective, and contiguous life and constitution of all things; not *a* heterogeneous force, but *the* intrinsic strength; not the concrete, but abstract; not relative but absolute, as to the principle."

I trust what I have said will go some way towards dispelling, in my readers' minds, those narrow ideas of a materialistic education which leads them to look upon the Deity as of a "*nature distinct*" from that of creation; a species of outward looker-on, instead of being, as He is, the intimate constitution, action, life, and intelligence of all things. It is not He who keeps Himself distinct from us, but *we*, who having divided our being *in* Him, have thus, as the unavoidable consequence of our self-degradation, chosen and cherished the principle which leads to death, and neglected that which leads to life. "*In Him was Life; and the life was the light of men.*" "*And the light shineth in darkness; and the darkness comprehended (received) it not.*" * * "*That was the true Light which lighteth every man which cometh into the world.*" What can this Light and Life mean, if it allude not to the higher qualities of the soul of man, such as it is in the undivided state, when every new-born infant comes into the world? * * * *

In specific answer to the question often put, as to "What the particular Spirit is which presides at our meetings?" I reply in the words given us that it is the *Spirit of our communion.* * * *

Jesus Christ prayed the Father that His disciples and all those who should believe in Him through their teaching, should be *one*, not only among themselves: but being one among themselves they should also be admitted as *one with Him and the Father*. (See Jno. xviii: 20, 21.) It is also stated in the same chapter that, although through their faith they were no longer of the world, He did not pray that they should be withdrawn *from* the world; which is plainly affirming that, although we are distinct persons bodily in the world, we could, nevertheless, be *one* together, and *one with Him and the Father*, notwithstanding that He and the Father were *not of* the world. * * * *

It is, therefore, manifest that the souls of two or more persons can, during their life on earth, unite and form *one* Soul. Union is strength; and when that strength is constituted upon the conditions laid down by the Christian Doctrine, it becomes divine power, omnipotent in its principles, and without any limitation in its effects other than that imposed upon it at the time by the degree of the faith of its constituents. * * *

The power of the elect, are we not told, is to be that of performing miracles, and their work that of healing, consoling, converting, and regenerating the common herd. "He saith unto him, feed my lambs." * * * * "Feed my sheep."

Such and many others are the teachings we have received in some 1,200 or 1,400 pages of manuscript from the intellectual side of the phenomenon, which first manifested itself to my family circle, in the apparently trivial form of *table turning and rappings* in the year 1853.

THE PLANCHETTE.—The whole of this information was not given to us through raps in the table, far from it. That process being by much too slow a one; the table indicated the use of a "*planchette*," which consists, etc. * * * * The hands of two or more persons are placed on the upper surface of the board, with the tips of the fingers lightly touching it, precisely in the same manner usually followed with regard to the table turning.

The planchette soon begins to move in different directions, and after a short time, the lines traced by the friction of the pencil on a paper placed under it, becomes intelligible writing, and with a little practice, or more correctly speaking, with the habit of "*laisser aller*" which the operators acquire, the speed in writing becomes sometimes far greater than that ever attained by the hand of the most rapid penman.

[Here follows a graphic description of some striking physical manifestations, which included most of those claimed as common in circles held for them by the Spiritists.—J. H. D.]

ANIMAL MAGNETISM, ETC.—Among other things which we have been told in the planchette writings was, that what is called "*animal magnetism*" is but a branch of this same great phenomenon; that the discoveries made by Cagliostro, Mesmer, and others, have been wrongly attributed to fluids as their cause; but that they were particular signs sent to mankind by Providence to prepare us for what was to follow, and to be used by us as the rudiments or means of developing the Spiritual faculties latent within us, by which we are to attain our regeneration and definite Redemption. * * *

However, after having received the most satisfactory and edifying instruction, through the channel of the planchette-writing, on the nature and divine origin of these facts, as also the proper use to be made of them, and the manner in which to proceed for obtaining the required results, so as to avoid all harm and obtain nothing but good,—from that time, under the constant guidance of our invisible Spiritual instructor, I undertook to try to magnetise the different members of our family. Although till then we had never seen any of those operations, nor received instructions as to how to proceed from any person whatsoever, it is astonishing how well and rapidly we succeeded in producing the majority of the effects known and spoken of, by others.

[At that time it was not known that all the effects obtained in the mesmeric sleep could be induced in the wakeful state, and that the trance itself, and induced, or "artificial somnambulism," are as readily produced without the process of supposed magnetism, as since demonstrated by Dr. Baird, of London, and Fahenstock and others in this country,—J. H. D.]

After some trials my young people were thrown into the magnetic sleep, and in that state could read in books with their eyes bandaged and well padded up—could see and hear things in far distant places—were made insensible to pain, and deprived of their memory on being wakened, or retained a perfect recollection of all that had passed during their somnambulic state. It was made known to us by the Spirit, that this power to obstruct or retain the memory could be vastly extended; that the memory with the faculties of perception could be so strengthened as to make the education of our young people the easiest of all things—an amusement, a real recreation—instead of being, as it is now a slow, tedious and fatiguing process.

In like manner the power of suspending all physical sensibility and that of creating every species of pain in any organ of the body, when under the influence of the magnetizer, by the mere expression of his will to that effect, was, we were informed, the basis of a new order of things, tending to a general diffusion of that blessed gift possessed by our Saviour and His original disciples, and ranked among the recompenses promised by Him for a future day to all who should put His teachings into practice :— that gift consisting in the power of performing miraculous and instantaneous cures, and of healing all the physical ailings to which man had become subjected through his original fall.

Another and most important revelation imparted to us, was that the acquirements of the somnambulic conditions could, with a little pains and perseverance, in a great majority of subjects, be transferred to their normal waking state ; and that, too, through very simple and easy processes, the actuating principle of which was the *Power of Faith* in those therein concerned, and great confidence on the part of the presiding operator.

INITIATION.—I will begin by exposing the development effected by us, of some of those latent faculties of the soul, common to all mankind, which tend principally to the education of the mind.

I. One object attained was "Clairvoyance" (or *"second-sight"*), in the SOMNAMBULIC OR SLEEPING MAGNETIC STATE; with a view towards fitting the organs of the body to subserve the same faculty in the normal condition.

II. READING.—Having once acquired the faculty of discerning objects, and distinguishing persons, positions, etc., a book was placed in the hands of the somnambule, whose eyes were covered with a bandage, and who could soon read in spite of this, correctly, line after line and page after page.

(NOTE.—In this operation it was made known to us that the more the external light was excluded, the more easily would the clairvoyance be developed at the outset of the trials, and also that the application of any cold object on the lids of the closed eyes in order to lull the action—to lower the intonation—of those organs, would greatly facilitate and improve the action of the inward or "*second sight*" upon them.)

III. READING IN THE MAGNETIC SLEEP FROM A CLOSED BOOK, at any named page.

IV. THE SUPPRESSION OF THE NATURAL SENSATIONS AND THE CREATION OF IMAGINARY ONES, during the magnetic sleep, at the bidding of the magnetizer, and subsequently the SUPPRESSION OR AUGMENTATION OF THE MEMORY, on being awoke, with regard to things that had taken place during the sleep.

The first of these two phases has led to the faculty in the patient, of being easily cured of all physical ailings by the *will* or *prayer and faith* of one or more of their fellow-creatures, seconded by their own.

The second phase has become the basis of a novel spiritual mode of most easy, rapid, instantaneous education, without the slightest fatigue to the natural system of the student.

V. THE next step indicated to us was that which constitutes the PASSAGE TO THE MAGNETIC (or somnambulic) CONDITION IN THE WAKING STATE BY THE ACT OF "VAGUE CONTEMPLATION."

It consists in *gazing intently* upon an uniform body or a fixed luminous object. This is done in order to deter or fruitlessly preoccupy the temporal reason of the *"outer man,"* acting through the brain, while the spirit of revelation appertaining to the soul or *"inner man,"* is operating upon the material organs of perception.

[This is simply shutting off the impressions of the outward world through the five physical senses—which focalize upon the front brain—by diverting the attention from the external, and opening the mind to corresponding impressions through the sixth sense by directing the observation to the inner light or medium of sight, sound, feeling, etc., sometimes called the *"astral fluid,"* *"luminous ether,"* etc., and concentrating the attention upon any given object in this light thus opened to the mind through the sixth sense. This sense embraces in its sphere of activity the whole realm of the occult. It is the border realm between the purely sensuous plane and that which is purely spiritual—the kingdom of God, or realm of the divine and heavenly—into which the seventh or highest sense of the soul when opened inducts man.

APPENDIX II. 353

Mediumship and magic belong to the plane of the sixth sense, and are a perversion of its normal powers.—J. H. D.]

The impressions thereon produced, when the subjects are left entirely to themselves, vary. They are sometimes those of actual facts or realities co-existent at the time, sometimes of those having taken place in the past, and sometimes of those belonging to a future more or less distant; while at other times they are what is termed "*purely imaginary or visionary*," when they cannot be traced to any known cause or pre-established order of things. After having succeeded in obtaining this condition, and rendered it familiar by practicing several times, my young probationers acquired next what may be called:

VI. THE DIRECT CLAIRVOYANCE BY VAGUE CONTEMPLATION, and which consists in seeing—while gazing into a bowl of water, upon a sheet of white or black paper, or any other *monotinted* surface—such objects alone as are indicated to them, those objects being under cover, placed at a distance, or otherwise kept quite out of sight. To this succeeded:

VII. THE READING IN BOOKS, closed or out of sight, by aid of the same process. At first words only, then lines, and definitely entire pages were read currently.

Then, after having varied the objects gazed upon, and also by degrees, the regularity and monotony of the surfaces, the faculty was developed by gazing vaguely upon *any object* that presented itself first to view.

The above auxiliary means served to render the organs of perception more supple and obedient to the direct action of the soul or "*inner man*," and freed them from the interference of the temporal, misguided reason of our present degenerate state. Hence the subsequent progress of our young novices was destined to be one into the higher intellectual and moral order of things; that of:

VIII. THE DIRECT UNAIDED CLAIRVOYANCE IN THE NORMAL STATE. By it distant persons and things are seen without the aid of "*vague contemplation*," or gazing upon any fixed object whatsoever, but simply BY THE PIOUS CONCENTRATION OF THOUGHT.

The power brought to bear here is that of FAITH, HOPE, and CHARITY. * * * * This is the most important period in the development of the probationers. After having well inculcated into their minds that it is requisite to proceed in these things with the highest sentiments of veneration, * * * * the novices should be made to place confidence in *their own spiritual abilities,* and be taught to understand and feel that all the gifts they have received, up to the present stage of their probation, are but the "*earnests*" from Providence for the entire fulfilment of the new covenant towards them, and given in order that they may regain the strength of their "*Inner man made in the image of God,*" to become IN REALITY "*re-born of the Spirit,*" members in Christ, the children of God, and inheritors of the kingdom of Heaven:" *i. e.*, Spiritual Power on earth.

Impressed with the truth and *efficacy* of these principles of THE DOCTRINE OF REDEMPTION, delivered to mankind through Jesus Christ, * * * * my daughters soon entered into this higher grade of their initiation: *The direct unaided clairvoyance in the Normal State.*

With a view to applying this important development to the easy improvement of their minds by a new mode of education, * * * they were enjoined to apply themselves assiduously to

IX. THE READING CURRENTLY THROUGH THE POWER OF THE PIOUS CONCENTRATION OF THOUGHT, *in their natural waking state*, the named pages of books closed or hidden from their view. This gift, combined with that mentioned at No. 4, was soon after applied in the most satisfactory manner to the education of my young students, as shown hereafter. They were then told that having eyes by which they were now beginning to see as man *ought* to see, inwardly as well as outwardly, eyes able to receive the inward and spiritual as well as the outward and material sight; they must concentrate their thoughts with *entire faith* in Christ and confidence in themselves through Him, together with expectant hope and a fervid sentiment of prayer, in order that they might also have ears by which they might likewise hear as they *ought* to hear. On doing as they were bid the *direct spiritual* action of the soul, or *power of the "inner man,"* was immediately extended in them to the organ of hearing, and they possessed the faculty of

X. CLAIRAUDIENCE IN THE NORMAL STATE, by which the initiated of this degree are enabled to hear the sounds of things, and voices of persons, not only far beyond the ordinary range of hearing, but indeed from the most distant places. They also receive as by a voice speaking to them, answers to all sorts of questions.

This faculty, which may be made good use of for an infinite number of purposes, is already employed by us to teach our students the pronunciation of foreign languages without the assistance of a competent master, the pronunciation when wanted being given to them by a voice that seemed as though it were speaking in the air.

* * * * With this foundation to work upon, and confiding in the revelations and spiritual guidance by which we had already attained the degree of spiritual strength shown in the preceding narration, I boldly withdrew my two younger daughters from the school they were attending; and in spite of the opposition and commonplace arguments of other parties, began their new mode of education in the manner indicated by our invisible spiritual conductor which was pursued much in the following order:

XIII. LESSONS WERE LEARNT BY HEART BY READING TO MY STUDENTS IN THEIR MAGNETIC SLEEP, ordering them to retain in their memory when they awoke, all they had heard.

XIV. LESSONS WERE NEXT LEARNED BY HEART, BY THE PUPILS READING THEMSELVES ONCE OVER, IN THEIR MAGNETIC SLEEP, one or more pages of a book. When this began to become familiar, and the organs of memory showed that they were in a fit state of rapid obedience, the action of the organs of outward perception upon the memory was submitted to the strong developing power of the soul's direct influence, and

XV. LESSONS WERE LEARNT BY THE SIMPLE INSPECTION OF (or staring at), THE OPEN PAGE OF A BOOK,—THE STUDENTS BEING IN THEIR NORMAL WAKING STATE. In the beginning, the inspection, or staring, was made to last a definite number of seconds, and that number being gradually reduced, after a short space of time, the duration of a single second or a mere glimpse at the page was sufficient for the pupils to retain in their memory the whole contents of it.

To those who possess the slightest degree of reflection or analysis, * * * * it will be manifest what immense advantages, what endless resources are offered by this extension of the intellectual powers, by this perfection of the organs of perception and memory.

This instantaneous *"Psychotyping"* on the memory—this instantaneous photographing of the Soul upon the heart of man, may indeed be considered as a commencement of the fulfilment of the promise of God towards His elect, *"I will be their God and they shall shall be my people, and I will place my laws in their hearts."*

XV. LESSONS ARE ALSO LEARNT BY A SIMPLE ACT OF PIOUS CONCENTRATION FROM BOOKS CLOSED OR TOTALLY OUT OF SIGHT.

In this case we have usually named the page where the beginning of the lesson is to be found, for we have, as yet, had recourse to the process less as a matter of immediate utility than as a practice of the powers of distant clairvoyance. It will be easily conceived that by a slight extension of this faculty, or rather by the special direction being given to it, it may be applied to obtain references from, and even the perfect knowledge of, works which are known to exist in certain libraries and other places, rendered either by their distance, or want of time or otherwise, inaccessible to us. * * * *

XVIII. MENTAL DICTATION.—In this case the pupils are made acquainted—by the *knowledge of their "inner man,"* and the *perfected obedience of the organs of the "outer man,"* with the contents of the page held open in a position visible alone to the eyes of the teacher,—and as the latter desires to communicate a phrase to the pupils, they hear a voice dictating it aloud to them in the air, although no person is speaking to them at the time.

[The clearly defined thought of the operator becomes vocalized to the inner ear of the attentive subject.—J. H. D.]

XIX. HISTORY.—THE DIRECT CLAIRVOYANCE gives the student a correct sight, WITH REGARD TO THE HISTORICAL PERSONS AND FACTS treated of in the lessons learnt by the inspection of books, either open, or closed, or at a distance,—as explained in the foregoing articles, Nos. 15 and 16.

XX. THE SIGHT OF THE PLANTS, FLOWERS, MINERALS, ANIMALS, etc., described or mentioned in their books on natural history and other branches of science, as also such other useful details as may have been omitted by the author, or belong to a more minute study of the subject, is enjoyed in the same manner. * * * *

XXII. THE STUDENTS ARE ALSO BY THE FACILITY THEY ACQUIRE FOR RECEIVING INSPIRATIONS SO PERFECTLY IDENTIFIED WITH EVERYTHING BELONGING TO THE PLACES SPOKEN OF IN THEIR STUDY OF GEOGRAPHY, THAT THEY FEEL AS THOUGH THEY WERE ON THE SPOT. So correct are the impressions made by the ubiquitous power of their souls on all the organs of the body in their temporarily perfected condition, that they appear to themselves to be, not where the lessons are going on, but in the very places therein referred to; seeing, hearing, and feeling all that they are required or desirous to see, hear, or feel.

XXIII. SOLUTIONS ARE GIVEN INSTANTANEOUSLY, BY INSPIRATION, TO ARITHMETICAL AND OTHER MATHEMATICAL PROBLEMS. * * *

Another very useful gift, which it would be difficult to designate as appertaining solely, either to the inspirational powers, or to the perfection of the natural organs; but most probably to both at once—is that of

XXIV. THE MICROSCOPIC, AND THE TELESCOPIC SIGHTS, by which the students are enabled to see the most minute and the most distant objects with the naked eye, as though they were looking at them with a microscope or a telescope.

[This experience of Bertolacci's initiates confirms our claim, that spiritual illumination and the development of the inner psychic powers, does not weaken or in any way injure any sense, faculty or function of the "outer" and physical man, but rather exalts and brings them to their highest degree of organic activity and perfection.—J. H. D.]

CURES.—The foregoing initiation for the development of our latent spiritual faculties, the strengthening of our faith [the one essential condition of success—J. H. D.], and the appropriation of the material organs of the probationers towards their becoming the perfected instruments of the soul's long-neglected higher powers—that initiation was not only intended to serve the purposes of education—as commonly understood—but those of memory, in fact, of all other useful objects.

The power of alleviating pain, of curing diseases, of healing wounds instantaneously is, no doubt, among the most important objects. At the outset of man's regeneration, it is, perhaps, the most essential of all, for it is more contributive towards his willing compliance with a higher order of existence than any other inducement which can be held out. It is that of which our Saviour made the most extensive use to demonstrate the efficacy of the doctrine he preached: a doctrine which had regard to the temporal regeneration of man, no less than to the salvation of his soul. * * * *

I have said that by a judicious application and combination of the effects obtained in the induced somnambulic state, the organs of the human body are made to obey the power of the will. BUT THE POWER OF THE WILL IS THE RESULT OF FAITH, FOR NO ONE CAN POSSIBLY WILL WHAT THEY DO NOT IMPLICITLY BELIEVE IN. And furthermore those organs are thereby prepared to yield the same obedience to the direct spiritual action of the soul, or superior "inner man," upon them, in the normal waking condition of the patient.

[The simple process of introversion which we have described, has proved equally effectual in awakening and bringing forth the inner powers, and mental illumination, without the abnormal conditions of trance, or induced somnambulism, and has proved effectual where the trance itself could not be readily induced. Had Bertolacci been free from the mental limitation which the impression that all those preliminary processes he adopted were a necessity, set to his efforts, and had he believed as fully that the last process—"THE PIOUS CONCENTRATION OF THOUGHT" for focalizing the psychic powers in the normal waking state,—was all that was needful to secure the full result,—as our own experiments have demonstrated—he would have been equally successful. The specific exercises for the development and training of the psychic powers in the several processes adopted was all that was essential to his final success. The simple process of introversion is equally effectual in focalizing the power of the mind over the body and its sensations, and the immediate and often instantaneous cure of disease and injuries.—J. H. D.]

* * * * Our Saviour was incessantly extolling the power of faith; in fact, his whole Doctrine was that of the unlimited power and wisdom to be acquired by man through Faith rendered effective by confiding Hope—fervid expectancy—prompting the action or will; that union of power and wisdom becoming divine and sanctifying those who purify it and practice it with charity. Not that degraded thing, which has blasphemously usurped the name of Charity, and which is nothing more than a cold-blooded, vainglorious ostentation of the superfluities of wealth exhibited in alms-givings, * * * * but the TRUE SUBLIME VIRTUE, whose roots are implanted in the LOVE OF GOD,—the sentiment of veneration for the invisible power of the one great and all-pervading Spirit—whose branches, fed with the "new wine" of Christianity, pours forth its fruit in the "LOVE OF THE NEIGHBOR" by sympathizing with the sufferings of our fellow-creatures, extolling their virtues, pitying their faults, and sharing our wealth with the needy—kindly, cordially, and without reluctance; and not as an obligation conferred, but with gaity of heart, or as a pleasure to ourselves.

Let it not be thought that, in exposing these sentiments, I wish either to hold forth the virtuous principles of my family circle, or to gain favor for ideas, theories, or philosophies of my own. They are but a part, a most minute portion of the teachings inspirationally given to us, in order that, by purifying our minds and elevating our aspirations, the organs of the body might become more fitted to be the channels of a higher order of things, and when in any way impaired, might be easily and promptly restored to that healthy and harmonious intonation of life which is to constitute the existence of man on earth in his regenerate state.

The powerful effects of the mind upon the health and energies of the human frame, is a thing too long and too immutably established to require any pleading here, * * * * but so great is the power of that renovated action of the mind, and so permanent, I should add, may become its effects, that in moments like these, the most miraculous cures can be, and have been lately performed upon persons whose maladies set at naught all medical science. Several times have I, in the midst of my family, experienced the indescribable joy—received the divine blessing—of being made with them, not only witnesses, but indeed instrumentally, the participants in the work of God's mercy to that effect.

When residing in Paris and its environs, during the years 1853 to 1858 inclusively, some intimate friends having been made acquainted with, and witnesses of, what was daily occurring in the family, soon requested the permission to introduce others, who were received on the following conditions: They were previously to be informed that as I held these things sacred, I would not allow them to be turned into ridicule; that in coming there, they must conduct themselves as they would at a religious meeting, putting aside, beforehand, every notion of fraud or legerdemain being practiced upon them. * * * * The course followed was very varied, as we had no methodical order for proceeding. My part consisted in seeing my company comfortably placed in a half circle or horse-shoe form round the room, a table being set at the open space with the planchette upon it, on which two of my young ladies, sitting opposite each other, held both of their hands. The planchette writing regulated the rest. * * * * * At times the planchette would ask for a Bible; and, the book being opened, and the chapter there presenting itself having been read, one or more verses were selected by the Spirit, and the four hands of the two young ladies being left upon the planchette, it would write with the greatest rapidity during a space of time, varying from half an hour to an hour, expounding the passage which had been chosen, and giving us the highest light, the most encouraging exhortations and explanations, with regard to the efficacy of the Doctrine of Christ, and the high aspirations it was destined to impart. * * * *

It was sometimes after a written *"seance"* of this nature—when all present were deeply impressed with the sublimity of the teachings they had received, and convinced that the intellectual influence making itself thus manifest to them must be of the highest and purest order—that some most wonderful and instantaneous cures were effected. * * * *

To the astonishment of many present, persons appearing amongst us for the first time, would be called upon by their Christian names, and others by their familiar nicknames, telling them their peculiarities of disposition, their favorite pursuits, and their thoughts at the very moment. * * * * If among those present any one was momentarily ailing, or in a state of permanent ill health, they were generally singled out, and desired to come to the table. When there they would often be told what their sufferings were, how long they had been ill, etc., although no previous mention had been made of the subject, and while under the surprise and awe which these unexpected communications generally created, they would be told that if they had faith in Christ they should be cured. * * * * Then God's blessing through Christ Jesus was called upon the ailing, in a few words of prayer written by the planchette, after which I do not think I could call to mind a single fact of any of the sufferers not feeling more or less relief, while in the majority of cases, the cures were complete.

In some circumstances the mode of *"laying on of hands"* has been prescribed; for that one of the members of our family, or a relation of the patient, has been at times appointed to officiate; at others, a certain number of persons have been selected to form a chain around the sufferer during a given time, a prayer being written by the planchette while the operation was being performed.

In particular and rare instances, where the faith of the patient has required assistance, as in the case of the blind man, on the eyes of whom mud was placed by our Saviour, certain remedies of a simple nature, and a short regimen were sometimes prescribed with wonderful success. * * * *

An intimate friend of mine who had been relieved of a troublesome rheumatic affection, begged leave to introduce a friend of his, who had for years been a dreadful sufferer from paralysis of the bladder, who had spent enormous sums of money in consulting the first medical men of all countries, and in following their prescriptions, to no other effect than the still greater ruin of his constitution by all the drugs he had taken, and who, although his case had been known to him as one which no medical science could overcome, still felt himself upheld in hope by an inward conviction, that he would be restored to health by some extraordinary or miraculous means.

On his first visit, after having witnessed some of our daily spiritual pursuits, and having had the principle on which the results were obtained briefly explained to him, the subject of his own malady was discussed between him and the *invisible power*, conversing by means of the planchette writing. He therein related how, of late, he had been sustained in hope by an inward conviction that Providence would ere long come to his aid; he also said that what he had seen and heard, in addition to the cure of his friend, had filled him with faith, and he felt sure he would be cured. He furthermore requested to be permitted to earn his own reward by following strictly and religiously whatever prescription should be ordered. In compliance with his request, some easy regimen and two simple remedies were indicated, as also certain hours of deep meditation on the teachings of our Saviour, in conjunction with all he had seen and heard; and he was enjoined *to have perfect faith in the efficacy of the prayers* he should address to God through Christ, for his recovery. On being told that on these conditions *he would, in three days,* receive back the full health and strength he had for years been deprived of, his tears of joy, his rapturous expressions of gratitude towards God, shared by all present, were such as to leave no doubt in our hearts but that these signs of his implicit belief were the seeds of that certain unerring power, which in its rapid development, would bring forth his perfect recovery. On the morning of the third day after that, and immediately after he had executed the last form of his prescriptions—that of drinking a small glass of magnetised water—an indescribable feeling came over him; all at once his full vigor returned to him; all his pains were no more; his very complexion, which, up to that time, bore all the marks of his shattered constitution, became at once that of the hale, re-invigorated man he felt himself to be, and that he, in reality, was from that hour.

Among those introduced to us was the family of Mr. and Mrs. K——d. * * * * Mrs K.'s health had been impaired to a very serious degree for several years past, from more than one of those organic affections for which the medical science has not yet found a permanent remedy; but with this we had not been made acquainted. During her second visit, when only a few persons were present, * * * * the *seance* had been most satisfactory, enlightening and impressive, and all present freely and unreservedly expressed their conviction that the light they had therein given was of the purest and most salutary, as also their complete faith in the teaching they had received. Among the most enthusiastic, the fervor and excitement of our new friend were signally predominant. Much passed between her and the Spirit in a direct manner, and when she began to calm down, to her fresh surprise, she was spoken to of her bodily ailings; and the precise spot and nature of the pains she was at that moment suffering from, were indicated, and she was told that if she persevered in the faith with which she was animated, she would, in answer to the collective prayer of our souls then in communion, be cured by the Spirit of Christ of all her maladies. She asked when that would be, and was answered through the planchette-writing that the inward prayer had been heard, and was already granted. At this moment the complete restoration of her health was effected in a most wonderful and permanent manner.

[Other cases equally remarkable are recorded of cures wrought at these "*seances*," among which were an aggravated case of stone in the bladder, it passing away in immense pieces without a particle of pain; and a case of the instantaneous healing of a lady suffering from complete paralysis "from her waist downwards," of "eleven months standing," resulting from a premature confinement, etc., etc. Passing over much interesting discussion of the principles involved in these facts of healing, by the author, we will only add a portion of the specific experience he gives of his own family as a further illustration of the transcendent advantages which the development and training of the higher psychic powers adds to our common life.—J. H. D.]

EXTENSION OF THE HUMAN FACULTIES, FITTING THE INITIATED TO RECEIVE MIRACULOUS CURES AS A PERMANENT GIFT.

Before I entered into the explanation which I have just concluded, I had related some of the cures that were obtained at our meetings. It will be remembered that they were all, more or less, operated under the influence of the surprise first occasioned by the manifestations which had just been produced. That surprise is felt by our reason. * * * * When that reason is confounded, and the aspirations of the mind are elevated, *faith* in the higher order of things takes the place of *doubt*, and faith is the first and main condition towards the acquirement of spiritual power. If our ill-bred reason is only temporarily vanquished, our faith will not be a permanent one. * * * *

This brings me back to other permanent advantages which we have obtained in my family, besides those of the new mode of education which I have described as one of the results of the spiritual initiation. Among these is the attainment of that *normal state* of the improved faculties of mind and body, in which the initiated can, at any time, be miraculously and instantaneously cured of all their ailings, without the use of any material remedy or any preparation or preliminary whatsoever, beyond a few seconds of mental concentration and confidence in the name of Christ, in conjunction (or communion) with any one or more of their brethren in the true faith.

The difference which exists between this normal state and that in which most of the cures I have described were effected, is that, instead of the misguiding reason being vanquished, for the time, to permit the mind, during its temporary elevation, to operate upon the organs of the body—the improved state of those organs admits of their immediate obedience to the dictates of the sane reason of an acquiescent mind, furnishing its proper contingent in the operations of the "inner man."

The means pointed out to us by our Spirit of communion through which this preparation of the material organs is effected,

APPENDIX II.

are those I have described in the "initiation" preliminary to the spiritual mode of education.

Without entering further into the details of the "initiation," which, under the constant guidance of our "Soul of communion," varied according to circumstances, suffice it to say that, in a very short time, my three daughters acquired that extension of the human faculties, mental and corporeal, and that degree of spiritual faith, by which they are, and have been for several years past, qualified to be cured of all ailings in a space of time seldom surpassing six or eight seconds. It is of the very rarest occurrence that the cures are not as permanent as they are rapid in their effects.

In such cases, which I am happy to say we seldom meet with, the cause of our failure is invariably attributed by our "*Soul of Communion,*" to a temporary ascendency of the mundane principle over the spiritual life in the patient, and declared to be the sign of a moral self-condemnation and reproach.

FACTS RELATIVE TO THE FOREGOING.—In the year 1857 the scarlet fever and scarletina were creating great devastation where we were then living (in France). One day my eldest daughter was suddenly visited with all the symptoms in a very violent manner. At the end of *eight seconds* of concentration and communion together with myself and some members of the family, the headache, fever, and every other unpleasant feeling had totally vanished. * * * *

Many other contagious maladies have, at various times, been instantaneously arrested in a similar manner, whenever the young people of our family have been attacked by them; and such has been the case with every one of them at different times. * * *

That part of the promise made by our Saviour in behalf of believers, which says that if they take poison "*it shall not hurt them,*" has also been accomplished towards us. * * *

When any of my girls cut themselves, or meet with any other accident, such as bruises, sprains, etc., not only is all pain immediately taken away, but indeed the healing is almost as rapid.

One day, one of them, in cutting a loaf of bread, gave herself a deep gash across the left hand, an inch long. The blood was flowing very copiously and had quite wetted a towel, which she had wrapped around it, through and through many folds, by the time she came to me, though she lost no time, however, in so doing. The towel was taken off, and I held the lips of the wound together, while those present joined us, during eight or ten seconds, in communion, the name of Jesus Christ being invoked. The blood ceased to flow, and the wound was closed. Not more than four hours afterwards, some friends having come to pass the evening with us, she played several long pieces on the pianoforte, and had totally forgotten that she had cut herself in the day. Nevertheless, the wound was sufficiently severe to leave a scar still very plainly to be seen, although it is now somewhere about seven years since the accident occurred.

On another occasion since that, one of her sisters cut the top of her thumb from one side to the other, down to the very bone, and was cured in the same manner, as completely and as instantaneously.

I have mentioned these two cases in particular to give my readers a notion of the efficacy of the cures; but, indeed, it is almost of daily occurrence with us; either for one thing or the other—a cut, a bruise, and the blistering of an arm from the effects of a poisonous plant, having, the very day on which I write this narration, been cured, each in the space of eight seconds. A few days back, it was a hand and wrist which had been pretty smartly scalded with boiling water.

Tooth-ache and caries are as effectually stopped, even to the destroying of the nerve in order to obviate any recurrence of the pain from extraneous causes.

On one occasion, when the request was made that the nerve should be destroyed, the most complete insensibility immediately succeeded; but we were told, that as the tooth was but slightly attacked, if it were stopped within a few days, in order to keep the air and moisture from it, it would be preserved; but that, if it were not done, in ten days it would begin to fall to pieces. It was *not* done, and on the tenth day, a large portion of the tooth fell off, and, in a very few days more, nothing but the bare root was left, which, however, was very easily extracted without occasioning the least pain.

HEAT AND COLD.—Among many other beneficial results obtained from the faculty of creating or suppressing the sensations of the body is that of obviating the inconvenience of climate. At any time when my children suffer from cold feet, not only can they be immediately warmed, but even by the will being expressed, they can be made unpleasantly hot. In the same manner, when suffering from oppressive heat, they are made to feel refreshingly cool, and are thus enabled to proceed in many occupations which, at the time, are intolerable to others.

FATIGUE.—When they feel fatigued from over-exertion, long walks, or any other cause, they can be, and constantly are, as completely restored to a perfect state of rest as if they had passed a good night's repose in sleep, and indeed the effect spiritually produced is still more perfect, inasmuch as that every degree of stiffness disappears together with the sensations of fatigue.

HUNGER AND THIRST.—It has very often occurred, sometimes for a particular motive, at others from involuntary causes, that the ordinary meals had to be considerably protracted, or totally suppressed. In such cases, the smallest piece of bread is divided equally among the members of the family,—each piece sometimes not exceeding the size of a walnut; these, distributed and eaten during an act of communion, or pious concentration of faith and inward prayer,—have caused the partakers of them to lose every sensation of hunger, and to feel as if they had enjoyed what is erroneously termed a "*hearty meal.*"

The power to create or excite an abnormal vitality in that order of things, which is, perhaps incorrectly, called inert matter [as water and other substances], is no less possessed by man with regard to the vegetable reign, as was plainly announced by our Saviour to his disciples when, by his anathema he withered the fig-tree.

A friend of my family, Madame ———, residing in Paris, was instructed in the Doctrine of the Spiritual Phenomena of the day at our meetings, and became very soon efficient in obtaining some of the faculties developed among us. To try her strength upon plants, she first began by sowing in a wooden box full of earth some mignonette seed, and having divided it by a piece of plank into two equal parts, applied herself to obtain an augmentation of vitality in favor of one of the halves, and to that purpose concentrated herself daily over the box, for a few minutes, in faith and prayer. The favored side of the box was luxuriant with a full growth of mignonette beginning to flower, when on the opposite half the seeds were only just showing the first signs of vegetation.

[Other striking exhibitions of this direct power over vegetation are given by the author, together with illustrations of finding lost articles through the inner sight, also of predicting future events, etc., etc., but these we will pass over to quote a few of his closing words of suggestion and appeal, simply adding here, that in this little school of spiritual development they seemed to have acquired in a satisfactory degree all the special Gifts described by St. Paul, viz., "The word of wisdom," "the word of knowledge," "faith," "the gifts of healing," "the working of miracles," "prophecy," "discerning of spirits," "divers kinds of tongues," and the "interpretation of tongues," and all these, as in the olden time, by the "working of the one and the same Spirit, dividing to each one severally as he will," which they recognized as the "Soul of Communion."—J. H. D.]

Now that I have said all that I mean to say for the present, one step of my duty toward God and my neighbor is nearly performed. I have to say, however, a very great deal more—with regard to the spiritual manifestations which we have received, both spontaneously and in answer to our wish of obtaining them; as also with the great principle which distributes them on our earth; and those *useful applications* of them by which so perfect an *extension of the human faculties* can be acquired as eventually to lead to the complete regeneration and redemption of mankind. But to accomplish this first *public* act of my life in the service of Christ Jesus, our Saviour, our "*first-born brother*," and "co-inheritor" of the God-head of man on earth, I have one or two more words to add for those who, in consequence of what I have herein exposed, may wish to become partakers of, or co-operators in this apparently new order of things.

In the first place, if you would succeed, you must begin by arming yourself against every idea of your own, as also the absurd theories and suggestions of others, which may tend towards making you believe that there is any peculiarity in my nature or that of my children, by which we are exceptionally qualified for the attainment of the gifts we have received. * * * * I most positively maintain that all can show as much if they choose. It makes no difference to what class of society you belong, what may be your mental acquirements or not, prince or pauper, you can do in the main what I have done. The secret is this; having received the FAITH, you must adopt the most determined WILL to persevere in that path of *"new life in the Spirit,"* in spite of all the opposition you will meet with in the world; you must not allow yourself to be disheartened, if at times you feel that the spirit of Mammon occasionally returns to your heart; or if, as it will often occur, you fail in your endeavors, either from your own weakness or the fault of others. I have had to arm myself with the most undaunted determination, and I trust it will prove undaunted to the end, to remain steadfast to that order of things of which it has pleased God to show me the Light and Strength, that I should therein employ all my energies and such faculties as it may have pleased Him to endow me with, in His service; with the view not only to accomplish my own redemption, but towards furthering that of my fellow-creatures. You indeed will have to bear in mind these impressive words of our Saviour, "No man having put *his hand to the plough, and looking back, is fit for the Kingdom of God."* * * *

CONCLUSION AND APPEAL.

Those things, which, in my isolation, I have had to labor and struggle for, through unforeseen difficulties and unknown obstructions, you may obtain for yourselves and your neighbors, with but a small share of the efforts I have had to employ. Together and united, men might far surpass these points, and attain, indeed, still higher grades to which our thoughts, at present, would hardly dare to aspire.

Instead of having to conceive the idea, draw plans and lay foundation with materials you know not yet where to find, my readers will, from the very outset, have my experience to guide them, as also the foundation I have laid, and the materials I have excavated, wherewith to begin building their spiritual house. If in material life, union is strength, it will be so still more with regard to the spiritual order of things. It is not only useful, but indeed indispensable, that the social principle be the very first and leading condition of any permanent or serious undertaking for the regeneration of mankind; for in it alone is there to be found that love, that charity, of which the man Jesus was the living type on earth, and which is the very soul of the great body of CHRIST,—"the POWER, the GLORY, and the WISDOM of GOD."

Were it necessary to produce still stronger and more practical proofs that the principle of association is that of spiritual power, they are to be found all through the life and actions of Jesus Christ and those of His true disciples. Did He not—immediately after He had received the baptism of John, * * * * forthwith, and in order to lay the foundation of His career of miracles and demonstration of the divine power of *"the re-born man,"* begin by calling around Him twelve men to whom He imparted in private, the truths and strength of His doctrine, by some, if not all of whom, He was constantly attended? Did not they after His bodily departure from among them, consider that principle of association so essential to the fulfillment of the mission with which He had entrusted them, that their first care was to complete the number He had chosen as that of the starting point of their future operations, by the election of Matthias, to fill the place left vacant by the treason and subsequent destruction of Judas Iscariot, *"the Son of perdition,"* that type of treachery, perjury, virtue-selling infamy, and false kisses which you must not allow yourself to forget, in the glorious enterprise of association, that I aspire to for our own, our neighbors', and for Christ's sake?

Was it not through that principle of association that the disciples, the apostles, and those whom they converted, received the in-pouring of the Holy Spirit, and laid the foundation of the future reign of Christ on earth? Let them, all those who call themselves Christians, to whatsoever sect they may belong, who really do *feel* that there is any truth in the gospel; who really do hold that Jesus Christ was neither the myth of a devised religion, nor an impostor, * * * * nor an imbecile visionary—as our detractors kindly pity us for being—put these things to proof. Let those examine for themselves who do not dare to think that He evinced a great defect of judgment in supposing, and a still greater imprudence in taking upon Himself to predict that there would be a future day of regeneration for man on earth; and that that day would be preceded by times of great trouble for those who should be opposed to the order of things He had established; "*men's hearts failing them for fear, and for looking after those things which are coming on the earth: for the powers of heaven shall be shaken.*" Let all those meditate earnestly on what is written who, * * * * after what they have read in the foregoing narration and explanations, are not quite so void of every sentiment of morality and veracity themselves, as to suppose me capable of having, all throughout, composed a blasphemous fable, for the sake of laughing at their credulity, or for the still worse purpose of turning it fraudulently to my own account. And if they are not wanting in the intelligence requisite to understand, from what I have explained, that in "*the application of modern spiritual phenomena according to the doctrine of* Christ," are to be found the means of regenerating mankind by the widest possible "*extension of the human faculties;*" let them, I say, if their faith be not a "*dead faith*," come forward and declare themselves openly in favor of the one side or the other on the great question of the day; for Mammon or for God. For the former, by continuing in their so long-trodden path of self, materialism and stagnation; or for God in the love of the neighbor, spirituality, and social progress.

Let all those who are or wish to be for Christ, for His fellowship, and for regeneration through Him, begin forthwith, by devoting their minds seriously to what has been disclosed to them in these papers. There remains much to declare and communicate from and under the same authority, but the time for that will come when these things shall have been examined, digested, discussed and received.

In the meantime let the willing hearts assemble, as much and as often as circumstances will permit, among such members of each family as do really believe, and also among small parties of intimate and truly congenial friends; in order to try to obtain those spiritual manifestations which may seem to them the most likely to lead towards any one or more of the useful applications herein pointed out. Let them ever bear in mind the words and works of our Saviour. Let them principally strive and *pray* to obtain the gift of miraculous and instantaneous cures, as also that extension of the latent human faculties, by means of which Providence has miraculously and mercifully shown us—for them as much as for ourselves—with a view towards fitting the organs of the youthful generation of our day to receive not only the faculty of relieving pain, but also the most rapid and easy acquirement of temporal knowledge and divinely moral truths. They have in these pages a ground-work for their labors which I had not, and I not only expect and am content to be surpassed, but pray, indeed, that it may be so, and I, in turn, taught by many of them.

Above all let such spiritual groups consider themselves, from the beginning, as members moving and toiling towards the formation, at an early future, of A GREAT SPIRITUAL ASSOCIATION OF PRACTICAL CHRISTIANITY, whose object shall be the continuation and completion of the work commenced by Jesus' first disciples and Apostles. Let them have ever in view, that by the endeavors of that spiritual Body, not only presided over and aided by, but indeed, identified with the plenitude of Jesus Christ's love, power and glory, the rising generations of this world shall receive at once their physical regeneration and moral redemption.

APPENDIX III.

The following from a work entitled "Statuvolism, or Artificial Somnambulism, by Wm. Baker Fahnestock, M. D., will give the reader some idea of his simple and original method of inducing the statuvolic condition, and its remarkable results:

OF THE PATIENT: I have never found any perceptible difference in what has been called the susceptibility of persons of different temperaments, * * * * nor have I observed much difference between the readiness with which it is entered by the different sexes. I have found some men of opposite temperaments to enter this state more readily than some women of the same temperaments, and *vice versa*, and believe that what is termed susceptibility, or a readiness to enter it, depends *more* upon the *state of the subject's mind* at the time of trial, than upon sex, temperament, or phrenolygical developments, etc.

Noise, being afraid of it, an over-anxiety to enter it, risibility, and in fact any other mental excitement, is unfavorable to its accomplishment, and should always be avoided as much as possible.

Very old persons, and children under eight or ten years, from a want of sufficient steadiness, knowledge and determination, cannot often be induced to enter it perfectly.

INSTRUCTIONS.—Various methods have been employed by different operators to induce this state. * * * * The most rational, certain, and pleasant way of inducing this state, which I have discovered, is the following:

When persons are desirous of entering this state, I place them upon a chair where they may be at perfect ease. I then request them to close the eyes at once, and to remain perfectly calm at the same time that they let the body lie perfectly still and relaxed. They are next instructed to throw their minds to some familiar place—it matters not where, so that they have been there before and seem desirous of going there again, even in thought. When they have thrown the mind to the place, or upon the desired object, I endeavor, by speaking to them frequently, to keep their mind upon it; viz.: I usually request them to place themselves close to the object or person they are endeavoring to see, as if they were really there, and urge them to keep their mind steady, or to form an image or picture of the person or thing in their mind, which they must then endeavor to see. This must be persevered in for some time, and when they tire of one thing, or see nothing, they must be directed to others successively, as above directed, until clairvoyancy is induced. When this has been effected the rest of the senses fall into the state at once or by slow degrees—often one after another, as they are exercised or not—sometimes only one sense is effected during the first sitting. If the attention of the subject is divided, the difficulty of entering the state perfectly is much increased, and the powers of each sense while in this state, will be in proportion as that division has been much or little.

* * * * Much patience and perseverance is often required to effect it; but if both be sufficiently exercised, the result will always be satisfactory—if not in one sitting, in *two or more*. I have had several to enter this condition after twenty sittings, and had them to say, "that if they had not interfered, and let things take their own course, they would have fallen into it at the first sitting." This shows that those who do not enter it in one or two sittings, must do something to prevent it.

Many persons have entered the state in the above manner who could not do so in any other, although repeated trials had been made to effect it. * * * *

I have found that persons always enter this state better without any contact, looking, passes, or anything of the kind, particularly when they are assured that they have some competent person to take care of and to converse with them while in it; and, by observing carefully the instructions which I have given, it is possible

APPENDIX III. 375

for any person to throw themselves into this state *at pleasure*, independent of any one; but it might not always be prudent to do so, for the *first time*, for *some*, upon entering the condition for the *first time*, become unconscious to all that is passing around them; and if such persons were to throw themselves into it independent of any one, and had not consented, or made up their minds before entering, to hear or to speak to some one, it is most likely that when in it and spoken to, they would not hear any one, and in all probability would sleep for a longer or shorter time, without doing anything, and when they did awake, would remember nothing, and scarcely know that they had been it at all.

* * * *

It is, therefore, always better for those who wish to enter it to place themselves under the care of some one; and he who understands the nature of the state best, and has had the most experience in its management, is the best calculated for this purpose. When they have entered the state frequently, and have had the proper instructions *while in it*, the case is very different; they are then able to move about with as much certainty and safety as if they were awake.

THE SENSATIONS EXPERIENCED BY THOSE WHO ENTER THIS STATE—are variously described by different subjects; but most commonly they agree that after the eyes are closed, and they have been endeavoring to see for a longer or shorter time, a drowsiness ensues, accompanied with more or less "swimming of the head," and a tingling sensation creeping over the whole body.

Some experience a feeling of sinking down as if they were passing through the floor; others, again, feel light as a feather, and seem to ascend or to be suspended in the air. Some start and twitch involuntarily in various parts of the body, while in others the breathing is more or less affected, but there is no necessity for their feeling unpleasant in any way. Some feel warm, others cold, but none of the sensations are described as being unpleasant; and when the state is entered perfectly the feelings are said to be delightful.

OF THEIR AWAKENING: All that is needful, when it becomes necessary that they should awake, is to ask them whether they are ready or willing to do so, and if they are, I direct them to do so at once, and they will awake at the word Now! in an instant. * * * * Before they awake, however, I commonly request them to remember how they felt and what they saw, etc., or they may not know anything about it when they do awake; particularly if it be their first sitting. With some this is not necessary after the first or second sitting, as they commonly make up their minds to do so of their own accord; yet I have seen some with whom it was always necessary. * * * *

Others, on the contrary, have the power of remembering whatever they please, or of forgetting what they please; or in other words, they can remember all that has transpired, only a part of it, or nothing at all, as they may feel disposed at the time.

This quality or power of the mind while in this condition, enables them to *create* pain or feel pleasant at will, and if they imagine or determine, that there is, or shall be pain or disease in any part of the body, that pain or disease will surely be felt, at the time and place designated, and will continue until the mind acts, or is directed so as to alter the condition.

[This is true also to a degree in the ordinary waking condition, and all that is needed to make it absolute—as in the concentration of trance—is an understanding of this law, and the art of inward concentration and control of the attention in the waking state.—J. H. D.]

This peculiar power of the mind while in this state, I have taken advantage of to cure diseases, and if the mind be properly directed while in this state, so as to make them to resolve to be well, pains, contracted habits or diseases are removed by an act of their will, as if by magic, and will last until the conditions are changed or altered by influencing causes, or by a positive act of the subject's will. * * * *

This state has also two conditions, viz.: A waking state and a sleeping state.

The former may be entered, without losing or forgetting themselves, and is generally entered first, particularly when the patient has been frequently spoken to while entering it.

The latter cannot be entered without losing or forgetting themselves, and is the state into which many subjects usually fall when not spoken to, while entering it, and out of which they would sooner or later awake, without any knowledge of having been in it, if not spoken to during the sleep.

It is generally expected that all persons who are said to be in this state shall exhibit the same phenomena.

This is true, so far as the state is perfect, but it must be remembered that all do not enter this state perfectly at the first sitting, and that there is such a thing as a partial state, in which only one, two or more of the senses are affected at the same time, while the rest remain in their natural condition, and of course cannot exhibit the peculiar phenomenon which they are capable of when such senses are truly in this state. * * * *

[It is highly important that the three leading senses, viz.: sight, hearing and feeling be fully focalized inwardly, whether in the statuvolic condition, or normal waking introversion, especially hearing and feeling, as without this the attention is liable to be diverted by sounds and sensations from the plane of the physical. The whole attention is required for the perfect exercise of psychic or inner sight, hearing, feeling, etc.—J. H. D.]

Some subjects are not clairvoyant, although they are perfectly in the state, and their not seeing in such cases is owing to their not knowing how to direct their mind, or their having no disposition to try. I have, however, succeeded in getting many to see who otherwise would not have done so, by persevering until I persuaded them to try, and instructing them to throw their minds to certain places where they were acquainted, or to hunt up certain individuals whom they were most anxious to see.

The reason why certain senses do not enter this state is owing to their not having been given up to it, or to a natural or constitutional wakefulness, which, however, I am persuaded can be overcome in all cases by perseverance, and a fixed determination on the part of the subject. * * *

CONSCIOUSNESS.—Consciousness and sensation are completely under the control of the will in most subjects while in this state, and are extremely active or entirely passive, as the will of the subject determines.

APPENDIX III.

ATTENTION.—When persons are in the sleeping condition of Artificial Somnambulism, all the senses and faculties lie dormant or inactive, and it requires an express action of their will to render any of them active. They can do this whenever they please, either partially or entirely, but they cannot see, and hear, and smell, and feel, etc., at one and the same time. But they can see or not, hear, feel, taste, smell, move, think, attend, perceive, be conscious, remember, judge, imagine, like or not, etc., as they please, or when they please, independent of any one.

In the waking condition of this state, their attention is commonly directed to the person into whose care they have entrusted themselves, not because they cannot do otherwise, but because they choose to do so, and often do not wish to be disturbed by others; and as it commonly requires an effort for them to do anything (particularly when they have entered it for the first time), it is necessary when an experiment is desired, that their attention should first be drawn and properly directed, and their full consent to do so before the experiment is attempted. * * *

PERCEPTION.—The powers of perception in this state compared with the same function in a natural state, are inconcievably greater, and it is impossible for those who have not seen or made the necessary experiment to conceive the difference. Language fails to express it, and our common philosophy is too circumscribed to explain the reality. * * * *

They can also translate their faculties to a distance, and I have had them to perform thousands of experiments correctly at various distances, varying from ten feet to eighty miles, independent of any previous knowledge or communication whatever, either personal or otherwise. * * *

JUDGMENT.—The judgment in this state is correct or not according as the thing to be judged interests them or not. When active it is extremely correct, and the reverse when the opposite is the case. * * *

WILL.—The will is paramount in this state, and controls the activity of all the functions. * * *

CLAIRVOYANCE.—When any of the senses are in the somnambulic condition, they become what I call, for want of a better term, clear-minded. Clairvoyance relates to the eye only, and is *internal perception, or perception without the aid of* the external eye. * * * *

HEARING.—When the sense of hearing is in this state, the subjects usually do not hear or listen to what is passing around them, unless directed to it by the person into whose care they have placed themselves, or there is an express desire on their own part to do so, and then they hear without any other communication.

When they are desirous of listening, they can translate this faculty to any distance, and hear what there transpires as distinctly as if the thing to be heard were in the same room. * * * *

Many individuals who are not clairvoyant often hear, and use this faculty at a distance very well.

I have had many subjects, two in particular, both gentlemen, in whom the sense of sight was not perfectly in this state at the same time that the hearing was; and who were both enabled to translate this faculty to a distance, and although they could see nothing, they could hear what was said or going on distinctly.

They have frequently told me what was spoken at a distance of several miles; and when taken [mentally] to a cocoonery at a distance of four miles, they declared that they could hear the worms feeding as distinctly as if their ear was within an inch of them.

Both gentlemen were sceptical, and entered this state out of curiosity. They have both lately entered the state more perfectly, and are now most excellent clairvoyants. One entered it perfectly on the tenth, and the other on the twelfth sitting.

[Many remarkable instances are related in the book in which this inner hearing, as well as sight, at both near and great distances, were critically tested and fully demonstrated by the Doctor, which we have not space to give.—J. H. D.]

If, therefore, when the mind has been properly directed, they can hear the exact words spoken, or the tunes played or sung at a distance so far exceeding the powers of this sense in a natural state, how can we limit their abilities? * * * *

FEELING.—The powers of feeling in distinguishing articles

whether by actual contact or at a distance, are as remarkable as those of the other senses. * * * *

They have also told the quality, size, shape, roughness, or smoothness, etc., of articles placed at a distance, or the temperature of solids, liquids, or of the atmosphere in different rooms or places, independent of any previous knowledge on our part, to the perfect satisfaction of those who at different times were engaged in the experiments.

When only a portion of the body is thrown into this state by the subject, say a finger, a hand, or an arm, etc., they still have *the power to feel or not, as they please, in these parts;* but it at first will be more difficult to do so than when the mind is also in this state.

The power of throwing any portion of the body into this state, independent of the rest, may be acquired by any person who will practise it under proper instructions; but it will be much more difficult for those to acquire it who have not been wholly in this state, than for those who have; but when they have once succeeded with one part, the rest becomes more easy.

The ability to do this is extremely useful in cases of injury, when the subject at will, by doing this, could relieve himself from the pain which he otherwise would be obliged to suffer, until a physician or surgeon could be obtained and the limb or part set or dressed, etc., according to the nature of the injury sustained.

After an operation, or where an injury has been sustained, I always request the patient to wake up, *with the exception of the affected part*, so that no pain may be experienced during the time necessary for its complete restoration.

It is remarkable that when a tooth has been extracted while in this state, if they have been properly managed by the operator, when they awake they do not miss it; or, in other words, feel the vacancy which has been created by its extraction, any more than they would if it had been out for years, and they had become used to its loss; the tongue, as is usually the case, is not thrust into the cavity, and the unpleasant feeling created by its loss is not experienced. * * * *

To give the reader an idea of the advantage of being able to enter this state quickly, or at pleasure, I will relate the following case of injury, which was entirely relieved in less than two minutes by entering the state at will:

Miss ——, in attempting to place a smoothing iron upon a high mantel-piece, stepped upon a chair, and in reaching up the chair tilted, and she fell across its sharp back, upon her right side, with her whole weight, injuring several of her ribs, etc. Somnambulism was proposed, but objected to, because she did not believe she could enter the state while suffering so much pain. * * * * I however insisted upon her making the trial, and, as she had been in the state frequently before, I did not apprehend any difficulty. She was suffering extremely at the time, yet, notwithstanding, she entered the state in about one minute; and, when interrogated respecting the pain in her side, she declared that she did not feel it at all, and kept pressing her side with impunity. She remained in the state about fifteen minutes, when, after being directed to leave that part in the state, she awoke entirely free from pain, and immediately went about her usual occupations.

Another case which was related to me by the gentleman himself, is as follows:

Mr. H——, whom I had previously taught to throw any part of the body into this state at will, having had his fore-finger mashed between two railroad cars, threw it, although suffering very much at the time, into this state readily, and declared to me that, from the very moment that he had done so until it was entirely healed, he had not experienced the least pain, although, at the time, he was obliged to press it into shape, etc., until the necessary bandages, etc., were applied.

Miss ——, of Philadelphia. * * * * I taught this young lady to throw any part of her body into the somnambulic or insensible condition at pleasure, and in about six weeks after I returned home, I received a letter from her father, stating that he would not take a thousand dollars for what I had taught his daughter, as she had lately met with an accident from boiling water, which so severely scalded her leg and foot that the skin adhered to the stocking when it was taken off. Yet notwithstanding the severity of the scald, she threw the leg and foot into the insensible condition in an instant, and kept it in that state during the time necessary for its restoration, which was not long in being accomplished, as the scalded parts seemed to *dry* up without any inflammation, pain, or suffering of any kind.

This is a remarkable case, and shows the use of being able to enter the condition at any time that it may become necessary, and as no possible injury can result, or habit arise, from the power of exercising it at pleasure, those who do not avail themselves of its blessings do not only "stand in their own light," but are slaves to prejudice, superstition, ignorance, or bigotry, and unnecessary suffering will exist, until a higher plane is assumed and its blessings realized.

* * * * Every man is liable to accident, and may become injured or ill, and if he has once been in this state he can enter it with more facility even while he may be suffering pain, and I give this as a reason why all who desire to enter it should do so under the care of proper persons, so that, if necessity requires it, the subject can accomplish it whenever it becomes desirable.

The oftener a person has entered it, the more readily he can accomplish it, and this shows the necessity of practicing it until the power to enter it sufficiently soon is completely acquired.
* * * *

[Striking illustrations of the inward development of taste and smell of distant substances, etc., are given, which need not be quoted, as the same principle is involved in their transfer.—J. H. D.]

PHYSICAL STRENGTH.—The physical strength of persons while in this state, compared with that when awake, can be much increased by them at will. I could relate many cases in which this has been successfully demonstrated, but it will be sufficient to state that I have seen some hold out at arm's length weights which, when awake, they could not possibly so extend.

Indeed I have seen some delicate young ladies lift, with apparent ease, weights which the strongest gentleman in the room had considerable difficulty in raising to the same level. * * * * The diseases relieved by the method I have proposed have been both of an acute and chronic nature. * * * * It can never retrieve an absolute loss, nor restore a function virtually destroyed; yet

APPENDIX III.

I have known it to relieve many cases of disease after repeated courses of medicine and the laying on of hands, etc., had entirely failed. Pain can always be relieved.

[Numerous instances of healing by this process are related in various forms of both acute and chronic disease, some of the latter being of an aggravated and supposed incurable nature. One of fever we will quote.—J. H. D.]

Miss A. P—— was seized with a high fever, accompanied with a violent headache, giddiness, and restlessness, * * * * which continuated unabated for three days and nights.

I was not sent for until the evening of the third day, and not being at home, word was left for me to visit her the moment I returned. I returned from the country about one o'clock the next morning, and visited her immediately.

I found her laboring under a high fever, was very restless, and described her head as being "ready to split with pain." As she was *very much* opposed to taking medicine, and had often, out of curiosity, been in a state of Artificial Somnambulism months before, I proposed that she should enter that state. She at first objected, as she said it was impossible for her to enter it as long as her head ached as much as it did at that time.

I told her she had but one choice besides and that was a dose of medicine. The thought of medicine decided the question, and, after a third attempt, she threw herself into it in less than a minute.

Upon asking her how she felt, she said she was somewhat relieved, but still felt the pain along the side and back part of her head. I directed her to throw her mind upon something else, and not to think of her head; and, as soon as she had done so, she was entirely relieved, and declared that she did not feel a particle of pain.

Five minutes had not elapsed since she was awake, sick, and suffering torments; now, she was well, lively, and, as usual, in health, began to laugh and talk as if nothing had been the matter with her, occasionally joking about the medicine, saying that "this medicine" (viz.: Somnambulism) "is very easily taken, and I shall, hereafter, prefer it on all occasions."

She remained in the state about half an hour, and after directing her to forget or throw off her disease, I requested her to awake with the understanding that she should remain well when she did awake. She awoke perfectly relieved and in fine spirits.

I saw her during the day, and found her as I had left her in the morning, well, sprightly, and ready for her usual vocations. She never had any return of the disease, and the only thing I regret, in connection with her case, *is* that the whole world did not witness, as I did, *the triumph of mind over positive disease.*

* * * * If a patient enters this state for the relief of disease, and while in it no allusion to his disease be made, or he does not think of it, or places his mind upon it of his own accord in a proper manner, no relief will be experienced when he awakes. * * * *

It is therefore *highly necessary*, when relief of any kind is desired by a subject, that *his mind should be placed upon the disease, and before he awakes* he should *resolve to forget it, or that it should cease to trouble him when he awakes.*

Early in my operations I observed the power of subjects while in this condition, to remember or forget what they pleased, or of correcting habits, etc., which were unpleasant, and soon after applied it to the relief of disease, and I have always since found that the firmer the resolution made in this state is, that the disease or habit shall cease, the sooner and more permanent will be the relief experienced when they awake. * * * * All unpleasant feelings will subside as soon as the mind is withdrawn or directed to something else, and this the instructor should always be careful to do as soon as they complain. I have taught many who have practiced the art to relieve themselves of pain or disease, even when otherwise perfectly awake. This, however, is not easily accomplished when they have never been in the state.

[The practice of normal introversion secures the same practical result in acquiring control of sensation as the artificial somnambulic state upon which Dr. F. so much depended. His own experiments would have demonstrated this had he not been so fully under the impression that the sleep was a necessity, and impressed his patients, or subjects with the same belief.—J. H. D.]

The following cure of *"Melancholia from Unrequited Love,"*

illustrates the power of banishing unpleasant and disturbing memories from the mind:

Miss ———— had been melancholy and desponding for several years. She was induced to try somnambulism for her relief. She entered the state perfectly the first trial, in less than ten minutes; and after she had been in it for some time, I asked her, as is usual in such cases, whether she did not think that it was better for her to forget an attachment which could not be returned? She said: "*Yes, I believe it would.*" I then asked her whether she was perfectly satisfied to do so, and to become lively and happy hereafter. She said: "Yes, and I am resolved that it shall be so." With this understanding I requested her to awake.

She awoke and retired with a friend. I have since been frequently informed that she has banished the circumstance from her mind entirely, and has been lively, contented, and happy ever since. * * * * The foregoing cases given in detail, have been selected from a number of others, who have been restored to health by the proper direction of the mind while in this state, within the last twenty-five years; and I will here again remark that the *mere entering this state will not relieve disease. It requires that the mind of the patient, while in this condition, should be directed to the disease, and a desire or a resolution formed on their part that it shall be otherwise when they awake. It is no matter whether this resolution be taken or be made independent of the instructor or not, the effect will be the same; but it is the duty of every person into whose care they intrust themselves, to see that it is properly done before they awake, or no beneficial effects will follow.*

[These remarks thus emphasized by the Doctor, apply with equal force and pertinency to natural sleep. If, on or before falling asleep, one will take up his disease, enslaving appetite, or any form of evil habit, fully in thought, with the understanding that he can thus dismiss it from his life, then focalize desire and resolution that he shall awake in freedom from it, if he do this with confidence, he will certainly succeed. Let any form of disease be resolutely cast out of the memory for one hour—for this purpose—it will lose its hold forever whether one sleeps or not;

but going to sleep under this impression gives the system a chance to become fully established in the changed and restored order. The reason why the forgetfulness of common sleep does not always suspend diseased action is because people go to sleep under the impression that the disease is there and will be there on awakening. "According to your faith be it done unto you," is the law of the mind's power over the body.

After describing some cases of surgery performed on subjects in the state, without pain or shock, the Doctor closes with the following:—J. H. D.]

I shall conclude my remarks upon this interesting subject, by stating, that in operations upon subjects while in this condition, it is not only beneficial, because the patient is not subjected to the pain usually experienced while under severe operations, but because the system under such circumstances receives no shock, the effects of which every surgeon is fully aware, are more to be dreaded than anything else.

[Again in giving his experience in securing painless child-birth by the same means, the Doctor jubilantly adds:—J. H. D.]

This desideratum, which I have long believed possible, I have, with but little difficulty, accomplished in many other cases, and the time is not far distant when prejudice, ignorance, and bigotry will be set aside, and the benefits which an improved science has brought to our doors, will be hailed with delight by a free and enlightened people, while all the ills that flesh has been heir to will live but in the memory of the past.

This idea may seem premature at this time, but if mankind had witnessed the perfect freedom from pain *in these cases*, they, too, would say: "Old things have passed away, and a new era is at hand." * * * *

In regard to the possibility of entering this state I have but to say, that the doing it depends upon the individual desiring to do so, as well as upon the instructions given, and it will be more difficult for those whose characters and prejudices are formed, than for those who are free from such hindrances. * * * * When the condition is perfectly understood by the masses, and properly taught by those who profess to do so, there can be no doubt that all will be able to enjoy its benefits. It does not require the gift of prophecy to foretell that the time is not far distant when Artificial Somnambulism will be taught in all the schools, lyceums, seminaries and institutions of learning. Then will this knowledge be truly appreciated, and the benefits to be derived from it realized by all who wish to escape the ills that ignorance is heir to.

It has been our object in presenting the above extracts from Dr. Fahnestock's book, to fairly represent his views, method, practice and experience, as they are among the most valuable and suggestive that experiment in this line has given us, especially in the matter of healing. As Clairvoyance was so fully illustrated in Bertolacci's experience, we have not quoted illustrative cases from Fahnestock.

The remarkable experiments of both these men furnish a complete demonstration of the claim for the higher psychic education put forth in this book. There are living witnesses in abundance to attest the truth of both the records. A personal friend of the author lived for years in almost daily communication with the Bertolacci family, and assures us that the facts of their experience were more marvelous indeed than he has reported them.

The one great law and principle which the remarkable experiments of both Bertolacci and Fahnestock demonstrate and emphasize, is that upon which our own doctrine, method and experience are based, viz.: that the full concentration of attention and desire with perfect confidence in any one direction, to the forgetfulness of everything else for the time, secures the result with absolute certainty. This applies to the relief of pain, the healing of the whole or any part of the body, change of bodily states, the illumination of the mind, the strengthening of a weak memory or the banishment of a hateful one, the attainment of any legitimate knowledge, or any physical, mental or spiritual good legitimate to man. "Therefore whatsoever things ye desire, when ye pray, believe that ye receive them and ye shall have them."

Apply this principle to securing all the results obtained by Bertolacci, Fahnestock, and others, by the normal process of introversion, without the suspension of consciousness, and it will be found still more practical and universal in its application.

Dr. Fahnestock's experiments were confined wholly to the plane of the sixth sense, without any reference whatever to the spiritual nature or the religious life. Bertolacci, on the contrary, recognized and sought first the supremacy of the spiritual nature; and hence the larger results and broader sweep of both his method and experience.

The mere matter of physical healing, however, and the control of sensation by mental supremacy, from the plane of the sixth sense, independent of spiritual experience, was fully demonstrated by Fahnestock's successful experiments. The complete subordination of the external senses to the higher psychic activities of the sixth sense, is secured by the focalization of these senses inwardly. A simple matter of mental discipline or control of attention.

The complete subordination of the animal nature and the law of the selfish life, however, to the spiritual nature and the law of the divine, can be effected only by the awakening of the spiritual nature, and the submerging of the personal will into the Divine Will.

One more and still different illustration of the inspirational method of education must close our appendix, which could be extended indefinitely with equally striking and suggestive experiences.

APPENDIX IV.

THE SPIRITUS MUNDI.

The following is taken from an interesting sketch by the talented spiritualist, lecturer and authoress, Emma Hardinge Britten, published in 1876:

A curious paraphrase of the Holy Ghost legend obtained currency amongst certain classes of European mystics during the great outpouring of Modern Spiritualism. During the early days of this movement, I met with a large number of intelligent persons in Europe who attributed very remarkable spiritualistic endowments, not as the majority of the Spiritualists claim, to the influence of their deceased friends, but to a mysterious, incomprehensible, impersonal sort of a personage, a somebody, yet a nobody, to whom has been given the comprehensive title of the SPIRITUS MUNDI. Vague and various as are the theories afloat concerning this last named mystic agent, there seem to be two which represent the sum of the whole. One class of believers infer that there is in the world an element aggregated of all the intelligence dispensed by humanity. Its operation on the mind is assumed to be something analagous to the influence of oxygen on the body, but in addition to its universal influence upon mentality, it is represented as susceptible of being *collected* and focalized by any concrete gathering of persons to such an extent that it can and does respond to questions, move tables, and, under the influence of WILL, *effect all the marvels* attributed to the spirits of the so-called dead.

* * * * The second class of believers in the action of an universal "Spiritus Mundi" simply substitute that term for the Apostolic "Holy Ghost." Unlike the credulous and unreasoning Christian, they do not pretend to impersonate their idea, but claim that it is the direct procedure from the Divine Spirit—the influx of God-like power, the action of the Supreme Being manifest to those who in faith and apostolic aspiration seek the gift. As an example of this class of believers, I shall here cite my own experiences with a very interesting family to whom I had the pleasure of an introduction during a hurried visit to France, some eight or nine years ago. The family in question is one of high rank, and occupy too exclusive a social position to permit of my naming them, although the peculiarities of their phenomenal experiences have become the subject of wide-spread rumor. The members of the family consist of the father, mother, and three children. The eldest, at the time of which I write, was a fine lad of fourteen, with a brother two years younger, and a little fairy sister of six summers. It was the custom of this family, once in each day to assemble together in what they called their hours of Pentecost, during which they were visited by the manifestation of the spirit in every conceivable form of intellectual development. Their exercises consisted of invocations, the singing of hymns by the assembled circle, the performance of fine music by hired musicians stationed without the place of gathering, trance speaking, drawing, writing, visions and eloquent improvisations. Their sessions were limited to two hours, and during that time they received prophetic addresses, medical prescriptions, business directions, and instruction for the younger members of the circle in reading, writing, elocution, languages, mathematics, astronomy, history, and every branch of knowledge necessary to perfect an accomplished scholar.

The father of this wonderfully trained band of mystics, a nobleman whose rank, standing and unimpeachable character would seem to forbid the possibility of deception or falsehood, himself assured me no teacher of any kind had ever given his children a single lesson. In the trance condition these little ones had themselves mastered every branch of knowledge with the most perfect facility, and that, commencing from their earliest infancy. It was their custom to employ themselves in useful and intellectual pursuits during the day, but whatever problems arose among them,

APPENDIX IV. 391

that their quick intuitions did not immediately solve, were reserved as matters of inquiry from the *Spiritus Mundi* at the next day's seance. Having the privilege of an introduction to this singular and accomplished family, I was courteously invited, before my departure for England, to be present at one of their seances. Joyfully availing myself of this opportunity, I repaired to the *chateau* at the time appointed in company with an intimate friend of the family's, by whom I had been introduced as "one worthy to share in their holy communion." Before entering the Oratory, which had been fitted up for, and was kept exclusively devoted to that purpose, I was gravely, though courteously, warned not to indulge in feelings of idle curiosity, or advance to that spot as a mere spectator of some remarkable phenomena. "If," said my host, "you are sincerely desirous of partaking of the high spiritual afflatus to which this sacred place is dedicated, I doubt not you will realize the presence and influx of the *Spiritus Mundi;* to no lesser motives will the divine power we invoke deign to respond." Somewhat daunted by this preliminary demand upon conditions of mind I did not dare to analyze, and certainly could not command, I nevertheless advanced with all possible desire for *truth*, if not for religious illumination, and this was the result :

The Oratory was built in a secluded grove, fitted up with vases of flowers, rare pictures, noble sculptures, gems of natural beauty and artistic skill everywhere greeting the senses. Soft music from invisible performers stole on the ear; a remote chime of exquisitely toned bells occasionally rung a sweet peal, and the distant chant of a beautifully intoned litany was answered by responses from the family, standing around the altar-shaped table within. That altar was simply adorned with a pure white cloth, supporting seven delicately perfumed lamps, and clusters of fragrant flowers. The family took their seats in a semi-circle close by the altar, on the further side of which were seats for invited guests, occupied on the present occasion by myself and the friend who had introduced me. Although not particularly prone to reverence or veneration for ecclesiastical displays, I was too easily psychologized by my surroundings to have required any further injunctions to yield myself up to the fascination of that deeply impressive scene. There was a serene and earnest air of aspiration too on each calm brow, that would have subdued the most rebellious or mocking spirit into courteous attention, if not sympathy with the principal actors. After the opening invocation by the master of the house, and the performance of the musical services, before mentioned, each member of the family, according to custom, proceeded to lay the special petition which filled their hearts before the invisible presence they invoked. The little girl lisped out a prayer that the Great Spirit would be pleased to inspire her with an understanding of how the flowers grew which she held in her hand. The younger boy wished for inspiration to continue the Roman history, in the study of which he was at present engaged, and the eldest offered a brief prayer for light upon the mathematical problems to which he was devoting his attention. These singular requests seemed to be presented in the most perfect confidence that they would be complied with, and addressed with as much good faith to the invisible *presence* as if spoken to their attentive father. As the children concluded their brief petitions, the mother arose, speaking evidently in a deep and unmistakable somnambulic condition. She reminded her children that there were strangers there who had honored them with their presence, and who, therefore, in Christian kindness should be preferred before themselves, and she called upon her husband and children to unite in desiring that such tokens of spiritual light and guidance should be vouchsafed to the visitors as should be best suited to their frame of mind and requirements. Instantly, as with a flash of mental lightning, the eldest boy, addressing me, said: "Lady! you are anxious to be informed of the fate of Sir John Franklin. Learn it now!" The boy had echoed my inmost thought—nay, revealed one of the secret purposes that was leading me to visit every available source of spiritual light and knowledge.

The moment the child had ceased to speak, and silence followed, a vision full of deep meaning and significance was presented to me. Like everything that transpired in that strange scene, it was given rapidly, clearly, without pause or halting. It came as the children spoke, upon the instant, and passed away almost as rapidly, and I have since had reason to *know* that brief as that vision was, it represented graphically the special points of the great navigator's life and death, upon which I sought to be informed. Directly it closed, each of the party described it, and though I had not had time to breathe a syllable of what I had seen, their words agreed in every iota with one another, and with my own visual experience.

"Dear lady," said the little girl, turning coaxingly to me, "I see you are wishing two things, and they cross each other in your mind just so,"—crossing her little hands over each other as she spoke; "you wish that I should have my question answered about how the flowers grow, and yet you want still more to hear about your *double* that was said to have appeared to a circle of people somewhere in the north of England. Now, don't you, lady?" This was strictly true; every word of it. I had felt a wish running through my mind, that the little fairy who had brought her flowers to show to "dear God," and ask him how they grew, should be satisfied, and yet I could not keep from thinking all the time about a tale I had heard of my "double" having appeared and communicated to a circle in Yorkshire. Before I could respond to my little querist she arose, and with a beautiful mixture of childish simplicity and spiritual dignity, recited some incidents known only to myself—on earth at least—went on to describe the circle where I had appeared, mentioned correctly several attendant circumstances, and wound up with a brief but deeply philosophical explanation of what the "double" or apparition of the human spirit really is. *My own future destiny* was my next fixed, though involuntary thought, and before it was fully framed into shape, the matron arose, and poured out in thrilling accents a prophecy, the details of which will never pass from my mind. Many of its predictions have been already fulfilled—some have failed—still I believe in them, for the memory of that inspired woman cannot connect itself with aught but truth and purity.

"Stonehenge!" cried the deep voice of our host, speaking seemingly in his normal condition, but with the same breathless rapidity in which each communication followed on the heels of the other. My companion was addressed this time, and our host fixed his piercing eyes upon him as he waited for an answer. "Yes—I was thinking of Stonehenge," replied my friend, "and wishing that I could receive some special information concerning the rites once practiced there." Instantly our host explained grandly, authoritatively, and philosophically, problems connected with that mysterious Druidical temple which must have been the echo of divine truth.

At length the closing moments of this wonderfully fascinating and instructive seance drew nigh. I had not been in that presence above fifteen minutes, before I felt that I was partaking in the illumination of the scene, and, realizing the wonderful mental lucidity of those who surrounded me, I was beginning to read them as they read me, when, to my regret, I perceived mentally—for I was all perception now—that the hour of parting was at hand. I wished for music, and *they knew my wish*, and obeyed it. I longed for further intercourse, yet felt the hedge of impossibility crowding upon me. They spoke my thoughts, expressing their deep regret that we should so soon be estranged. I *knew* they were sincere in those regrets, knew, as they said, that we should never meet again.

I knew the points of difference between their belief and mine, when we soared away to heavenly knowledge, but perceived our perfect agreement on points that concerned our mortal existence.

We all enjoyed in those two brief, wonderful hours, perfect clairvoyance of mortal things. Each of the family responded to my unspoken wish by improvising a verse of song, then all joined in a choral of benediction. The sweet bells pealed out, and the invisible musicians gave us a parting pæan, and so closed the seance with this strangely gifted family. I subsequently learned from the friend who had introduced me,—himself the most intimate associate of these persons,—that they regarded with abhorrence the idea of communion with the spirits of the dead; indeed they *strenuously denied* even its possibility. I have some reason to think they wished to convert me from my heretical belief in this respect.

The nobleman whom we visited had in early youth, it seems, received his "illumination" through visions, and the visitation of what he deemed to be "an angelic messenger" from the Most High. He had selected his wife, and reared his children, entirely under this heavenly guidance, sometimes conversing face to face with the same "angel" who had at first conferred his mission upon him, but still oftener conducting his whole scheme of life by the influence of the *Spiritus Mundi*, which he regarded as the Holy Ghost of apostolic times, not as the material God of the Christians, but as a direct procedure from the Most High, or the Spirit of God poured by influx into the minds of those who in humble faith and high aspiration put themselves in the Pentecostal attitude of waiting for his coming. At times the walls of their Oratory were shaken, the floors quivered, exquisite perfumes were wafted through the chamber, and deeply occult meanings were revealed to them in the philosophy of color, tones, and perfumes. I could write a volume on the significant and instructive ideas derived from these persons, did space permit. At present I can but add that though there was a specialty in the sublimity and exaltation of these persons' spiritual views, I have met many other highly endowed persons in Europe, who attributed, as they did, their great gifts, not to individualized spirits, but to the *Spiritus Mundi*, or Soul of the World, communicating to mortals through influx. Such were the opinions cherished, I believe, by the interesting family of the Bertolacci, the friends of William and Mary Howitt. Like the French nobleman above referred to, Mr. Bertolacci claimed that much of his childrens' education was obtained at their seances, and in a little pamphlet put forth on the subject of their experiences, more marvels are related of them than I should care to repeat, yet all the phenomena which fell in such abundant profusion on this family were attributed, as in the former case, to direct influx from God, and not in any way to the agency of spirits. Numerous other instances have been presented to me of the same kind; indeed I can recall the experiences of some of the most remarkably endowed families and individuals of my acquaintance in Europe, as being believers in the direct agency of the *Spiritus Mundi*, and utter disbelievers in the influence of spirit friends, or the souls of humanity.

* * * * Whilst admitting the constant ministry of our angel friends, are we so very sure that there is no higher power than them capable of reaching us? No higher being controlling them and influencing us through these nameless intuitions? Are we so sure that there is no collective soul-element in the world, operating upon and through matter, as the soul acts through the body, infilling men and spirits both with more than finite perception, and gleams of more than finite wisdom?

* * * * * * * * * * * *

Whilst I gratefully, lovingly attribute to my precious angel-friends all care, guidance and watchful ministry that they are capable of rendering, I am day by day, hour by hour, more and more startled by gleams of the wonderful powers of the human spirit itself, and I have yet to learn that the singular realms of intelligence we so vaguely attempt to define as intuition, instinct, presentiment, or even spiritual impression *alone*, are not due in a great measure to our contact with the ocean of spiritual life over which our barques are drifting from the shores of time to eternity.

CONTENTS.

CHAPTER.		PAGE.
	Preface,	v
I.	The Possibilities of Man,	1
II.	Is Christ to be Superseded?	15
III.	Christ the Perfect Way,	35
IV.	True Basis of the Higher Education,	45
V.	Man a Microcosm and what it Involves,	68
VI.	Elements of Christian Theosophy,	87
VII.	The Law and Basis of Mental and Faith Healing Practically Considered,	111
VIII.	The Law and Principle of Mental and Faith Healing Practically Applied,	147
IX.	The School of Christ, or the Higher Education Based upon the Spiritual and Psychic Powers of Man,	201
X.	Method and Specific Processes of the Higher Education,	246
XI.	Spirituality the only Basis of a Normal and Perfect Life,	292

APPENDIX.

I.	Nature and Aims of Theosophy,	337
II.	Bertolacci's Views and Remarkable Experiments,	343
III.	Dr. Fahnestock's Views and Experiments; Statuvolism,	373
IV.	Spiritus Mundi. A School of Prophets,	389

www.ingramcontent.com/pod-product-compliance
Lightning Source LLC
Chambersburg PA
CBHW050851300426
44111CB00010B/1215